MIDDLE-GRADE TEACHERS' MATHEMATICAL KNOWLEDGE AND ITS RELATIONSHIP TO INSTRUCTION

SUNY series, Reform in Mathematics Education
Judith T. Sowder, editor

Middle-Grade Teachers' Mathematical Knowledge and Its Relationship to Instruction

A Research Monograph

Judith T. Sowder,
Randolph A. Philipp,
Barbara E. Armstrong,
and
Bonnie P. Schappelle

STATE UNIVERSITY OF NEW YORK PRESS

Published by
State University of New York

© 1998 State University of New York

For information, address State University of New York Press,
State University Plaza, Albany, NY, 12246

Production by Cathleen Collins
Marketing by Patrick Durocher

Library of Congress Cataloging in Publication Data

Middle-grade teachers' mathematical knowledge and its relationship to
    instruction : a research monograph / Judith T. Sowder ... [et al.].
        p.   cm. — (SUNY series, reform in mathematics education)
    Includes bibliographical references and index.
    ISBN 0-7914-3841-4 (alk. paper). — ISBN 0-7914-3842-2 (pb : alk.
paper)
        1. Mathematics—Study and teaching (Middle school)—United States.
    2. Mathematics teachers—Training of—United States.   I. Sowder,
    Judith T.   II. Series.
    QA13.M525   1998
    372.7'049—dc21   97-34910
                                                                CIP

10 9 8 7 6 5 4 3 2 1

We wish to dedicate this book to a very special person. Barbara Ellen Armstrong, our colleague, fellow author, and dear friend, showed us that to respect teachers includes trying to understand the complexities of their worlds. When working with teachers, we frequently find ourselves asking, "What would Barbara do in this situation?" Losing Barbara is more than a personal loss; it is a loss to our profession.

Judy, Randy, and Bonnie

Contents

Chapter 1

INTRODUCTION

The research described here was undertaken as a 2-year investigation of two sets of related questions:

1. How does teacher understanding of rational number, quantity, and proportional reasoning influence the manner in which teachers teach? That is, what changes and shifts, both subtle and overt, can be noted in the way these topics are treated by the teacher as the teacher becomes more familiar with the mathematics involved and comes to understand better how students learn this content? After teachers have opportunities for study and reflection, how does a teacher's decision making change? How does a better understanding of the mathematics and the ways in which students come to learn this mathematics influence teachers' views about what it means to teach mathematics?
2. As teachers' understanding of rational number, quantity, and proportional reasoning develops and as teachers become more aware of how students learn this mathematics, how is their students' learning enhanced? How does student understanding change over the course of a year?

ORIGIN AND BACKGROUND OF THE STUDY

This research was carried out as a project of the Teaching and Learning Rational Numbers and Quantities Working Group, one of the seven working groups of the National Center for Research in Mathematics Education (1990–1995). This Working Group was composed of members representing many different orientations and theoretical perspectives, but all members had research interests that focused, at least in part, on various aspects of the multiplicative conceptual field. The orientations

1

and perspectives of the individual members guided them to undertake research that varied widely in the types of questions addressed, the methodologies used, the interpretation of data, and the manner of disseminating and sharing results. Overarching these differences were commonalities of interest and agreement that included, at a minimum, consensus on the complexity of the field under study, the need to come to a fuller understanding of these complexities and how they should be addressed in a classroom setting, and the need to provide teachers with stronger pedagogical understandings of the mathematical content in question. The initial meeting of this Working Group was held in May of 1991. Four local middle-grades teachers also attended the meeting. One of the outcomes of this meeting was the recommendation that research be undertaken to investigate the relationship between middle-grades teachers' knowledge of mathematics and their instructional practices within the area of the multiplicative-structures domain.

This recommendation was formulated into the research questions stated at the beginning of this section and was undertaken by some of the Working Group members located at San Diego State University. A 1-year preparatory investigation into these questions focused on the four teachers who had attended the initial Working Group conference. These teachers were well known to the researchers from their participation in past projects and in graduate coursework, from their excellence in teaching as noted by observation and through awards received, and from their leadership in mathematics education in San Diego. The purpose of this initial year of work was not only to explore the research questions with excellent teachers, but also to develop both the conceptual framework and the procedural plan for our long-term study. Results of our work with these teachers is reported elsewhere (Flores, Sowder, Philipp, & Schappelle, 1995; Philipp, Flores, Sowder, & Schappelle, 1994; Philipp, Sowder, & Flores, 1992; Philipp, Sowder, Flores, & Schappelle, 1995; Sowder, Philipp, Flores, & Schappelle, 1995), and is not further discussed here. These four teachers assisted us in designing the research project represented in this monograph.

AN OVERVIEW OF CONTENTS

In the chapter following this introduction we present the conceptual framework for this investigation. This framework is a refinement of the original framework (J. Sowder, 1992), prepared at the beginning of our planning year. By attempting to define the content domain in terms of what teachers need to know, we expected the boundaries of that domain to change during the course of our work. In this case, several researchers associated with the Working Group presented to the teachers seminars in which they described research-based principles and projects related to content topics relevant to this project, to be used to guide classroom instruction. The seminars and associated papers, together with further discussions of the presentations during other seminars, came to define, for the teachers, the bulk of the content domain focused on by this project. The revised conceptual framework reflects this influence. (The papers, by Armstrong and Bezuk; Harel; Kieren; Lamon; Mack; J. Sowder; L. Sowder; and P. Thompson, are available in another project publication, edited by J. Sowder and Schappelle, 1995.)

The third chapter provides details on the methodology of our study. We describe there the selection of the teachers, the content of the seminars with the teachers over the 2-year period, and our data collection, which consisted of interviews of the teachers, tests of the content knowledge of the teachers, protocols of seminar interactions, many classroom observations throughout the 2-year period, and tests of student understanding of the mathematics being addressed by this study. We also discuss the manner in which we handled our concerns about matters of validity, reliability, and ethics. Finally, we attempt to articulate our own assumptions and biases, here and throughout the chapters, insofar as they might have an effect on the investigation undertaken and described in this report.

Chapters 4 through 10 directly address the two research questions that guided our work and that appear at the beginning of this chapter. In chapter 4 we explore the effects of our seminars with the teachers on their development of both mathematical understanding and understanding of how students learn this mathematics. Chapters 5 through 9 are case studies of five of the teachers associated with the project. Chapter 10 contains an analysis of the student data we collected.

There were results that we had either not anticipated or that we had chosen not to investigate, but which, in retrospect, we deemed worthy of discussion. These results are discussed in chapter 11. We take the opportunity in this chapter to reflect on the effects this project had on us as researchers and as teachers and to make some recommendations about teacher professional development, both preservice and inservice.

THE CASE STUDY APPROACH

Case study is a method of choice when the purpose of a study is to examine the interaction of significant factors associated with a phenomenon. In this study, many factors influenced teacher change over the 2-year period, and any attempt to examine these factors and place them in perspective demanded a multileveled approach both to the kinds of data collected and to the data interpretation. An interpretive case study (as opposed to a descriptive or an evaluative case study) depends on rich, thick description to develop conceptual categories and to illustrate and support (or challenge) assumptions held at the beginning of the study (Merriam, 1988). This approach appeared to us to be an appropriate way to analyze and present data we collected relative to the teachers. We assumed, in particular, that our intervention would positively influence instructional practices and student learning, that the teachers would themselves come to understand the mathematics better and would effect deeper conceptual understanding on the part of their students. Most of the data we collected were qualitative in nature: seminar protocols, interview protocols, and classroom-observation data. This type of data is regarded as more likely than quantitative data to yield insight into changes that occur (Merriam, 1988). Some of our data were quantitative (a content understanding test given to the teachers; tests of fraction understanding and ability to reason proportionally given to students); but these data were used primarily to support the qualitative data analysis.

Our choice of composition of this case-study approach also deserves comment. Among written forms of multiple-case studies, there exist the possibilities of presenting cases (teachers, in this study) singly as individual case narratives or focusing on cross-case issues with information on individual cases dispersed throughout the chapters (Yin, 1984). The second format was very attractive to us because it allowed us more protection of the identities of the teachers involved in the study. However, this approach simply did not work for us. When we attempted to follow the second format, we felt that we lost too much of the information needed for interpretive analysis, and we found our-selves returning in our writing to a focus on the individual case narratives. We therefore decided on the individual case-study format. Individual case studies have been used successfully by other researchers interested in teacher change (or lack of it). These include, for example, the case studies by researchers at the National Center for the Study of Teacher Learning intended to document the effects of policy on elementary mathematics teaching (Ball, 1990; Cohen, 1990; Peterson, 1990; Wiemers, 1990; Wilson, 1990) and case studies by Schifter and Fosnot (1993) in their investigation of teacher change resulting from SummerMath.

Stake (1994) has said, "A case study is both the process of learning about the case and the product of our learning" (p. 237). Developing case studies of these teachers has been a long and fruitful process for us, and we hope that the product we provide here adequately portrays what we have learned.

Chapter 2

CONCEPTUAL FRAMEWORK

Eisenhart (1991) described a conceptual framework as follows:

> A conceptual framework is an argument including different points of view and culminating in a series of reasons for adopting some points—i.e., some ideas or concepts—and not others. The adopted ideas or concepts then serve as guides: to collecting data in a particular study, to ways in which the data from a particular study will be analyzed and explained, or both.

> Crucially, a conceptual framework is an argument that the concepts chosen for investigation or interpretation, and any anticipated relationships among them, will be appropriate and useful, given the research problem under investigation. Like theoretical frameworks, conceptual frameworks are based on previous research and literature, but conceptual frameworks are built from an array of current and possibly far-ranging sources. The framework may be based on different theories *and* various aspects of practitioner knowledge, depending on exactly what the researcher thinks (and can argue) will be relevant and important to address about a research problem, at a given point in time and given the state-of-the-art regarding the research problem. (p. 209)

The conceptual framework discussed here was developed to guide the long-term investigation into the research questions contained in the previous chapter. The first set of questions dealt with teacher change, the second set with subsequent student learning. This framework borrows from several theories and points of view, primarily those of researchers associated with the Rational Numbers and Quantities Working Group. Some of our sources are themselves frameworks for studying particular aspects of the research agenda we adopted. The manner in which they were intended to guide our work is discussed, and rationales for adopting some theories or frameworks and not others are offered. While the research evolved, so did the framework. A primary source of change was the reformulation of the content domain that resulted from presentations to the teachers by members of the Working Group. By attempting to define the content domain in terms of what teachers need to know, we expected the boundaries of that domain to change during the course of our work. This aspect of our work is in keeping with the notion of a conceptual framework: "Conceptual frameworks . . . should reflect the current state-of-affairs regarding a research problem. . . . [They] may have short shelf-lives; they may be revised or replaced as data or new ideas emerge" (Eisenhart, 1991, p. 210). It is also in keeping with the notion that research is fundamentally collaborative, with teachers sharing in the content analysis and the definitions of the domain of the knowledge they need in order to be effective.

TEACHERS' KNOWLEDGE OF THE MULTIPLICATIVE CONCEPTUAL FIELD

The *multiplicative conceptual field* (Vergnaud, 1983, 1988) consists of all problems and situations calling for the analysis or application of the interrelated concepts, procedures, and representations that encompass multiplication, division, fraction, ratio, rational numbers, linear functions, dimensional analysis, and vector spaces. One way to view knowing and learning in this conceptual field is to use an environmental metaphor such as Greeno (1991b) did in the context of the acquisition of number sense. Knowing the domain means knowing one's way around in that environment, including knowing what resources are available and how to find and use them. In the particular landscape we call the multiplicative conceptual field, the environment is complex and multidimensional. Numbers and operations are resources, and navigating the environment calls for reasoning that is at times multiplicative, at times quantitative, at times proportional, and at times some combination of the three. Greeno pointed out that this metaphor

> is quite suggestive regarding the role of a teacher. As learning is analogous to acquiring abilities of finding one's way around in an environment, teaching is analogous to the help that a resident of the environment can give to a newcomer. (p. 197)

A number of researchers, including the members of this working group, have been studying and continue to study various aspects of this conceptual field and the interrelatedness of these aspects. The individual aspects, however, have frequently received more attention than has their interrelatedness. Although this choice may reflect the current state of research in this field rather than signifying the status researchers accord the topic of interrelatedness, it also seems reasonable that a deep understanding of the various aspects is needed to understand fully the ways in which they relate to one another. This attention to components first and relatedness second seems particularly appropriate when considering what teachers need to know about the multiplicative conceptual field. In terms of the environmental metaphor, we might say that we must first have some knowledge of the resources before we can begin to analyze how they relate to one another.

In this study we restricted the multiplicative field to aspects of rational number, of the multiplicative operator, and of what it means to reason multiplicatively, quantitatively, and proportionally. After we consider these notions separately, we begin to explore some of the fundamental interconnections within the field.

Rational Number

Since it appeared in 1976, Kieren's early analysis of rational number in terms of subconstructs has been the backbone of most rational number research. Other researchers (e.g., Behr, Harel, Post, & Lesh, 1992, 1993; Behr, Lesh, Post, & Silver, 1983; Marshall, 1993; Ohlsson, 1988) have accepted or in some way extended Kieren's subconstructs in their own analyses. Recent work (Behr et al., 1993; Marshall, 1993) has focused on five subconstructs as exemplifying the concept of rational number: part-whole, measure, quotient, ratio, and operator. According to Kieren (1993), the different subconstructs need to be accounted for when designing problems that will allow a teacher or researcher to study children's cognitions of rational number.

In our own thinking about the subconstructs, we borrowed from several of these researchers. Marshall (1993) analyzed the subconstructs in terms of her schema theory, and in so doing provided a way of assessing different levels of understanding of each of the subconstructs. In order to clarify our references to her work, it is necessary to first take a brief detour to review her theory. We then consider each subconstruct separately by attempting to synthesize Marshall's work with that of many others.

For Marshall (Marshall, 1988, 1993; Marshall, Pribe, & Smith, 1987), knowledge of a domain is represented in memory as a large semantic network of nodes (features) and links (relationships) between nodes. The network can be decomposed into smaller (linked) networks, each of which might be considered a schema. The schemas can be decomposed into smaller networks, each containing a specific type of knowledge. When applied to instruction and assessment, schema theory provides assistance in choosing the appropriate level on which to focus:

> It clearly would be inappropriate to restrict teaching and testing to the maximum macro level—students would fail to develop the specific details needed to work within the domain. It is equally inappropriate to restrict teaching and testing to the maximum micro level [since this would] not facilitate the higher level connections necessary for building the broader domain knowledge understanding. (Marshall, 1993, p. 265)

Instruction focused on schemas as the organizing structures creates a cohesiveness that allows an entire schema, instead of individual, unconnected elements, to be retrieved from memory thus allowing access to all relevant schema knowledge in order to deal with a problem situation.

In her development of a schema-theoretic approach to a content domain, Marshall identified four types of knowledge associated with the application of a schema to a situation. *Feature knowledge* is general descriptive knowledge of the situation, containing examples and abstract characterizations of the situation. *Constraint knowledge* is the set of rules or conditions to be met before the schema can be applied to a situation. *Planning knowledge* is instantiated through the setting of goals to solve the problem, and includes making plans for implementing the schema and making inferences about its use. Finally, *execution knowledge* includes knowing the algorithms, rules, and procedures necessary for implementing the schema. Marshall now refers to feature knowledge and constraint knowledge as *identification knowledge* and *elaboration knowledge* respectively (S. Marshall, personal communication, October 25, 1994). The two latter terms are better descriptors of these kinds of knowledge and will be used here.

Marshall contended that most present assessment tasks measure execution knowledge only, and she focused on the other three kinds of knowledge in her discussion of the subconstructs. We in turn found identification knowledge and elaboration knowledge most useful in clarifying our own thinking about the identifying features and the elaborations associated with each of the subconstructs. In the ensuing discussion our delineations of identification and elaboration knowledge closely follow her delineations of feature and constraint knowledge (Marshall, 1993).

Rational Numbers as Parts of Wholes

The partitioning of a continuous quantity or a set of discrete objects into equal-size parts is, for most students, their first encounter with rational numbers. For many, it remains the strongest (Kerslake, 1986) and for some the only (Silver, 1981) type of situation they associate with rational numbers in the form of fractions. The act of partitioning is an intuitive thinking tool (Kieren, 1993) that leads many individuals, both children and adults, to treat almost all rational number problems as whole number partitioning problems (Mack, 1993).

According to Marshall (1993), identification knowledge of part-whole situations includes knowing visual representations of the manner in which we both symbolize the situation as $^a/_b$ and partition regions or sets, and also includes knowing the meanings of the a and the b appearing in the symbol. Elaboration knowledge includes understanding the nature of the whole and the manner in which it may be partitioned. This understanding differs from discrete to continuous cases; for example, in discrete cases equality of parts refers to the number of elements in a partition, whereas in continuous cases equality of parts refers to the size of the parts. Also, depending on the level of partitioning, the parts need not be equal. Marshall presented the example of Billy having three marbles, Troy four marbles, and Joe nine marbles. One could illustrate this situation as a partitioning into 16 parts, or as a partitioning into parts of sizes 3, 4, and 9, leading to fractional amounts of $^3/_{16}$, $^4/_{16}$, and $^9/_{16}$. Finally, elaboration knowledge includes knowing (in the case of a single unit) that the number of parts being considered can not be more than the number of parts into which something is partitioned. Elaboration knowledge in this interpretation of rational number is related to understanding the role of the unit: "The unit is the context that gives meaning to the represented quantity, but often it is implicit rather than explicit" (Hiebert & Behr, 1988, p. 3). According to Kieren (1995), moving away from a single-unit counting scheme to one in which whole numbers are seen as decomposable units marks a critical growth change in children's thinking. Moving from whole number to fractional situations calls for a shift from counting to measuring as a primary activity.

An additional element of elaboration knowledge identified by Mack (1995) as critical for the development of understanding addition and subtraction of fractions is that the more parts the whole is partitioned into, the smaller the parts become. This idea also leads to the ability to order unit fractions and to build on this understanding to order many nonunit fractions; that is, a student knows that $^9/_{10}$ is larger than $^8/_9$ because $^9/_{10}$ is $^1/_{10}$ away from 1, whereas $^8/_9$ is $^1/_9$ away from 1, and since $^1/_{10}$ is smaller than $^1/_9$, $^9/_{10}$ is closer to 1. This ability is essential to developing rational number sense (J. Sowder, 1995).

Rational Number as a Measure

By a measure we mean the number assigned to some measurable quantity. This notion of rational number occurs when we want to measure something but the unit of measure does not fit some whole number of times in the quantity to be measured. In such cases, the whole is partitioned into b parts, and a/b is used to measure a parts of size $1/b$. This interpretation of rational number demands that the rational number be understood as a number, as a quantity, as how *much* of something. "The focus here is on the arbitrary unit and its subdivision rather than on part-whole relationships" (Kieren, 1980, p. 136). Kerslake (1986) discovered that children (and some teachers) found it difficult to think of a fraction as a number, preferring instead to think of it either as two numbers or not as a number at all. Mack (1995) has argued that this understanding of a fraction as a quantity is critical for meaningfully adding and subtracting fractions.

Thinking of a fraction as a measure of quantity provides a foundation for reconfiguration of a unit. Iterating and combining subunits, for example, reconfiguring three ¼ units as one ¾ unit, allows one to view fractional numbers as amounts that are sums of other amounts (Kieren, 1995). Thus, to use Marshall's (1993) terminology, the identification knowledge in this case includes understanding how $1/b$ is being used repeatedly and cumulatively to determine the size of something.

Two other notions fundamental to understanding the additive nature of fractions (Mack, 1995) also flow from viewing rational number as a measure of a quantity. The first is that the measure of a quantity can be expressed in more than one way. Two ⅙s yield one 2/6; it is also one ⅓. (This understanding will also be developed through viewing fractions via a part-part-whole relationship and through understanding ratios as unit-rate fractions.) Dual representations of fractions as measures of quantity lead to the second fundamental notion: In order to combine quantities expressed as fractions, a common measure is needed (M. Behr, personal communication, September 30, 1994). So to combine one third and one half, one possible common measure would be one sixth: One ⅓ is two ⅙s, and one ½ is three ⅙s.

The primary component then of identification knowledge in this case includes understanding how $1/b$ is being used repeatedly to determine the measure of something. Elaboration includes understanding that a/b is but one way of naming a particular quantity. There is no constraint on a, indicating that a/b does not need to be less than 1. According to Marshall (1993), the main constraint here is the necessity for understanding that there must be a meaningful zero and that the intervals of the scale must be the same size. The constraint of a meaningful zero is a particularly serious one, requiring some knowledge of ratio scales.

Rational Numbers as (Indicated) Quotients

A fraction a/b can also represent the quotient $a \div b$; that is, a and b are integers satisfying the equation $a = bx$. A quotient denotes the relationship between two measure spaces: When five candy bars are fairly shared by two children, then each gets $5/2$ candy bars (Kieren, 1995). Kerslake (1986) found this interpretation of rational number to be unfamiliar and not readily accepted by students. Of all the inter- pretations of rational numbers, this is perhaps the most mathematical in that it is this interpretation that leads to the construction of rational numbers as a field. Kieren (1993) pointed out that the existence of rational numbers as quotients is guaranteed by the field property that each nonzero integer b has a multiplicative inverse, $1/b$ (or b^{-1}), which, it should be noted, is a unit fraction. Partitioning therefore plays a role in this interpretation of rational number, just as it did in the part-whole interpretation.

The identification knowledge required to understand rational numbers as quotients includes understanding that although a situation can again be symbolized as a/b, the a and the b probably represent different things (e.g., candy bars and children in the example above). The a represents something to be partitioned into b parts. One constraint in this situation is that the partitions must result in equal-sized parts (in the continuous case) or sets of equal cardinality (in the discrete case). If something is shared, it is to be shared equally. However, sharing equally can be done in different ways. In the problem above, each child might get two whole candy bars and an additional half bar, or might instead get five halves of candy bar. If the candy bars are different, the method of sharing might matter to the children.

Rational Number as an Operator

A rational number acting as an operator maps a set or region multipli- catively into another set or region (Kieren, 1980). Now a/b has an algebraic interpretation; it is a function that can operate on a continuous region as a stretcher or shrinker or on a set as a multiplier or divider, in either case serving as a "function machine" that operates on one value to form an output of another value. This interpretation is particularly valuable for studying multiplication of rational numbers, which can be viewed as a composition of functions (Behr et al., 1983). Fraction equivalence (and equivalence among different forms of a rational number, such as $3/5$, 0.6, and 60%) must be understood since there are many forms of an operator that will do the same thing as a/b. Iden- tification knowledge includes, in addition to an understanding of the role of equivalence, an understanding of the size transformation notion that underlies this construct of rational number. Elaboration knowledge includes knowing whether an operator interpretation is appropriate and whether, in a continuous situation, the relationship between the beginning and ending states is proportional in nature. Planning knowledge requires understanding of composition of functions (i.e., one operation followed by another), reversibility (the "undoing" of a stretch or shrink by applying the inverse operator), and, in the case of an operation on a continuous quantity, proportionality.

The Ratio Interpretation of a/b

A ratio occurs when two quantities are compared multiplicatively; it is usually expressed as an ordered pair (the ratio of boys to girls is 3 to 2, or ⅔) or as a relation between a quantity and a unit (if 2 pounds of nuts cost $9.00, resulting in a 9 to 2 ratio of cost to pounds, the nuts are said to be $4.50 per pound). A ratio is intensive by nature; that is, it is not measured or counted directly. No partitioning is involved. The ratio interpretation of a/b is quite different from the part-whole, quotient, and measure interpretations in which rational numbers are additive entities, extensive in nature.

The identification knowledge of this interpretation requires understanding the comparative relationship of a and b. Equivalence is involved: A ratio of 3 to 4 is equivalent to a ratio of 6 to 8. According to P. Thompson (1993), a constant ratio, reflectively abstracted, is a rate. This notion of rate gives prominence to the notion of the constancy of a comparison. Identification knowledge also includes knowing how to abstract a rate associated with a ratio and recognizing implications for proportions. Thus, if 12 pizzas are shared by 8 people, a rate of 3 pizzas per 2 people is implied; if 12 pizzas are shared by 8 people, each will get the same as if 6 pizzas are shared by 4 people. The symbolization of the proportion ¹²⁄₈ = ⁶⁄₄ is also a part of identification knowledge.

One important aspect of elaboration knowledge is that combining ratios results in a weighted average. This operation is sometimes confused with addition, which is defined for extensive quantities. Another aspect is that comparisons can be made in several different ways. If orange juice calls for 4 cups of water for each cup of concentrate, we could consider the ratio of water to concentrate, of concentrate to water, of water to total liquid, or of concentrate to total liquid. Finally, elaboration knowledge includes knowing that a ratio can be used also as a measure of an attribute, such as steepness of a ski slope (Simon & Blume, 1994). In such situations a ratio expresses a quantitative relationship between two quantities.

Forms of Rational Numbers

The common forms of rational numbers include fractions, decimal numbers, and percents. Understanding the symbolism used for each of these forms and understanding the relationships that exist among these forms are important components of rational number sense (J. Sowder, 1995). For example, in decimal numbers, it is important to realize that the one's unit, not the decimal point, is the focal point of the system. The decimal number 34.56 is *34 ones and 56 hundredths of one*. It is also 3,456 hundredths; it is 345.6 tenths; it is 3.456 tens.

Although all three forms of rational numbers are sources of difficulty in the curriculum, fractions are the most troublesome for students. Streefland (1991) described two sources of difficulty: "extreme underestimation of the complexity of this area of learning for children" and "the mechanistic approach to fractions, detaching it from reality and focusing on rigid application of rules" (p. 11). Much of the focus of instruction on rational numbers is therefore rightfully on fractions.

Knowing Rational Numbers

Teachers also need to understand how children come to know rational numbers in a more general sense. This more general knowing has been explored by Kieren (1993), who has characterized knowledge of rational number in terms of four kinds of knowing: *ethnomathematical, intuitive, technical-symbolic,* and *axiomatic-deductive* (see Figure 2.1), in which each kind is increasingly more sophisticated. One comes to possess ethno-mathematical knowledge through interacting with the environment. For example, children have shared continuous and discrete quantities and described such shares; they have seen measurements being made using fraction numbers. Kieren noted that they might even be able to place fractions on a ruler from having used one, although not being able to place fractions on a number line. Their language is not standard. Kieren used as an example a 7-year-old's description of a share of pizza as "a half and a bite."

Intuitive knowing "entails the use of thinking tools, imagery, and the informal use of fraction language" (Kieren, 1993, p. 68). A child who completes the task of determining pieces that form a whole pizza by choosing pieces from three pizzas divided into halves, quarters, and eighths uses the notions of dividing up equally and of equivalence, of carrying out an action, and of using language to describe that action. Technical-symbolic knowing, in which students work with only the symbolic expressions of fractional or rational numbers, is too often the only level focused on during schooling, with the result that students

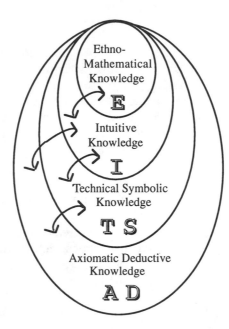

Figure 2.1. **Kinds of knowing.** Adapted from *Rational Numbers: An Integration of Research* (p. 67), by T. E. Kieren, 1993, Hillsdale, NJ: Erlbaum. Copyright 1993 by Erlbaum. Adapted with permission of the author.

have no way of connecting the symbols with meaning. The last level of knowing, axiomatic-deductive, is arrived at through deductive reasoning within an axiomatic system. Kieren claimed that each of these kinds of knowing successively embeds the previous kinds, and that therefore the outer kinds cannot be achieved independently of the inner ones. Instructionally, this model is useful in generating knowledge-building activities at different levels and for understanding students' actions on rational number problems.

Coming to know rational numbers at the ethnomathematical and intuitive levels should quite naturally lead students to develop rational number sense. Number sense, a well-organized conceptual network that enables a person to relate number and operation properties (J. Sowder, 1992), develops gradually through involvement in sense-making situations. An important characteristic of number sense is a disposition to make sense of number situations. Students are unlikely to develop such a disposition if their exposure to rational numbers takes place primarily at the technical-symbolic level. If students are provided with opportunities to explore rational numbers in a variety of situations that lead first to the development of ethnomathematical and intuitive knowledge, they will be more likely to develop the confidence necessary to seek sense in the problems they solve, and they will have developed a foundation for working with rational numbers in a technical-symbolic manner.

Kieren's approach to knowing fractions has similarities to that of Mack (1993, 1995), whose work has focused on the informal knowledge that students bring to the learning of fractions and the sense they are able to make of realistic examples presented to them in appropriate contexts. Mack claims that such experiences, particularly within part-whole situations, can provide a basis for developing a flexible concept of unit. Her work suggests that if initial instruction, based on partitioning and the part-whole notion of fraction, is carefully undertaken to exploit students' informal knowledge, then it may not be necessary or appropriate to address other rational number subconstructs until students are able to relate symbols and procedures to their informal knowledge.

Kieren's and Mack's approaches to coming to know and operate with fractions were predominant in our work with the teachers in this project. Kieren (1995), in his presentation on creating spaces for learning fractions, showed how the design of spaces could take into account the notions of fractions discussed here as subconstructs in terms of their different phenomenal bases. For example, for a child the phenomenon of measuring length in meters is different in character from measuring eggs in dozens. Mack (1995) considered the critical ideas involved in adding and subtracting fractions. Both emphasized the necessity of building on students' intuitive notions and creating environments that allow children to move between less and more sophisticated levels of activity while they are coming to understand fractions.

The Multiplication Operator

As discussed at the beginning of this chapter, the adopted ideas within a conceptual framework can serve as guides for a research study, but these ideas may be revised or replaced for a variety of reasons. In this study, we actually took a quite different route from the one we initially selected to consider multiplication and division, as shall become clear in the following discussion.

Multiplication and Division Situations

The analysis of multiplication and division we undertook with the teachers was based on presentations to the teachers by two members of the Working Group, L. Sowder and Harel. L. Sowder (1995) discussed all four operations in terms of their links to the real world through word problems and provided teachers with different types of real-world settings that lead to different ways of conceptualizing arithmetic operations. He described six types of multiplication situations: equal groups or amounts are put together (with a whole number as multiplier); a fractional part of a group or amount is described; multiplication is used to describe Cartesian product situations; multiplication is used to describe general rate situations; distinct quantities are compared (e.g., finding parts of similar geometric figures); and multiplication is used as part of a scientific relationship (e.g., find force, given mass and acceleration). In the second of the six types, mixed number multipliers are viewed as a combination of the equal-groups-or-amounts and the fractional-part-of-a-group-or-amount settings. A division situation is present when a group or an amount is shared equally (called the partitive model in our work with the teachers), when a group or an amount is put into groups or amounts of a particular size (called the quotitive model in our work), or when a missing factor needs to be found. (The third of these three division situations could be seen as containing the other two, mathematically speaking.) L. Sowder advocated treating these multiplication and division situations as links to operations, that is, as providing a way of finding operations appropriate to problems and thus coming to understand *when* a particular operation is appropriate. A student who can make the appropriate choice is operating at the highest of the seven levels of understanding L. Sowder (1988) described on the basis of his interviews with students solving story problems. At this level students choose the operation related to the situation; that is, they show relational understanding of the situation. All earlier levels described by Sowder (i.e., using whatever operation was being studied, random guessing, guessing on the basis of the size of the numbers, using key words, trying all operations then choosing the best answer, and choosing the operation on the basis of whether the answer should be larger or smaller than the numbers involved) could sometimes result in a correct answer when one operation was involved but could not successfully be used when more than one operation was called for by the situation.

Thinking Multiplicatively

Harel (1995) analyzed the "nonconservation of operation" phenomenon that occurs when individuals do not recognize that changing the numbers in a multiplication problem should not change the choice of the operation used to solve the problem. The conceptual conflict that can be associated with such problems (e.g., through teacher questioning) can lead the student to invent ways of thinking multiplicatively. Harel claimed that this phenomenon shows the harm in the common instructional practice of telling students to substitute "friendly" numbers for "nasty" numbers in a problem, solve the problem, then solve it the same way with the nasty numbers; that is, providing students with a ready-made *conservation formula*. Harel instead encouraged teachers to allow students to reach the point at which they could understand this formula, because in so doing they would probably have invented it for themselves. He claimed that prior to this point, use of the formula could cause harm to a student's mathematical development, particularly in the area of coming to reason multiplicatively. Harel's analysis was intended to lead to a better understanding of what multiplication is and what is involved in the transition from additive to multiplicative thinking.

Greeno's Analysis of the Multiplication Operator

Our initial analysis was one developed by Greeno (1991a). His framework for "thinking about semantic interpretations of rational number and the multiplication operator" (p. 1) was intended to be compatible with the earlier addition and subtraction schemas of quantitative combination, change, and comparison. The study by primary teachers of similar schemes for addition and subtraction has proved to be very successful in the Cognitively Guided Instruction project in terms of leading teachers to be able to recognize and evaluate the thinking of the students in their classrooms (Carpenter, Fennema, Peterson, Chiang, & Loef, 1989).

We did not actually introduce the teachers in our study to Greeno's analysis for two reasons. One was time; the analysis would be very new to teachers who had not already been made aware of the similar framework for addition and subtraction. The second reason was that the framework is theoretical in nature, and there are few data available on children actually analyzing problems according to the types described by Greeno. As we progressed in our work with the teachers, it quickly became apparent that when the mathematics being considered was linked to children's thinking, teachers took it more seriously and were more willing to grapple with it. We discuss Greeno's analysis here, however, because of its influence on our own thinking as we designed this project.

Although the analysis of the multiplication operator provided by Greeno did not guide us directly in our work with the teachers in the way we had first intended, we decided to include it here for two reasons. Its inclusion provides a clearer picture of ways in which a conceptual framework evolves over time in a long-term research study. The second, more compelling reason is that Greeno's analysis, developed for this working group, is attractive from the standpoint of following up on earlier analysis of the addition operator. A study using this analysis as a basis for examining children's thinking about multiplication and division could produce data and protocols that would make it more amenable to use with teachers.

Greeno proposed four general schemas for multiplicative quantitative relations. These schemas, called *replication and partition*, *multiplicative change, multiplicative comparison*, and *bidimensional transformation*, are intended to cover all semantic interpretations of situations involving multiplicative quantitative relations. The basic concept of multiplication, that is, the relation of three numbers such that the product of two of the numbers produces the third, is maintained throughout the schemas. The discussion that follows closely parallels Greeno's development of the four schemas and contains examples that originated with Greeno. When situations correspond to those described by L. Sowder (see the previous section on multiplication and division situations), they are so noted.

Replication and partition.   Greeno intended this first schema to be analogous to the additive schema of combination, that is, the joining and separating of sets or other measurable quantities. Simple replication covers situations in which there are n number of parts, with p amount in each part, giving a total of $w : n \times p = w$. In this instance, multiplication can be considered as iterative addition. (This would be L. Sowder's "equal groups are put together" situation, described earlier.)

Example: 5 bags of peaches ($n = 5$), 3 in each bag ($p = 3$).

So there are 15 peaches ($w = 15 = 5 \times 3$ or $3 + 3 + 3 + 3 + 3$).

(The numbers p and w need not be whole numbers, and usually will not be in texts at the middle grades.)

Suppose we change the focus to consider a whole being divided into a certain number of equal parts. We know w and either n or p. Depending on which we know, we are led to one of the two basic notions of division. If we know n but not p, we basically have a sharing problem: If w is 15 peaches and n is 5 bags, the bags must equally share the peaches: $15 \div 5 = 3 = p$. (L. Sowder called this a division situation in which an amount is shared equally.) If we know p but not n, we have an iterative subtraction or a *measuring out* problem: $15 - 3 - 3 - 3 - 3 - 3 = 0$; 3 has been subtracted 5 times: $15 \div 3 = 5$. (L. Sowder, too, called this a measurement division situation.)

Alternatively, we can think of 15 peaches equally shared by five bags as each bag having $\frac{1}{5}$ of the peaches, so there are $\frac{1}{5}$ of 15 peaches in a bag: $\frac{w}{n} = \frac{1}{n} \times w = p$. Here, the rational number r (with $r = \frac{1}{n}$) corresponds to partitioning the whole, w, into n parts. (This is an alternative way to look at sharing situations described earlier by L.

Sowder.) But suppose we are to ask, If 15 peaches are placed three in a bag, what part of the peaches is in each bag? Now we partition w into p parts to obtain $1/n$, that is, $1/n = p/w$. This kind of simple partition is frequently students' first encounter with rational numbers. (L. Sowder called this a fractional part of an amount.)

Greeno presented a more complicated version in which we replicate the unit fraction in our partition: w is partitioned into n equal parts and we take m of those parts to obtain an amount that has measure p, with $p = m/n \times w$. For example, we have 15 peaches ($w = 15$) put into five ($n = 5$) bags with an equal amount in each bag. If two of the bags ($m = 2$) are put into a picnic basket, how many peaches are in the picnic basket? Now $m/n = 2/5$; we want $2/5$ of 15, or 6 peaches ($p = 6$). A conceptually more difficult problem would be We have five bags of peaches ($n = 5$), and two of the bags ($m = 2$) are in the picnic basket. There are six peaches in the picnic basket. How many peaches are there in all? Now $w = n/m \times p$ that is, $5/2 \times 6 = 15$. Most children would not at first see this direct way of getting the answer, and would instead find the number of peaches in each bag, then multiply by 5: $5 \times (6 \div 2)$, which is equivalent to $5/2 \times 6$. (According to L. Sowder, 1995, they might say $2/5 w = 6$, so w is 15. L. Sowder called this a missing-factor situation.)

Greeno also showed how this type of partitioning could be used in a continuous situation: Suppose four people share two pizzas. Three of the people eat theirs. How much pizza was eaten? Now n (the number of equal parts) = 4, m (the number of parts we are considering) = 3, w (the total quantity) = 2, and p (the amount we are considering) = $m/n \times w$, or $3/4 \times 2 = 3/2$. Or we could say that four people each get an equal share of the two pizzas. After three of the people had eaten, $3/4$ of the two pizzas, or $3/2$ pizzas, had disappeared. How many pizzas were there to begin with? Now $w = p \times n/m$, or $3/2 \times 4/3 = 2$. Again, children would be more likely to solve this problem by partitioning $3/2$ into three parts, then taking $4 \times 1/2$, that is, $4 \times (3/2 \div 3)$.

Multiplicative change. In multiplicative change situations, something gets larger or smaller by a multiplicative factor. If b represents the measure of a quantity before a change and c represents the change factor or the measure of the quantitative change, then a is the measure of the quantity after the change: $c \times b = a$. Now c, the change factor, is the rational number a/b. In many multiplicative change problems, a/b is a stretcher or shrinker; that is, a/b is interpreted as an operator. (See the earlier section on fractions as operators.) For example, a photocopy machine might shrink originals to give images $3/4$ of the original size. If an original picture was 6 inches along one side, what would be the length of that side of the image? Now b is 6, c is ¾, and a is ¾ × 6 = 9/2. If the other edge is 8 inches on the image, what was it on the original? $b = a ÷ c$, or 8 ÷ ¾ is 10⅔. Multiplicative change situations clarify the role of the multiplicative inverse; if the image is ¾ of the original, then the original is 4/3 of the image, so $b = 1/c × a$. Situations involving multiplicative change are often students' first encounters with problems in which multiplication "makes smaller" and division "makes bigger."

Some authors have interpreted multiplicative change problems more narrowly than Greeno did. For example, Greer (1992) considered this problem to be a part-whole problem (as did L. Sowder, 1995): A college passed the top ⅗ of its students in an exam. If 80 students took the exam, how many passed? According to Greeno, this problem could be considered a replication-partition situation: $w = 80$, $n = 5$, $m = 3$, and $p = {}^{m}/_{n} × w = 48$. It could also be considered a change situation in which the quantity before the change is 80, the change factor is ⅗, and the quantity after the change is $a = c × b = ⅗ × 80$. "Many situations are easier to think about with one schema than the other, but many (if not all) situations that can be schematized with one can also be schematized with others" (Greeno, 1991a, p. 4).

Multiplicative comparison. In multiplicative comparison situations two quantities are compared in terms of a multiplicative factor (the ratio between the two quantities). For example, a father is twice the height of his son, or there are ⅔ as many apples as oranges. Comparison situations differ from the previous two types of situations in that there are only two quantities and a numerical relation between the measures of the quantities, whereas in replication-partition and change situations there are three quantities. Comparisons can be made between quantities with the same units, such as inches to inches, or between quantities with different units, such as the number of forks to the number of spoons. Ambiguities will exist between change and comparison situations, but just as in additive situations, change situations are dynamic, whereas comparison situations are static.

Bidimensional transformation. Greeno used this designation to refer to situations in which one quantity provides a transformation between two other quantities. Such situations can be represented as $y × t = z$, in which y and z are measures of extensive quantities and t is an intensive quantity that expresses a relationship between y and z. Familiar examples include rate situations such as speed, unit price, temperature, and density. (L. Sowder referred to these as general rate situations.) As we saw earlier, some situations can be considered within different schemas. A unit price problem such as How much will eight packages of cupcakes cost if the cost per package is 69¢? can be considered as a replication problem in which $n = 8$ and $p = 69¢$, with $w = n \times p = \$5.52$. One could also think of this as a comparison problem by saying that the price of the total is 0.69 times the number of packages. Finally, this could be considered a rate problem, in which the extensive quantities eight packages and \$5.52 are related by the intensive quantity 69¢ per package. In other situations, such as with density, speed, and temperature problems, the replication schema does not seem to fit. These situations seem to be harder to think about than situations that fit the replication model. For example, speed is a property of a moving object within some framework, and so is not replicated.

It might also seem that situations can be thought of as both comparisons and bidimensional transformations. Greeno presented the following example: The ratio of two eggs to five cups of flour in a recipe means that the number of eggs is ⅖ of the number of cups of flour. As noted earlier though, a rate can be thought of as a generalized ratio, so if we generalize this situation to one in which ⅖ egg per cup of flour is thought of as a property of all cakes with this ratio of eggs per cup of flour, the situation fits better into the bidimensional transformation schema.

Greer (1992) categorized this problem as a product-of-measures: "If a heater uses 3.3 kilowatts of electricity for 4.2 hours, how many kilowatt-hours is that?" In Greeno's analysis of this problem, 3.3 kilowatts is seen as the transforming quantity, converting number of hours into the number of kilowatt-hours; that is, the rate would be 3.3 kilowatt-hours per hour. Or the time of 4.2 hours could be considered the transforming quantity that converts kilowatts to kilowatt-hours; that is, time would function like a rate of 4.2 kilowatt-hours per kilowatt. In either case this problem and others like it, foot-pound problems, for example, fit as situations covered by the bidimensional schema.

Relating the Semantics of Rational Number and of the Multiplicative Operator

Greeno noted that rational numbers are either relations between measures of quantities or measures of relations between quantities. The earlier discussion of five interpretations of rational number dealt with this distinction to some extent. A fuller discussion of this distinction can provide a way of relating the different interpretations of rational number to L. Sowder's multiplication situations and to Greeno's four schemas of multiplicative quantitative relations.

First, when do rational numbers denote relations between measures? In a part-whole situation, a rational number $^m/_n$ is used to describe the relation between the part and the whole. Similarly, a ratio expresses the relation that results when two quantities (usually not a part and a whole) are compared. In a change situation, a rational number is used as an operator and denotes the relation between the prior state of some quantity and the final state of that quantity.

Rational numbers are used directly as measures of relationships between quantities in situations in which the number is assigned to some measurable quantity, such as length. If we say the length of a segment is ¾ inches, then the rational number ¾ indicates the measure of the relationship between the segment and a unit of 1 inch. A quotient, too, can be considered as a measure "after the fact." If four friends share three pizzas, each friend gets three fourths of a pizza, so ¾ is a measure of the pizza eaten by each friend, a measure of the relation of friends and pizzas.

Rates can also be considered as measures. Density is the assignment of a number to a quantitative property of a substance, and that number denotes the relationship between mass and volume. Speed, when generalized to indicate the measure of a property of a moving object, denotes the relationship between distance and time. However, these quantities are intensive, whereas length and amount of pizza eaten are extensive quantities. Schwartz (1988) pointed out that "it seems odd to refer to a relationship as a quantity" (p. 43) but that we do so because it is possible and because arithmetic operations can be carried out on these quantities.

Greeno suggested that one way to think of the relational issue is to consider the reference quantity in each situation, that is, the quantity to which the other quantities are referred. In replication and partition situations the reference quantity is the quantity we referred to as the whole. The rational number measures the multiplicative relation between the whole and the part of the whole. In change situations, the reference quantity is usually the beginning quantity, but could be the end quantity, and the rational number measures the relation between the two. In comparison situations, one of the two quantities serves as a reference quantity, and the measure of the other quantity is the second term of the ratio. Finally, when a rational number is the measure of a bidimensional transformation, the referenced quantity is the one following "per" in the name of the measure of the relation. The notion of referenced quantity is closely related to the notion of the unit. This relation needs to be explored more carefully, particularly in terms of instructional implications.

Postscript

Greeno's framework developed the semantics of the multiplicative operator and the semantics of rational number simultaneously. In fact, he considered the semantics of one to be the semantics of the other, because rationals are the numbers that multiplication works on. He noted that he had been influenced by a course he taught with Henkin, in which Henkin's formal approach to rational numbers did not assume integers. The two approaches have been contrasted by Lesh, Post, and Behr (1988), who said that the tradition of building rational number concepts in accordance with lower order whole number-based concepts, as followed by Vergnaud (1988), had its origins in the mathematics of ancient Greece, whereas other mathematicians, such as Schwartz (1988) and Kaput (Kaput, Luke, Poholsky, & Sayer, 1986), based their work on a mathematics of quantity as a way of linking rational number concepts to higher order topics. This second position is far more influential within this working group. Greeno's framework captured this thinking.

A Focus on Reasoning

Finding one's way around the multiplicative conceptual field calls for multiplicative reasoning, that is, reasoning in multiplicative situations. Additive reasoning plays a major role in the early grades, and children return to additive reasoning in multiplicative situations when they are not sure how to apply multiplicative reasoning. For example, if one candy bar weighs 4 ounces and another weighs 8½ ounces, children will sometimes say that the second bar weighs 2½ times as much as the first bar, thus combining multiplicative and additive reasoning in an incorrect fashion. In the literature there are many instances of children reasoning additively in multiplicative situations (Hart, 1984; Karplus, Pulos, & Stage, 1983; Noelting, 1980).

When children move from additive situations to multiplicative situations, they are forced to reevaluate, refine, and extend their earlier strategies, and sometimes to abandon them for new, more effective strategies. Both multiplicative quantitative situations and proportional situations offer special opportunities for the children to reason multiplicatively. (Proportional situations will necessarily also invite quantitative reasoning together with proportional reasoning, but quantitative situations need not be proportional in nature.) Understanding the reasoning involved in these situations can provide teachers with the knowledge they need to provide instruction that can build upon children's intuitive notions and can lead to productive mathematical thinking.

Quantitative Reasoning

Recent work on quantitative reasoning, most notably by P. Thompson (1993, 1994), has been influential in guiding the thinking of the San Diego researchers. In characterizing quantitative reasoning, Thompson (1994) first defined the terms *quantity*—the conception of a measurable quality of an object—and *quantitative operation*—the conception of a new quantity in relation to already conceived quantities. If, for instance, two quantities are compared additively, a difference is created, whereas if they are compared multiplicatively, a ratio is created. Thompson (1993) argued that when one reasons quantitatively, one analyzes a situation as a network of quantities and quantitative relationships. He further proposed (1995) that helping children *see* the world quantitatively is what leads them to understand the big ideas in mathematics and that seeing the world quantitatively means conceptualizing "aspects of objects as things to be *measured*" (p. 203). The comprehension of a situation as containing quantities and quantitative relationships is intrinsic to a quantitative operation. It is nonnumerical. To evaluate a quantity, one uses a numerical operation. Thompson argued that in simple situations it is sometimes difficult to distinguish between quantitative and numerical operations; however, the distinction is important in more complex situations. His analysis of the following example (1993) helps clarify these distinctions:

> Team 1 played a basketball game against Opponent 1. Team 2 played a basketball game against Opponent 2. The captains of Team 1 and Team 2 argued about which team won by more. The captain of Team 2 won the argument by 8 points. Team 1 scored 79 points. Opponent 1 scored 48 points. Team 2 scored 73 points. How many points did Opponent 2 score? (p. 208)

He explained that this problem was difficult for students because they did not distinguish among the numerical operation actually used to evaluate a quantity, the quantitative operation used to create the quantity, the kind of quantity being evaluated (in this case a difference), and the operation of subtraction used to evaluate the quantity.

A further example from P. Thompson (1995) illustrates that understanding "the relationship of part to whole as a two-way relationship is at the heart of understanding fractions" (p. 217). In this example, which Thompson used with the teachers in this project, he presented the following diagram:

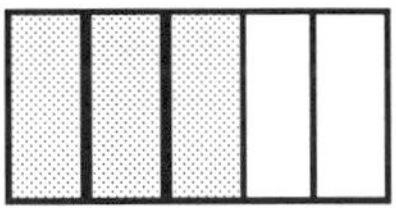

He then asked several questions: Can you see $\frac{3}{5}$ of something? Can you see $\frac{5}{3}$ of something? Can you see $\frac{5}{3}$ of $\frac{3}{5}$? Can you see $\frac{2}{3}$ of $\frac{3}{5}$? Can you see $1 \div \frac{3}{5}$? Can you see $\frac{3}{5} \div 2$? Can you see $\frac{5}{4} \div \frac{3}{4}$? He argued that this task required reasoning about objects and their measurements, that is, quantities and the relationships among these quantities. As with many complex quantitative reasoning situations, this task requires multiple identifications of quantity.

P. Thompson's conviction of the importance of addressing the distinction between numerical and quantitative operations at the elementary level echoes a concern expressed earlier by Kaput (1985): "The elementary mathematics of school should not be, as tacitly assumed, exclusively the mathematics of number with applications regarded as separate, but rather should begin with the mathematics of quantity, so that the mathematics and its 'applications' are a piece from the very beginning" (p. 13). Obviously, the numerical operations remain an important aspect of elementary school mathematics. There exists convincing documentation (e.g., L. Sowder, 1988) that too little attention has been given to developing meaning for numerical operations by coming to understand the situations calling for arithmetic operations. P. Thompson (1995) echoed this concern: "Before students can make sense of numbers and operations . . . they must first make sense of the settings themselves" (p. 217). Thompson and Kaput have extended Sowder's concerns by showing us that teachers need to be able to attend to both numerical and quantitative operations and that they must understand how the two types of operations are the same and how they are different before they can attend to both types during instruction.

Proportional Reasoning

Proportional reasoning is, according to Lesh et al. (1988), a pivotal concept that is both the capstone of elementary school mathematics and the cornerstone of what is to follow. Students reason proportionally when they are able to recognize and validate the type of relationship that is formed when two ratios are equivalent (Lamon, 1995). Lesh et al. claimed that the ability to reason proportionally develops over several years, with competence initially mastered on restricted classes of problems and gradually extended to larger classes of problems. It is well known that children's early encounters with problems involving proportionality almost invariably call forth an additive strategy.

> This strong preference for additive relationships among numbers produces a pattern of development for ratio reasoning that lacks the smooth character that seems to prevail for the development of addition and subtraction knowledge. . . . This means that school practice very likely plays a more definitive role in the development of ratio reasoning than in earlier mathematical development. (Resnick & Singer, 1993, p. 126)

When one considers the formalism with which proportion problems are traditionally introduced and taught and the lack of instruction that builds on intuitive knowledge of proportion, one wonders what could be achieved if instruction involving proportions were situated in familiar contexts.

In her recent research, Lamon (1991, 1993a, 1993b, 1995) has built on work by Steffe (on unitizing) and Freudenthal (on norming) to analyze children's thinking about proportional problems through consideration of a unitizing or norming process, that is, the construction of a reference unit and the reinterpretation of a situation in terms of that unit. She has claimed that ratios can be interpreted as the result of unitizing. For example (Lamon, 1993a), if we have a ratio of nine people to two cars, we can consider both 9 and 2 as composite units: Nine is 1 nine-unit, a unit of 9 one-units. Similarly, 2 is a single two-unit. A new unit, 9:2, is formed by relating the 9 and the 2. This new 9:2 unit can be used to create new, equivalent ratios.

> Unitizing and norming encompass some of the critical relation-
> ships we would like children to understand about ratios and
> explain their development in terms of a conceptual process that has
> been evolving since early childhood. Thus, they have the potential
> for suggesting an important mechanism for the growth of mathe-
> matical thinking as well as for providing some implications for
> content-related pedagogy. (Lamon, 1993a, pp. 137–138)

Lamon (1995) advocated looking for phenomena that "might compel the student to constitute the conceptual understandings required to mathematize a situation using a proportion" (p. 168) rather than beginning with the formal notion of ratio and then building up applications of proportions, and she further advocated beginning this process in the early grades, recognizing that proportional reasoning ability develops over a long period of time. In her work with the teachers on this project, she identified phenomena from many types of situations, and in so doing she highlighted critical mathematical components of proportional reasoning, including the ability to analyze change in both relative and absolute terms, the ability to recognize when situations call for ratios and when they do not, and the ability to understand that although the quantities composing a ratio may vary, the relationship between the quantities remains invariant. Her framework, together with her analyses of student thinking, offered the teachers in our investigations insight into the development of proportional reasoning.

Interrelations in the Multiplicative Conceptual Field

Although we have introduced the elements of the multiplicative conceptual field separately in the preceding sections, the very notion of a conceptual field implies that the concepts, schemas, and forms of reasoning are closely interrelated. It was our contention that these interrelationships would exhibit themselves during the ongoing content analysis with teachers participating in our investigations, particularly through the analysis of problem situations offered in our seminars.

The notion of a *situation* implies a multifaceted setting, and understanding a situation requires recognizing how its facets are related. An appropriate framework in which to consider studying the learning of the field is the one offered by situated cognition. Within this framework, individuals must be able to generate mathematical meaning and solutions of problems in the situations they encounter before their mathematical knowledge can be active and useful (Greeno, 1991b). These considerations lead us full circle to the starting point for this discussion: the physical metaphor of an environment to describe knowing the multiplicative conceptual field. Greeno claimed that this environmental metaphor fits well with the view that cognition is situated in contexts and that perception and reasoning are relations between the learners and the social and physical situations they are in. "In the environmental view, knowing a set of concepts is not equivalent to having representations of the concepts but rather involves abilities to find and use the concepts in constructive processes of reasoning" (Greeno, 1991b, p. 175).

A FRAMEWORK FOR
CASE STUDIES OF TEACHING

We were interested in investigating the interactions of teacher knowledge, teaching activities, and student learning, within the context of the multiplicative conceptual field, that is, within the contexts of rational number, the multiplicative operator, quantitative reasoning, multiplicative reasoning, and proportional reasoning. We focused these investigations on the teaching-learning process, using a case-study methodology coupled with intensive collaborative work with the teachers involved in the study.

Discussions of teacher knowledge often center on pedagogical content knowledge (Shulman, 1987); we prefer here to use Harel's (1993) extended analysis of the components of a teacher's knowledge base: mathematics content, epistemology, and pedagogy. *Knowledge of content* refers to the breadth and the depth of the mathematics knowledge the teachers possess. *Knowledge of epistemology* refers to teachers' beliefs and understandings of how their students learn mathematics. *Knowledge of pedagogy* refers to the ability of the teacher to relate knowledge of content and knowledge of epistemology, that is, to teach the content in accordance with their understandings of how students learn that content. For good teachers these types of knowledge develop as rich, integrated, easily accessible schemas about teaching (Livingston & Borko, 1990), schemas that summarize information about particular cases and their relationships, about students, content, and instruction.

We investigated the expansion of knowledge of content through our seminars with the teachers, the knowledge of epistemology and pedagogy through our interviews with teachers, and all three kinds of knowledge through classroom observations. We hypothesized that as teachers came to understand the multiplicative conceptual field as a rich network of interrelated schemas, as they themselves came to a deeper understanding of these schemas, as they came to understand the learning of these schemas as interdependent and developing over a long period of time, these content schemas would become part of their teaching schemas and would be reflected in observable changes in their teaching.

Our study of the development of effectiveness and expertise in teaching middle school mathematics should reflect our values (Brown, 1993; Silver, 1985). In the mathematics education community, those values have been most recently expressed in the *Professional Standards for Teaching Mathematics* (National Council of Teachers of Mathematics [NCTM], 1991). The section on standards for teaching mathematics covers four areas in which teachers make important decisions about their teaching: (a) the nature of mathematical tasks that are worthwhile addressing in the classroom, (b) the nature and tools of classroom discourse that will lead to the learning, (c) aspects of the classroom environment that enhance learning, and (d) the type of ongoing reflective analysis of instruction and of student learning needed to "ensure that every student is learning sound and significant mathematics and is developing a positive disposition toward mathematics" (p. 63). These standards focus on the major aspects of how the mathematics education community defines good mathematics teaching.

Leinhardt and Greeno (1986) characterized teaching as a complex cognitive skill requiring the construction of plans and the making of rapid on-line decisions. We view these two aspects of teaching, planning and decision making, as central to our investigations. Teacher planning influences opportunity to learn, content coverage, grouping for instruction, and the general focus of classroom processes (Clark & Peterson, 1986). Planning is reflected in the manner in which teachers implement the first, third, and fourth standards discussed above: in the "worthwhileness" of the tasks selected, in the type of climate that exists in the classroom, and in the reflective analysis of instruction and student learning. The on-line decision-making ability of a teacher is particularly reflected in the quality of classroom discourse, the focus of the second standard. Discourse affects the thought processes of students and thereby the nature of what is learned (Cazden, 1986). The metaphor of improvisation is a useful way to think about the interactive and responsive characteristics of discourse in the mathematics classroom (Livingston & Borko, 1990).

A. Thompson (1991) proposed a framework that describes a pattern of development in teachers' conceptions of mathematics teaching. The framework consists of three levels of development, each of which is characterized by conceptions of (a) what mathematics is, (b) what it means to learn mathematics, (c) what one teaches when teaching mathematics, (d) what the roles of the teacher and the students should be, and (e) what constitutes evidence of student knowledge and criteria for judging correctness, accuracy, or acceptability of mathematical results and conclusions. These conceptions are basic to mathematics teaching, and they afford us a lens through which to study teacher planning and decision making. In our investigations we did not intend to categorize teachers as being at a particular level. However, Thompson's descriptions of teacher conceptions at each of the three levels helped us to formulate instruments for measuring growth on the part of the teachers. The following is a brief paraphrase of her descriptions of teacher conceptions at each of the three levels.

Conceptions of teachers at the first level are "based on perceptions of common uses of arithmetic skills in daily situations" (A. Thompson, p. 9). The teachers therefore focus on the development of skills through repetition and memorization, as sequenced by the textbook. The role of the teacher is to demonstrate procedures, and the role of the student is to imitate and practice the procedures and to obtain correct answers. Ultimate authority lies in the teacher, the text, or both. Problem solving is perceived to mean working word problems using techniques such as key words rather than examining quantitative relationships in order to choose appropriate mathematical operations.

Teachers at the middle level of A. Thompson's framework have come to appreciate the role of understanding, even while continuing to perceive rules as "predetermined and as governing all work in mathematics" (p. 10). The teachers are beginning to understand the role of instructional representations in the learning process. They place a high value on manipulatives, but for affective more than for cognitive reasons. They view teaching for understanding as a matter of possessing a "collection of unique pedagogical techniques" (p. 11). They are beginning to appreciate some of the complexities of the mathematical content. Problem solving is perceived as important, but generally unrelated to the mainstream curriculum. Pedagogical decisions are frequently based on perceptions of what others say is desirable.

At the highest level, teachers go beyond teaching for understanding to viewing understanding as growing out of engaging in the processes of doing mathematics: specializing, conjecturing, generalizing. Tasks are carefully designed to allow exploration of ideas and student generation of procedures. Major long-term goals guiding and shaping instruction include the intention that students develop an understanding of the connectedness of mathematics, and the importance accorded various topics is based on the inherent centrality of mathematical ideas. The teacher's role is to pose questions that will stimulate, guide, and focus students' thinking in mathematically productive ways, to provide opportunities for students to express their ideas, to assess students' reasoning, and to shape instruction so that cognitive obstacles inherent in the mathematical ideas ultimately clarify rather than confuse.

> The hallmark of this level is the presence of cognitively based principles that are explicitly used to guide instructional decisions. Cognitive objectives of instruction are also explicitly used in selecting and designing instructional activities. Criteria for judging the soundness of instruction are stated in terms of student outcomes consistent with broad goals that drive instruction. (A. Thompson, 1991, p. 13)

Thompson noted that advancing to the third level requires a reconceptualization of fundamental ideas, restructuring conceptual schemas rather than expanding or broadening them. She hypothesized that the difficulties inherent in reconceptualizing one's teaching might be the reason so many teachers remain at the middle level.

CONCLUSION

Our framework has undergone a transition during the 2-year project. One way to describe this transition is to say that the final framework is closer to the Cognitively Guided Instruction (CGI) framework (Carpenter et al., 1989). In CGI, teachers are provided opportunities to come to understand mathematical content from the perspective of the student. This understanding, over time, becomes the basis for teachers' curriculum planning and assessment of understanding. In this project, the teachers' introduction to the mathematical content took place through the seminars with members of the Working Group. In reviewing the transcripts from these seminars and the papers prepared for the teachers, we noted that the presenters consistently used student work to help teachers understand the mathematics and to understand how students come to know the mathematics. One outcome, discussed in chapter 4, was that the teachers began to really listen to their students, which is also characteristic of CGI teachers.

The mission of the National Center for Research in Mathematical Sciences Education was to provide a research base for the reform movement in school mathematics. The framework for research outlined here focuses on teaching and learning number and quantity in the middle grades. This content is highly interrelated and is referred to here as the multiplicative conceptual field. Middle school teachers typically are not familiar with the content except at a rather superficial, disconnected, and symbolic level. They have not themselves had opportunities to explore this content through a careful analysis of individual aspects of the content, the relatedness of these topics, and the ways in which these topics and relations are learned. If we can provide such opportunities and document the resulting changes teachers make in their instruction and the effect these changes have on student learning, we will then be in a position to make recommendations to guide the reform of middle school mathematics.

Chapter 3

METHODOLOGY

In this section we first describe the planning year. We then describe our work with the project teachers: the selection process, the content knowledge assessment, the interviews, the observations, and the interactions with the teachers from the planning year. To provide the reader with an understanding of the mathematical content of the seminars, a long summary description is next provided. Summaries of our staff meetings and of the testing of students follow this description. Finally, we discuss issues of ethics and of validity.

THE PLANNING YEAR

In the year prior to the study described here, we worked with four teachers who were known to us because of their reputations as excellent teachers committed to the reform of school mathematics. They agreed to assist us in developing the project details and to serve in a pilot project. We held six 3-hour seminars with these teachers during which we focused on content understanding. The teachers completed a Content Knowledge Assessment instrument, and our long discussions with the teachers on the items on this instrument lead to the revision that we used the following year with the project teachers. We interviewed these pilot teachers, then discussed with them the interview format and the questions asked. We observed the teachers several times and discussed the observation instrument with them. Our work with these teachers helped us plan the activities and instruments for the project we describe here. Our pilot work with these four teachers led to several publications (Flores et al., 1995; Philipp et al., 1992; Philipp et al., 1994; Philipp, Sowder, & Flores, 1993; Philipp et al., 1995; Sowder et al., 1995). (Note: Alfinio Flores left San Diego after the pilot study; Barbara Armstrong joined us for the remainder of the project.)

PROJECT TEACHERS:
SELECTION AND DATA COLLECTION

Selection of Teachers

In the spring of 1991, we sent letters to local middle schools and local mathematics projects asking for names of potential teacher participants. The letter explained the purpose of the project and asked for teachers who were interested in changing the way they teach mathematics, but felt that they needed a better mathematical background to be successful in changing. We interviewed several prospective participants by phone and provided additional details on project participation: a required 2-year commitment, the approximate amount of time they would need to devote to the project, the administrative support required, and our need for access to their classrooms for observation and student testing. We asked for information on their backgrounds and the reasons for their interest, and some candidates were eliminated on the basis of the interview. We then visited classrooms of the remaining eight candidates, and all were told we were interested in having them join our project.

An introductory seminar with the group was held in June of 1991, and a 2-day workshop was held in the fall before classes began. We lost three of the eight teachers within the first few weeks. A Hispanic teacher was reassigned to an all Spanish-speaking class, so it was not possible for any of us to observe her. Another had been assigned to assist in several mathematics laboratories a day, but no longer was teaching a mathematics class that we could observe. Then an African American female who taught sixth grade was reassigned and no longer taught any mathematics. Of the remaining five teachers, one African American female taught sixth grade in an inner-city school, one female taught fifth grade in a middle-class neighborhood school, one female taught sixth grade in a rural school highly populated with Native American and Hispanic students, one male taught fifth grade in an inner-city school, and one male taught sixth-grade mathematics at a rural school with a diverse mix of ethnicities. Both inner-city schools were attended primarily by African American and Hispanic students, with a strong minority of Asian (many Thai and Vietnamese refugees) and Somalian students. Many of these students spoke little, and sometimes no, English.

Assessing the Content Knowledge of Teachers

At the beginning of the first year, the teachers completed a written content analysis instrument, a revision of the instrument used with the pilot teachers. A copy of the instrument is included in Appendix A. In addition to this assessment item, the results of which were used to plan several of the seminars, there was an ongoing assessment of the teachers' knowledge during seminars and during interviews of the teachers.

Interviews of Teachers

Each teacher was interviewed at length during the beginning weeks of the project. The 17 questions that guided these interviews are included in Appendix B. All interviews were transcribed, and results were used in our project planning and in our work with the individual teachers.

At the end of Year 1 the teachers were asked to reflect on the year's activities by responding orally or in writing to a set of questions. A selection of transcriptions of seminars was provided for them to read in order to aid the reflective process. This set of questions is provided in Appendix C.

During Year 2 the interviews focused on the classroom observations. As before, teachers were interviewed after we had observed in their classes. In some instances very lengthy interviews took place with one or more researchers and a teacher viewing videotapes of that teacher's classes. The final seminar was what might be called a "group interview." (See the section below on seminars.)

The interview transcriptions served as a rich source of data in our ongoing analysis of the teachers and was used to inform the writing of chapters 4 through 9 of this volume.

Observations

Each teacher was observed five or six times during the first year. Each observation was of an entire mathematics class, and was audiotaped. The faculty researcher who observed the class then completed an observation form (see Appendix D). Lengthy selections of the audiotapes were transcribed and appended to the form. Each observation was followed up with a brief interview with the teacher. The questions used to guide the interview are also in Appendix D.

Each teacher was observed teaching mathematics several times during the second project year, ranging from 6 to 15 times. The variability was primarily because we had selected some of the teachers for more extensive study. The number of observations was also somewhat dependent on whether or not the teachers were teaching content relevant to the project at times we could visit their classes and on whether we were informed when such content was to be taught. All classes were audiotaped; a few were videotaped. As before, teachers were interviewed after each lesson, and parts of the lesson were transcribed and attached to an observation form completed by the visiting researcher.

Interactions With Other Teachers

The teachers were encouraged to observe classes of the pilot-project teachers and of each other. Four of the five teachers took advantage of this opportunity during the first year and observed one or more classes of other teachers. One of the pilot-year teachers spent a day observing in classes of two of the project teachers. To encourage teachers to reflect on their observations of other teachers, we asked the observers to complete observation forms (included in Appendix E) and paid them small stipends for doing so.

SEMINARS

Overview of the Seminars

A brief summary of the seminars over the 2-year period is provided so that the readers will have some understanding of the mathematical content to which the teachers were exposed and how they responded to the content.

An introductory meeting in the spring of 1992 was intended to acquaint the teachers with one another and to give them an indication of what to expect from the seminars, and to give us an indication of what to expect from the teachers. During the session, the teachers were given an excerpt from a lesson on fractions (Borko et al., 1992). In the ensuing discussion, one teacher said

> Maybe I'm way off the wall, but I don't teach kids to flip numbers upside down. . . . So we review multiplying fractions. . . . Then I put up a problem with division. (The teacher wrote a division problem on the board and drew two large Xs through the fractions while reciting the following.) I say, "Follow these lines and multiply, and you got your answer. Just go "I hate math; I hate math. Boy! Do I really hate math!" (See chapter 8 for more detail.)

The other teachers responded positively to this method. They felt that teaching fractions was extremely difficult; any "gimmicks" would be useful. They indicated that they did not think it was possible to "teach fractions with understanding," and some also used Explorer calculators for multiplying and dividing fractions. They felt that students' demands for the answers prevented them from teaching conceptually.

Year 1. In the fall of 1992 we held 2 full-day seminars for the teachers. We began by discussing data on how children compare decimal numbers (from Resnick et al., 1989), then worked on place value with decimal numbers via the Blocks Microworld (P. Thompson, 1992). In the afternoon of the first day the teachers completed the Content Knowledge Assessment instrument. We made copies of the completed tests and discussed them among ourselves in terms of the areas on which we should focus our efforts. The tests were returned to the teachers unmarked, and the second day was devoted to discussing the items on that test. The teachers became very involved in considering their own responses and those of the others, then thinking about how their students would react to some of the items. Some of the items had been used with students (Armstrong & Larson, 1995), and the ways in which students thought about those items and solved them were discussed with the teachers. (When relevant, each teacher's work on this assessment is discussed in the individual case studies.)

For the remainder of the year, approximately half the seminars were presentation-focused—that is, a researcher prepared a presentation based on research with children. The presentations were informal, and there were questions and discussions throughout the presentations. When the presentations were made by visiting researchers from outside the university, a few additional teachers were invited, so that the audience was approximately a dozen. (The presentation-based seminars were substantially the same as the written versions of the presentations appearing in *Providing a Foundation for Teaching Mathematics in the Middle Grades* [J. Sowder & Schappelle, 1995] as chapters by Armstrong & Bezuk, Harel, Kieren, Lamon, Mack, J. Sowder, L. Sowder, and P. Thompson.) The remaining seminars focused on follow-up discussions of these presentations, on discussions on topics selected by the investigators on the bases of their knowledge of the teachers' content understanding, of results of tests and interviews of the students of the teachers, and of questions raised by the teachers. (A more detailed presentation of the teacher interactions and struggles to understand the content of these seminars is presented in chapter 4 and also in J. Sowder & Philipp, 1995.)

The first two seminars were intended to lead the teachers to see the value of sense-making as part of the enterprise of teaching. A presentation on rational number sense led to practice with mental computation and estimation and to examination of sense-making with operations and algorithms.

The next four seminars focused on developing the teacher's understanding of fractions and fraction operations. Presentations by Mack, Armstrong, Bezuk, and Kieren provided the teachers with research-based ways of presenting critical ideas about fractions and fraction operations. Examples of students' thinking and working with fractions challenged the teachers to think about their role in teaching fractions in meaningful ways. The fourth seminar was devoted to discussion of the results of the teachers' students' work on the Fraction Understanding Test (provided in Appendix F). The items tested for conceptual under-standing rather than algorithmic skill. The teachers were surprised and distressed with the results. Although they recognized that they were not responsible for the poor performance (the tests were administered after students had been in their classes for less than 2 months), they also realized that until this seminar they had little comprehension of what their students knew and did not know, thus making it difficult for them to base instruction on students' knowledge. (This seminar was summarized and analyzed in Armstrong, Philipp, & J. Sowder, 1993.)

A more holistic look at both whole number and rational number operations was the subject of the presentation "Addressing the Story-Problem Problem" by L. Sowder. He discussed the connections between the operations and the real-world applications, focusing on what elements in a situation lead to choosing the correct operation.

The next three seminars were informal; they focused on critical incidents in the teachers' own classrooms and on discussion of the previous presentations. The teachers compared ways that their own planning for instruction on fractions was changing.

In the two following seminars we turned to the topic of pro-portional reasoning; the discussion was based on a presentation by Lamon. Proportional reasoning as multiplicative reasoning was dis-cussed in some detail. These seminars led into Harel's presentation in which he outlined students' progress through additive reasoning into multiplicative reasoning. The final presentation of the year, by P. Thompson, focused on quantitative reasoning in both simple and complex situations.

For the closing seminar of the first year we chose several transcript excerpts from the seminars during which teachers had struggled with mathematical concepts and had finally come to a deep understanding of them. The teachers were given the assignment of reading excerpts and providing written reactions to them at a later date. To set the stage for this assignment, the investigators each earlier wrote reflections on the year's work and shared them with the teachers at this seminar. For the remainder of the seminar, the teachers talked informally about what they had learned and how they had changed over the course of the year. The conversations focused on the seminars, our classroom observations, their own planning and insights, and their classroom interactions with students.

Year 2. During Year 2, several of the topics introduced during the Year-1 seminars were revisited, sometimes through discussions of (sometimes videotaped) segments of the participating teachers' classroom rational number lessons that had been observed by the researchers and sometimes through revisiting the papers written by the presenters of Year 1. The first seminar of the year was devoted to eliciting individual teacher reflections, partly to determine ways to provide seminars of most benefit to the teachers at this stage in their participation in the project. Teachers spoke about their mathematical goals for the year, their mathematical expectations for their students for the year, their roles as teachers, perceived obstacles in teaching mathematics, the growth of students from additive to multiplicative reasoning, changes they were making or would like to make in their mathematics teaching, and what each hoped to gain from the project during the coming year.

In seminar discussions of observed teachers' classroom lessons (sometimes with videotaped segments presented), the importance of consistently relating the part to the unit was an issue in both the fractions and decimal lessons being discussed; all of the teachers recognized this as an issue in their own classrooms. Issues related to the use of models for rational numbers also arose in these seminars. Before one seminar, two researchers had visited the same teacher a few days apart; the second had the opportunity to see implemented the first's suggestion to incorporate proportional reasoning into a lesson. Describing this lesson sparked a discussion of teachable moments—awareness of situations in which opportunities to develop important ideas, in this case proportional reasoning, arise.

The one topic tested on the initial Content Knowledge Test but not addressed during Year 1 was that of weighted average in rate problems. This difficult topic was approached in Year 2 through the use of P. Thompson's *Over and Back* (1994) microworld.

Just as in Year 1, most of one seminar was devoted to discussion of students' fraction-understanding-test and interview results. The teachers appreciated the limitations of the pencil-and-paper instrument, even though it focused on conceptual learning, and the greater richness of the responses in interviews in which answers could be probed for reasoning and in which misinterpretations of the problems were evident.

During these Year-2 seminars, even more than in the Year-1 meetings, the teachers often raised questions or shared classroom experiences that led to extended discussions (e.g., Darota gave students a problem to do individually so that she could work on report cards, but the problem instead turned into an extended lesson on ratio). Issues about standardized tests and textbooks were raised repeatedly. The importance of the teachers' having deep understanding of the content, the big ideas within a topic, the connections among topics—instead of merely presenting interesting problems that are not necessarily part of a bigger, overall picture of rational numbers—was recognized by the teachers and was raised by them more than once during the Year-2 seminars.

Year 2 concluded with a seminar in which we, the researchers, explained that we would now be trying to tell what had been learned from this project, and the teachers were asked to reflect on their participation and to tell what had been learned from their points of view. The teachers spoke quite passionately about how much they had learned and about the need for all teachers to have more opportunities to focus on mathematics during professional development.

STAFF MEETINGS

The four researchers met a total of 15 times during the first year and 12 times during the second year for approximately 2 to 3 hours each time. The meetings were devoted to planning for the seminars, reporting on observations, analyzing information from teacher assessment and from teacher interviews, discussing the progress of individual teachers, and planning project reports and presentations. Extensive notes were kept for each meeting.

STUDENT LEARNING

Students in the participant teachers' classes were tested at the beginning and end of the first year, and again at the beginning and end of the second year of the study. The test items focused on rational numbers and on proportional reasoning. We felt that data on these two topics would be sufficient to give a valid indication of what students were learning from the teachers. Data from the first year were used to inform teachers about their students' understanding. The teachers found this information interesting and useful, and we reported on this discussion with the teachers in Armstrong et al. (1993). The test was refined, on the basis of the responses, and was administered at the beginning and end of the second year. Results of this pretesting and posttesting are discussed in chapter 10. Test items and student responses can be found in Tables 1 and 2 in chapter 10. The test appears in Appendix F.

ISSUES OF VALIDITY AND RELIABILITY

Validity is traditionally considered in two ways: *External validity* refers to the generalizability of research results; *internal validity* refers to the question of how well the research results match reality. External validity is a thorny issue in qualitative research (Eisenhart & Howe, 1992) and more particularly in case study research (Merriam, 1988) because of the difficulty, if not impossibility, of generalizing from one or few cases.

Cronbach, as early as 1975, said, "When we give proper weight to local conditions, any generalization is a working hypothesis, not a conclusion" (p. 125). Merriam (1988), drawing from several sources, suggested that the researcher can improve the generalizability of case study findings by providing thick descriptions that allow the reader to make judgments of generalizability, by describing what is typical in a case so that the reader can compare it with other cases, and by conducting cross-site or cross-case analysis when possible. In later chapters we attempt to provide rich and thick descriptions as far as is possible within the limits of protecting confidentiality. We are, of course, also concerned that we do not provide information beyond what is necessary in the interests of time and space limitations. We discuss our work with five teachers and attempt to make comparisons that establish typicality or clarify differences.

Merriam (1988) also provided suggestions for assuring internal validity for case study research. The most important of these is the use of triangulation—"using multiple investigators, multiple sources of data, or multiple methods to confirm emerging findings" (p. 169). As described above, we have gathered data on the five teachers in multiple ways: through interviews, group seminars, classroom observations, written responses and reflections, and pretesting and posttesting of their students. Classroom observations were undertaken by all four researchers; many times two researchers visited a class together; each teacher was visited by at least three different researchers. The researchers met on a regular basis to discuss and compare observations, conclusions, and questions, and to make decisions on next steps.

Other suggestions made by Merriam (1988) included member checks (taking data back to the participants) and long-term observation or repeated observations. Many times our data were shared and discussed with the teachers, singly or together, particularly student data, classroom observation data, and seminar transcripts. Our repeated observations and continued interactions with the teachers over 2 years proved invaluable in helping us formulate results we believe to be valid for the teachers in this study.

Reliability in case study research should not depend on the assumption that replication would yield the same results, because by definition the case study is multifaceted and contextual and therefore idiosyncratic by nature. Rather, reliability in case study research can be better thought of in terms of the consistency of results. Reliability can be achieved by clarification of the assumptions and theory behind a study, by careful description of the data collection and procedures used to analyze the data, and by multiple methods of data collection and analysis (Merriam, 1988). Thus, in case study research, reliability is closely aligned with internal validity, and attending to one is in effect attending to the other.

ADDRESSING ISSUES OF ETHICS

Ethical concerns have to be addressed in any research in which human subjects are involved, and it is for this reason that universities have institutional review boards charged with the responsibility of over-seeing that research undertaken by people affiliated with the university follows certain guidelines when the research is with humans. These guidelines, however, were designed primarily for quantitative research, and they need to be reconsidered when research is qualitative in nature. Qualitative researchers conceive of the research process, and conse-quently their role within that process, quite differently from more positivist-oriented researchers (Deyhle, Hess, & LeCompte, 1992). The relationships they form with participants can often be best described as friendships, with all of the shared interdependencies a friendship con-notes. The ethical problems that arise are both personal and professional in their nature (Soltis, 1990). Cassell (1982) has pointed out that in qualitative research, participants are more likely to be wronged than harmed and that merely obtaining informed consent is not sufficient to prevent the possibility of wronging participants.

In our case, it is this stage, the reporting of the research, that we find most problematic in terms of ethical issues involved. This concern has lead us to do a full review of issues of ethics (J. Sowder, 1998). There are two major issues we have undertaken to address in our reporting. The first is the issue of our interpretation of the data. We are fully aware that our own theoretical positions and biases have acted as a filter as we analyzed the data we collected. In this regard we have followed advice from Diener and Crandall (1979):

> There is simply no ethical alternative to being as nonbiased, accurate, and honest as is humanly possible in all phases of research. In planning, conducting, analyzing, and reporting his work the scientist should strive for accuracy, and whenever possible, methodological controls should be built in to help experimenters and assistants remain honest. Biases that cannot be controlled should be discussed in the written report. (p. 162)

The researchers undertaking this project share some basic assumptions about the teaching and learning of mathematics. Our notions about the curriculum and about teaching can best be described by saying that we are in strong agreement with the reform efforts in school mathematics represented primarily in the two *Standards* documents (NCTM, 1989, 1991). Three of us have been intimately involved with the Cognitively Guided Instruction project out of the University of Wisconsin (Carpenter et al., 1989), and the philosophy guiding that work describes views we all share of student learning, particularly learning that takes place in classroom settings.

The second major issue regards the preservation of confidentiality. In qualitative research, preserving anonymity during data collection is not possible, and so the preservation of confidentiality becomes paramount, albeit difficult. Our decisions in this regard are to use pseudonyms for the teachers, to describe schools only in terms of important specifics but without names provided, and to delay the publication of the manuscript until at least 2 years past the time we worked with these teachers. Certainly the teachers in the project will recognize themselves; this cannot be prevented. But we have attempted in all cases to write with sensitivity and respect for these teachers. In cases in which we had any concerns that our respect for these teachers might not show, we asked teachers both in San Diego and elsewhere to read and suggest alternate wording in order to minimize any harmful effects the case studies might have on the teachers.

We have tried to follow advice from Johnson (1982) in which he provided guidelines for writing about people: We have attempted to use nonjudgmental words, and to allow judgmental descriptions only when we find it necessary to do so. We have attempted to be as objective as possible in our descriptions. We have warned the participants that it is not easy to read about oneself as described by others. We have asked other teachers both in San Diego and elsewhere to undertake ethical "proofreading" of the case studies. We have sent the project teachers a letter informing them that the monograph is finished and that they are invited to read their own case studies, in the context of the other chapters, and to discuss the case study with the researchers afterward. This decision was based on the belief that a serious ethical dilemma occurs when researchers insist on sharing with participants information that they may not necessarily welcome. We strongly feel that the project teachers have all benefited from their work on this project, that we have afforded them opportunities to learn, have provided feedback when appropriate, and that reading this research monograph would probably not do them any harm, but neither would it provide them any additional insights or other benefits. Thus, although we have given them the option of reading it, we did not request that they do so.

We have attempted to be responsible and sensitive in our decisions regarding ethical issues. Diener and Crandall (1978) have nicely summarized what this effort entails:

> Ethical decisions are made by concerned and knowledgeable people who realize the value implications of their choices. The ethical researcher is concerned about the well-being of research participants and about the future uses of the knowledge, and he accepts personal responsibility for decisions bearing on them. The basic ethical imperatives are that the scientist be concerned about the welfare of subjects, be knowledgeable about issues of ethics and values, take these into account when making research decisions, and accept responsibility for his decisions and actions. (p. 215)

Chapter 4

RESULTS: EFFECTS OF SEMINARS
ON TEACHERS' KNOWLEDGE

In chapter 3 we briefly described the seminars we held with the teachers over a 2-year period. In this chapter we wish to describe the mathematical growth of the teachers during this period, as indicated by their interactions and responses during the seminars. We describe this growth by focusing on just a few topics, and we provide and discuss some seminar excerpts dealing with these topics over a time period that allows for examination of changing attitudes and conceptual under-standing. Our first focus topic is the mathematical operation of division. Two major areas of division were considered several times during the seminars—division of fractions and division of whole numbers with remainders. Our second focus topic is proportional reasoning. We conclude this chapter with a description of how teachers themselves relate the seminars to their instruction.

TRACING THE DEVELOPMENT OF
UNDERSTANDING OF DIVISION OF FRACTIONS

In May of 1993, before officially beginning the project, we visited each of the classrooms of the teachers and interviewed them about their views on teaching mathematics. When each was asked to describe a recent lesson he or she thought to be exemplary, one of the teachers described a lesson on the division of fractions. This description served as a spring-board for a discussion the following month at an introductory seminar designed to introduce the teachers to one another and to the project. Tom was asked to show the group how he taught division of fractions, and the ensuing discussion follows. (Note: All of the author-investigators are designated as Inv. in transcripts of seminars.)

Tom: Maybe I'm way off the wall, but I don't teach kids to flip numbers upside down. I tell them what a reciprocal is. I say, "The reciprocal [is] the two numbers you multiply and it comes out to 1." So we review multiplying fractions. . . . Then I put up a problem with division. . . . I say, "You know, a lot of people will tell you to turn this [second fraction], turn it upside down, but it's gonna confuse the heck out of you because when you see it on a piece of paper, you're gonna say, 'Which one do I turn over?'" I could say, "Some of you can remember it if you say, 'Flip it good; flip the right one good.'" Or I could say, "Follow these lines and multiply, and you got your answer. Just go 'I hate math (Line 1); I hate math (Line 2). Boy! Do I really hate math! (Lines 3 and 4).'"

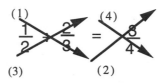

Inv: But what if a student says, "But why is that division?"

Tom: Well, I say, "Well, look, we multiply. What's the opposite of multiply? Divide. . . . You know, if this is multiply, we have to do something different. So what's the only way different? You can't multiply these two numbers. You have to multiply the other numbers." So I kinda explain, I say, you know, "opposites." I tell them, "You know, this reciprocal thing is ridiculous because you're gonna get confused.". . .

Cynthia: Well, why do you go straight across when you multiply?

Tom: It's easy that way. So when you teach them to multiply, you say, "Okay, it's easy to go straight across, because you got this nice line."

Inv: I'd like to ask the others, "What do you think of Tom's approach?"

Sharon: I'd have Explorer calculators, and that's how I'd take care of it.

Cynthia: To tell you the truth, I wouldn't really be able to—it was my student teacher who was teaching this at the end of the year, and one of my students said, "Why do you flip it, and why are we multiplying? This is division." And she says, "Because I just told you to do it." And I sat there and thought, "Boy that was a wonderful question, and that was a very common answer—'because I told you to do it.'" And I don't know how I would—you know, I would have to really sit down and think about it to give more concrete examples.

Linda: To me this [Tom's method] looks like another, almost like another algorithm, just like saying, "Flip the number"—this is, to me, the same thing. You have to remember where to put the Xs. That works. I would teach that.

Cynthia: Kids love gimmicks.

Linda: Yeah. Kids would love that. The kids would really like that, and I could see teaching that.

The excerpt vividly shows the thinking of the teachers, particularly Tom, to be procedurally oriented at the beginning of the project. There are several points of interest here. Tom was a very popular teacher in his school, and his comments here give some indication of why he was popular. He tried very hard to make mathematics as easy as possible for his students by teaching them procedures he thought they would find easy to remember. Moreover, he catered to the "gimmicky" approach that can be so attractive to students at this age level (sixth grade). Other teachers at this grade level recognized that their students also liked gimmicks, and the "I hate math" expression, coming from a math teacher, was just such a gimmick, however much the researchers in the group silently shuddered at this ploy.

Although the researchers pushed Tom to explain why his procedure worked, the teachers, even though one stated that this was "like another algorithm" did not seem to feel any need to understand the process—it worked, and that was enough. Only Sharon seemed to feel that her solution to dividing fractions might be better, that is, allowing students to use the Explorer calculator (on which operations on fractions can be performed). She did not indicate that she found it necessary for students to understand division of fractions; rather, they simply needed to know some way of finding the quotient.

The next excerpt is from a seminar the following January. We had met eight times since the introductory seminar, and division of fractions had come up, at least briefly, in some of these seminars. For example, in December Larry Sowder's presentation included a description of how each operation could be taught meaningfully. The teachers were exposed, probably not for the first time, to the partitive or sharing interpretation in which the question asked is "How many does each one get?" and to the quotitive or measurement or repeated-subtraction interpretation in which the question asked is "How many of these are in here?"

The following excerpt marks the first time we dealt in depth with division of fractions. The discussion began with a researcher's description of a preservice teacher who had struggled with the idea of referent units in terms of multiplication and division of fractions. She would use drawings to show $3/4 \div 1/2 = 1\frac{1}{2}$. (In this case the $3/4$ refers to a unit; the $1/2$ refers to the same unit. The referent for the $1\frac{1}{2}$ is the $1/2$.) After carefully and repeatedly working through the referents for the operands and results, she felt that she really understood multiplication and division of fractions. But she expressed anger that she had not learned these concepts while in school. The researcher followed the description with a question:

Inv: An interesting question we seldom ask is "What's the difference between the units, (that is) the referents for the operands, in $3/4 \times 1/2$ and $3/4 \div 1/2$?"

Cynthia: I don't think that I ever have thought about this because I'm sitting here. . . .

Inv: Well, if you take $3/4 \times 1/2$ . . . .

Cynthia: I understand that.

Inv: Then what are the referents? What does the $3/4$ refer to? What does the $1/2$ refer to?

Cynthia: Yeah. Exactly. What do they refer to?

Inv: Let's talk about what that means.

Tom: I would put $3/4 \times 1$; $3/4 \times 2$.

Inv: You might, yes. But at some point students should be able to do this and know what it means. So what would you expect, after you've done that kind of teaching, that they would understand this [$3/4 \times 1/2$] to mean?

Linda: You mean like $3/4$ of one half of a whole.

Inv: Yes. If you wanted to draw a picture of this, where would you start?

We drew a diagram to represent $3/4$ of $1/2$, and showed why the answer was $3/8$. We then talked about the referents: The $3/4$ refers to the $1/2$; the $1/2$ refers to some whole; the product, $3/8$, refers to the same whole, or unit.

Tom: You always have to reference back to the unit.

Inv: Does this one [quotient of $3/4 \div 1/2$] reference back to the unit?

Cynthia: Okay, now that's the one I want you to do. Give me the manipulations for this one.

Inv: You can see why this is confusing. Why is it that this answer [product resulting from $3/4 \times 1/2$] refers back to the whole unit and this answer [$1\frac{1}{2}$, the quotient resulting from $3/4 \div 1/2$] doesn't? [$3/4$ of a circle is shown on the board; $1/2$ in the $3/4$ is shaded. Below is written $3/4 \div 1/2 = 1\frac{1}{2}$.]

Tom: But I think it does refer back to the unit.

Inv: This [quotient]?

Tom: Yeah, because you've gotta say this means one half of the unit. We want to know how many of these halfs . . . I would go through the groups of whatever . . . I would say, "Here's a colored piece of paper. This is 1 three fourth. Here's a half, different color. How many of these would fit in here?" I would say, "Refer always back to the 1, the unit."

Darota: No, because the unit is. . . . You don't refer. . . .

Inv: If you look at a drawing, you don't see one and one half of a unit at the end. That's what's confusing.

Tom: What's really confusing is if you try to explain this in pizza: How can you have a three-fourths of a pizza, divide it in half, and get 1½ pizzas?

Darota: Because you're not giving a whole pizza. You're giving halfs of pizzas—1½ halfs.

Inv: When you divide into a half, you're really dividing by two.

Tom: So is this how Jesus fed the multitudes?

Inv: So what does the answer refer back to? It's very difficult to apply these to word problems. . . . Cynthia, are you comfortable or not?

The remaining part of this excerpt deals with Cynthia's confusion. Although the other teachers allowed Cynthia to have the floor, they too were struggling with these notions, as they later told us. But now we return to Cynthia, who was very persistent in her questions. She recognizes here not only that she has been teaching division of fractions without understanding it, but also that it *can* be understood.

Cynthia: No, I'm not. I'll be real honest. I'm not comfortable. And I can see where my students wouldn't be comfortable because it's the complete opposite of whole numbers.

Inv: Okay, let's look at the ¾ ÷ ½.

Cynthia: Yes, thank you.

Inv: I'm asking the question How many halves are in three fourths? So to ask that question means I have to start off with three fourths, to look at the number of halves in it. [Draws a square with three fourths shaded.] My question is How many halves are shaded? How many halves are in that part? What's here is one of the basic meanings of division—that when you're dividing, you're asking a question: How many of these [halves] are there in here [three fourths]?

Cynthia: See I haven't dealt with that. To be able to even explain that to them, I was just sitting here going. . . . It makes sense now. But I can see that, to a child, I think that they would look at one whole and one half and wonder. . . .

Inv: I wouldn't even show them this notation at the beginning. After they've shaded in three fourths, ask, "How many halves do you have shaded here?" It's like Tom's example of the pizza. You have three fourths of a pizza. How many halves of a pizza do you have in that three fourths?

Tom: I guess another approach would be measuring cups. If you had two measuring cups—one was three fourths of a cup and one was a half cup. If the ¾ was full, how many times am I going to be able to pour the ¾ into the half? One and a half times.

Cynthia: This is probably the most clearest [*sic*] thing that I've seen (Laughs). It is; it's very clear. This is something that's always confused me. Here *I* am.

Inv: Then you could say, "The way the mathematicians symbolize this is. . . ." I would never introduce those symbols until they had the concept down.

Cynthia: I agree with that because they're gonna relate this [¾ ÷ ½] to division and think it gets smaller: I'm gonna do three fourths and I'm gonna put it into a half; I'm gonna cut it in half. So if you have three fourths and you cut it into half, it would be smaller.

Inv: Then you would be getting half of three fourths; now that's multiplication.

Cynthia: Okay. Thank you. I've never received that information before.

Inv: That's exactly what the preservice teacher was saying. She never learned it before. And many teachers never have.

Cynthia: Yeah, and now I'm angry. No one explained it to me. . . . I guess the thing that bothers me was that I was the low-end kid when I got into high school, and I think it was because I was lacking in the experience of connecting it. . . . I wasn't the strongest student, but I think that . . . I really am beginning to believe that I needed the pictures; I needed the hands on; I needed the things that I could relate to.

Even when Cynthia thought she understood—was sure she did—she stumbled and confused division of fractions with multiplication of fractions. This understanding was still fragile and in need of reinforcement.

Cynthia, too, was angry that she was encountering these ideas for the first time. She had had difficulties in mathematics while in school and now began to believe that the reason for her difficulties was that her teachers had not focused on understanding. During subsequent observations in Cynthia's class, we saw her focus more and more on helping students understand procedures.

Although the other teachers did not say much during this episode, the few comments here, and comments made later in this seminar and in the following one, indicate a receptivity to the idea that it is important for teachers to understand the procedures that they teach; indeed, they should be teaching their students to understand what it means to multiply and to divide fractions. Even Tom, who had earlier claimed his "I hate math" method as an exemplary way to teach division of fractions, provided here an example that helped Cynthia understand. (Tom did, by the way, state in the following seminar that he had thrown his old method for teaching division of fractions "out the window.")

Our teachers appreciated our discussion on division of fractions. The reader might assume that we consider fraction division to be more important than many other topics covered in the middle school curriculum. We do not. We chose this topic for two reasons. First, most middle school mathematics teachers are expected to teach this topic to their students, so they are interested in reconsidering it. Second, division of fractions lies at the intersection of two mathematical concepts that many teachers never have had the opportunity to learn conceptually— division and fractions. When teachers begin to realize that division of fractions *can* make sense, they become very excited, and this excitement is sometimes followed by anger that their own instruction did not help them make sense of dividing fractions.

Division of Whole Numbers With Remainders

There exists a rich literature (e.g., Silver, Shapiro, & Deutsch, 1993) on children's difficulties with interpreting remainders when dealing with division. Our first excerpt shows that this difficulty also exists for teachers. The following excerpt was from a seminar in September of the first year. The entire 3-hour seminar was devoted to issues surrounding division—division by zero, student solutions to word problems involving division, the long-division algorithm, and the meaning of remainders in division. We noted several difficulties the teachers had with these issues. The excerpt below begins with a teacher's description of a student who, instead of writing the whole number remainders for division problems, wrote the fraction but still used R for remainder with the fraction (e.g., $37 \div 5 = 7 R \frac{2}{5}$). Tom is confused about the correctness of this student's work.

Tom: I was forcing kids to doublecheck their answers. I told [the student] that when he doublechecked his answer, "You get your answer; you multiply by the divisor and add back your remainder. So if you do that, you would get 35 and $\frac{2}{5}$. So if I ask you for a remainder, don't tell me 'remainder $\frac{2}{5}$' even though it's right." It was kind of hard to explain to him that he had the right answer and if he had multiplied both numbers by the divisor he would get the right answer.

Inv: Are those two the same: 7 remainder 2 and 7 remainder $\frac{2}{5}$? . . . For $35\frac{1}{2} \div 5$ is 7 remainder $\frac{1}{2}$ correct?

Tom: Yes.

Linda: But that's not the remainder.

Tom: But the thought process is. . . .

Inv: Let's talk about the difference between 7 remainder 5, 7 remainder $\frac{2}{5}$, and $7\frac{2}{5}$ and what they all mean. Could they all be correct or not?

Tom: $37 \div 5 = 7\frac{2}{5}$. Wouldn't that be the same as 7 remainder $\frac{2}{5}$?

Inv: Is it? $7\frac{2}{5}$ is a number. It is a quantity. It is the answer. If you say 7 remainder $\frac{2}{5}$, then does it mean the same thing? If I parceled out 5 groups of 7 and had 2 left, do I divide the 2 up and share them? If I do, the answer is $7\frac{2}{5}$. Or do I just put the two aside and not consider them a part of the sharing situation? Then it's 7 remainder 2.

Tom: But the real answer, the correct answer would be 7 and $\frac{2}{5}$ of 5 because that would be 2. In other words if you had a 5-unit candy bar. . . . This is the first time a student came up to me and said I did this. I had to think about it first. It was hard because I see the reasoning, but you shouldn't have it as a remainder. It was tempting to say, "You're right. Okay, I'll let you go."

Darota: This was a real confusing thing for me when I first started teaching division and we got to remainders. When I moved from elementary school to middle school, our teacher said that *Remainder 5* was for babies. We should always use fractions or put the decimal point and divide it out. So when I had a class and they wrote the *R*, I'd say, "You're babies." So I started having to really think about this and what it means, and it still—because the book gives the answer *Remainder 5*, and then when we get into a word problem where we need the remainder to be expressed in another way, it is hard for students to understand. The book doesn't give enough examples for you to be able to determine what's the most appropriate way to write the remainder and what does it mean in the context. Thinking about that now, I'm going to approach it a lot differently.

Tom's confusion about remainders was shared by the other teachers, as continued discussion during the seminar showed. Darota's comment indicated that she was, for the first time, beginning to think through the implications of division remainders. The difficulties teachers encountered during this seminar were noted again when we reviewed the entire seminar transcripts during planning for the Year-2 seminars. We decided that this topic deserved a return, and we presented the following problem again a year after the above excerpt.

> For 37 ÷ 5, make up a word problem for which the answer is 7;
> for which the answer is 8;
> for which the answer is 2;
> for which the answer is 7⅖;
> for which the answer is 7.4;
> for which the answer is 7 remainder 2.

When we enter the discussion, a situation is being sought that would appropriately yield the answer 7⅖.

Cynthia: Something with a pie that you're dividing up. How much pie would we eat altogether? If you can serve 5 people from one pie and there are 37 people in the class, how much pie will we need?

Shey: There are 37 inches of ribbon. We need five bows. How long could each bow be? It's still not a good problem because you wouldn't have a bow that's 7⅖ inches long. It's not long enough to make a bow.

Darota: If the idea was to get the fullest skirt, and we have 37 yards of material, what's the most material each person could use for a skirt?

Inv: Why is it that the earlier problem situations involving kids aren't working for 7⅖?

Darota: You can't cut kids in half.

Shey: You can't have ⅖ of a person.

We next discussed situations for which the answer would most appropriately be written as 7.4, then problems for which the answer would be stated as 7, *remainder* 2. Even though for students this is perhaps the most commonly given answer to 37 ÷ 5, the teachers found that it is the most difficult to interpret within a context. It is in this portion of the discussion that we also return to the problem from the earlier seminar.

Inv: So when is the answer 7 remainder 2?

Shey: It would be like the bus problem, 37 kids and 5 buses—7 remainder 2—How many are left over?

Inv: But then wouldn't the answer be just 2?

Cynthia: But when you're talking about division, that's the most common answer you'll get—7 remainder 2. You hear that more often, 'cause that's how we taught kids to say it.

Shey: Unless you're using a calculator. Maybe it's not as common now that kids have calculators.

Inv: What's the difference between 7⅖ and 7 remainder 2? I'll put it in context. We have 37 cookies. We're going to share them among five girls. You could say the answer is 7 remainder 2 or 7⅖. What would be the difference?

Darota: In the ⅖, you're going to take what's left over and split it up among all the girls. When you have *remainder* 2, that means those two you're just going to leave for the teacher.

Inv: So in the case of 7⅖, tell me what the 7 means.

Shey: In that case it means that five is your thing that you're trying to distribute the 37 into. That's the number of pieces. And you can do that seven times.

Inv: Are those two [in the remainder] being distributed or not?

Shey: They're not being distributed in the first case [7 remainder 2]. Whereas in the other one, they are.

Inv: So in the second case, this 7 and the ⅖, it sounds like they. . . .

Cynthia: Everybody gets 7⅖.

Tom: If you've put up 37 ÷ 5, and your answer's 7.4, what's the difference between that and 7⅖?

Darota: There's no difference.

Tom: So these two [7⅖ and 7.4] are a lot different than the other one [7 remainder 2].

Inv: Tom, do you remember last year when we discussed this? We talked about whether the answer to 37 ÷ 5 could be written as 7 remainder ⅖.

Tom: But ⅖ is part of the quotient. It's not the remainder. If we say 7 remainder ⅖, then each person got 7 cookies, and there was ⅖ of a cookie left. But there are 2 cookies left. Why? What did I say before?

The teachers have now distinguished clearly between 7⅖ and 7 remainder 2 as answers to 37 ÷ 5, and they realize that 7 remainder ⅖ is not an answer to 37 ÷ 5. Although this excerpt shows progress compared to the confusion shown a year earlier, there is still much to be understood, as further selections from the seminar show. The conversation turned to the interpretations of division. Two interpretations had been discussed in several previous seminars. A problem with a partitive, or sharing, interpretation would be one such as 12 candies being shared by three children, with the question being the number of candies each child received. A problem with a measurement, or repeated subtraction, interpretation would be one such as 12 candies shared so that each person received 3 candies, with the question being the number of children receiving candies (i.e., How many times can 3 be subtracted from 12?). The new element in what follows is now the meaning of the remainder in the two types of situations.

Inv: When you think about the interpretations of division, measurement and partitive, which is this? Thirty-seven cookies shared among five?

Cynthia: That's partitive.

Linda: Yeah. The other would be 37 cookies, give 5 to each student.

Shey: How many students can get 5 cookies?

Inv: Now there really is a remainder 2, isn't there? Can the answer be 7⅖ now?

Linda: No, because that would mean you have 7⅖ people.

Inv: Does 7 *remainder* 2 make some sense now?

Darota: Yes. You know, I really appreciate the insight you have given me on measurement and partitive division. It's something I really didn't think about before. But it's so important.

Inv: Suppose we go back to the bows. Let's say they are going to be 5 inches long each, what do the two numbers mean—the *remainder* 2 and the 7 in that problem?

Shey: The number of bows you make is the 7. And the remainder is how much is excess.

The final segment of this seminar transcript deals with the referent units for the quotient and the remainder. The group had discussed referent units in other contexts, illustrated in the seminar excerpts in the previous section. The teachers had come to realize that many of the errors made by their students were made because they did not understand referent units.

Inv: So there's an interesting question about the referents here. The remainder and the quotient refer to two different things completely. The 7 refers to the number of bows, the 2 to the number of inches left.

Linda: And ⅖ could mean something there. You can write ⅖ or *point 4.*

Darota: But if you were talking about ribbon, you would say, "And I have 2 inches that I can't use." I don't think you would say, "I can make 7⅖ bows."

Inv: The point being made is worth repeating. If we have 37 cookies and we're sharing them among five people, we have 7 cookies for each person and 2 cookies left. In both cases the units are cookies. In this case [7] , this is how much each of us gets, and this [2] is how much is left over. But if we talk about how many bows can be made with 37 inches, you end up with 7 bows and 2 inches of material left. They don't even refer to the same units of measure anymore. Let's go back to cookies and cookies, giving each person 5 cookies. It seems that when you're doing a partitive division, then you come out with the same unit of measure, and that's why they can be combined into 7⅖ or 7.4. But when you're using the measurement interpretation. . . .

Linda: But it can still be combined. You can still have 7⅖ bows.

Shey: But people don't think like that. When you're using that measurement model, the unit itself is what's most important, so that anything that's left over is not one of those. Because 5 is what makes it, so what's left over—you don't even talk about it. I wouldn't say "two fifths of a bow," because that's meaningless.

Cynthia: If this were flour, you could combine parts of cups together, but you can't combine pieces of fabric and have one piece of fabric.

Inv: This discussion that we're having now can only be had if you're talking about a situation. It can't be had if you're just dividing numbers. And most of the time the kids in school just have numbers; they don't have situations to talk about. So there's really nothing to talk about at all.

Shey: That's true of any computation that you do out of context.

Inv: But it's especially troubling with division because of the remainders. Kids don't have any idea what to do with those.

The seminar excerpts in this section portray not only the struggle to understand the meaning of the quotient and the remainder in a number of contexts; they also show how teachers can begin to connect ideas of quotients and remainders with different interpretations of division and to consider the role of the referent units within the problem. Finally, the point is made that setting problems within contexts helps to clarify many of the issues. The discussion in the first-year seminar on remainders lacked context, and so the interpretation of the remainder was more difficult then.

Dividing Fractions With Remainders

The last excerpt we provide on division is from a seminar in May of the first year, during which Patrick Thompson was presenting to the teachers a problem that called for understanding multiplication and division of fractions. We include it here not only because it illustrates a deepening understanding of division of fractions, exemplified by a higher comfort level than was apparent in previous seminars on division of fractions, but also because at the end of the segment the teachers (Shey in particular) are forced to deal with remainders resulting from division by a fraction.

Pat had introduced the following drawing and had asked teachers if they could see $\frac{3}{5}$, $\frac{5}{3}$, $\frac{3}{5}$ of $\frac{5}{3}$, and $\frac{2}{3}$ of $\frac{3}{5}$. In each case the teachers were expected to describe what each fraction referred to (e.g., the shaded area, the unshaded area, the whole square). We enter here at the time when the teachers have been asked questions about division. We begin with Shey's response. Although he appears to understand the division that has taken place, he does not at first understand Pat's prodding to define the referent unit.

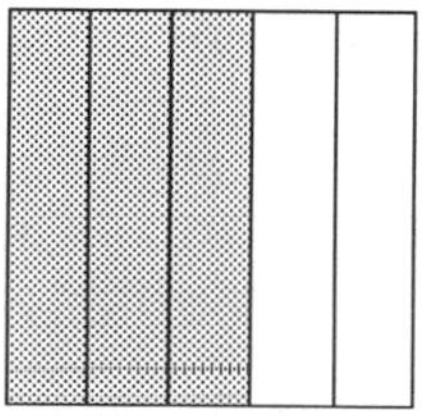

Pat: Can you see $1 \div \frac{3}{5}$? (Pause) One of the things that is very helpful is if you make explicit what you mean by *divide*. One way of thinking about that is "How many three fifths are there in 1?" Can you just read it off the diagram?

Shey: I just changed it all into thirds again. I saw there's three thirds and two thirds.

Pat: Three thirds of?

Shey: Of the whole thing.

Pat: What are you calling the whole thing?

Shey: The big part. I looked to see how many three fifths were in there. And there's one set of three fifths that are shaded, which is three thirds, which is one.

Pat: Three thirds of?

Shey: The part that's shaded is three fifths of the whole thing. But I also knew that was three thirds.

Pat: Three thirds of?

Shey: (Laughs) Well, that's what I couldn't. . . .

Others: Three thirds of three fifths.

Mick: Three thirds of the part that's shaded.

Shey: The three thirds there that's shaded, that's one, and the two strips, which is two thirds, I'm saying that's $1\frac{2}{3}$. I don't know what. . . .

In the next segment, Pat returns to an earlier conversation during the seminar, in which the meaning of remainders had already arisen and been discussed. It is in this segment that we see the complication of dealing with remainders within fraction division and of keeping straight the referent unit in each case.

Pat: Does this have anything to do with your earlier conversation about remainders?

Shey: I don't know. About remainders?

Pat: Suppose we said, "It's 1 remainder 2." So what does the 2 represent?

Shey: The two thirds.

Pat: Of?

Shey: The three thirds. (Laughs) Okay. The way I'm thinking of it as two thirds.

Pat: Two thirds of? But it's always two thirds of something.

Shey: Two thirds of the 1. No, it's two thirds. . . .

Pat: You can call it the shaded part if you want.

Shey: What's the question?

Pat: I'm changing $1 \div \frac{3}{5}$ into "How many three fifths are there in 1?" Okay, I see one $\frac{3}{5}$—that's the shaded part—remainder 2. And so the question I asked was "What does the 2 stand for, the remainder 2?"

Shey: Well, the way I had it in my head, each one of those strips was one third.

Pat: One third of what? Of the whole thing?

Shey: No, when we used the first five thirds. We changed the unit to three thirds.

Pat: You're calling one of these [strips] one third of something.

Shey: When we use them as in the second case, it's five thirds.

Pat: All right, but. . . .

Shey: So I was looking at how that was divided. You've got five fifths there, and divided by three fifths. I don't know. This is totally wrong, but I think the three fifths—I looked at how many three fifths there were. And I saw that there was one, and somewhere further back is thirds. So I said those three thirds are one whole. And the other two strips are two thirds. But the reasoning doesn't seem right.

At this point Pat turns to some of the other teachers, and it is during their explanations that Shey clarifies his thinking about the relation between two thirds and remainder 2.

Pat: Linda, how did you do it?

Linda: I look at the whole square as the whole. Then I looked at three fifths as the shaded part. And I said, "How many shaded parts are there in the whole?" And I could see that there was 1. Then there was the two extras, and I realized each one of those is a fifth.

Shey: So that's two thirds of the 1.

Linda: So there was 1, and I saw it as 1⅖.

Cynthia: Umhmm.

Darota: I didn't even think numbers; I just looked at it spatially. I saw the whole and then the shaded part as three fifths of the whole, and then I just looked at how many shaded parts would fit into that. And there was 1, and two thirds of a shaded part left over.

Shey: Yeah.

Darota: And it just came out 1⅔, but prior to that I hadn't thought. . . . It didn't seem like I was even thinking about numbers. I was just looking at the area.

Shey: So in that example, that three fifths, once you're dividing, that becomes the unit.

Pat: So 3 one fifths becomes 1 three-fifths.

Shey: So 1 three-fifths, okay, and then the other two was two thirds of that three fifths.

Pat: Yes. So that's right. And that's what I was trying to get you to say was that it's two thirds of three fifths.

Shey: Well, I knew that.

Pat: But you weren't saying it. You were just saying it was two thirds, without saying two thirds of what.

Shey: Yeah. I understand.

The notions discussed in these seminars call for careful reasoning that is based on conceptual understanding of the meaning and process of division. The discussions that took place during seminars late in Year 1 and in Year 2 are profoundly different from the discussions during the initial seminars. Yet there continues to be struggle with the ideas. This struggle is to be expected—each time we encounter a new twist to ideas we think we understand, we need to reason through the twist. What we note here is that as the concepts become less fragile and more robust, this reasoning is more likely to lead us in ways that avoid errors. This was certainly true for these teachers. However, we do not claim that at the end of the second year all of their mathematical knowledge was as robust as their knowledge of division, as illustrated in the preceding example. We could note growth in (a) areas in which we considered topics in very concrete ways, always on the basis of developing deep understanding, related whenever possible to what the teachers did or could at least envision themselves doing in the classroom; (b) in areas in which our questioning led to exploration of the nuances associated with the topic; and (c) in areas in which the topic was returned to several times, in many ways, over the course of the seminars.

"HOW MANY?" VERSUS "HOW MUCH?": DEVELOPING PROPORTIONAL REASONING

Susan Lamon's presentation late in the spring of the first year focused on developing proportional reasoning beginning in the early grades. She pointed out distinctions between relative and absolute thinking as well as between additive and multiplicative reasoning, distinctions that struck a chord with our teachers. They found the seminar to be very useful in helping them understand at what point they should begin instruction that would lead to proportional thinking. A couple of months later, we asked the teachers to read a transcript of the seminar and Susan's accompanying paper (for a final version, see Lamon, 1995). The presentation and paper led to a rich discussion, some of which is excerpted here. We begin with a question from one of the researchers.

Inv: Were there any points in the paper or in the transcript of the talk that were especially important to you when you thought about teaching ratio and proportion?

Linda: The thing that I remembered most and that I thought about the most was where she said, "Another simple but overlooked tactic to encourage relative thinking is to ask the student "How much?" instead of "How many?" It made me think a lot about, as I ask questions, which one do I want to know?

Inv: What happens to the kids' thinking if you ask one of those questions rather than the other?

Linda: When you ask "How many?" like when you think of a case of coke, the kids think of them as broken up little hunks. But if you ask "How much?" they can think of a 6-pack as being how much. Instead of six individual cans, they can unitize it as one thing [the pack].

Inv: What does *unitize* mean?

Linda: Unitize is "consider *that* the unit," not the can of coke, but the 6-pack or the 12-pack.

Tom: One pack of gum.

Inv: So if you had a case of coke and you took out a 6-pack, what is one question you could ask?

Linda: "Here's a case of coke. I'm going to give you this much. How much of the case did I give you?" So I gave you one-fourth [case], not six cans.

Inv: So if you ask "How many?" you're forcing them to think about individual cans. Have you tried thinking about that as you're teaching?

Linda: Yes. Because I've been more careful when I'm talking—about pizzas for instance. How *much* of the pizza did they eat? I don't want to hear that they ate two pieces. I want to hear that they ate a quarter of the pizza. If I want to know how many pieces, that's different than "How *much* of the pizza?"

Inv: So you can have a pizza divided into four pieces, and a child may not be thinking about fractions at all. The child will say, "There are four pieces," which has nothing to do with fractions. So it's in the mind of the child where that notion of fraction has to develop.

The teachers seemed to recognize that although proportional reasoning was not the point of these questions, the required re-unitizing and the focus on fractional pieces were fundamental to the later development of proportional reasoning. The next comments led to a discussion of instructional implications.

Inv: Susan says, "The development of proportional reasoning depends on more than the child's collection of past informal experiences. Those are important and we're going to build on those. There is evidence that proportional reasoning, at least in part, is the result of a mediated learning process." That means that somebody has to ask those kinds of questions that are going to get the child to look at this from another perspective.

Darota: That was what I was thinking earlier when I was talking about how the kids just initially respond based on their additive experience, just their experience with whole numbers, so I think you really have to create this artificial situation, in terms of their thinking, to have them think about "How much?"

Inv: Another way of putting that is that you have to, rather than say "create an artificial situation," is that you have to constrain the situation so that the students will be oriented toward thinking in a way that they might not have otherwise thought. Because my experience is that people will always continue to think in old ways as long as those old ways are perceived to be working. It's only when they don't work that they'll stop thinking in those ways.

Shey: But isn't that one of the techniques of a good teacher in everything—to put those constraints on? Because the teacher is looking for something from the kids usually. And our job is to kind of lead them to the conclusion. I think teachers do that all the time—well, adequate teachers do it most of the time.

Inv: So when kids say, "I see four pieces of pizza," how can you constrain that so they see it a little differently? What can you ask them that will then allow them to see this in a different manner? The "How much?" versus "How many?" is one way to accomplish that.

Tom: Are you saying that the one is more important than the other, though? To me, if a student could go back and forth with that, that to me shows more mathematical power than if they could only tell me how many. "How much?"—Does that mean that the student knows more?

Darota: I think so. Because if you can answer "How much?" you have a deeper understanding. "How many?" is just counting, and "How much?" implies that you understand some concepts of parts and wholes and the relationship of parts to a whole, which to me is a more analytical and a more highly developed understanding.

Tom: I like the combination of the two questions, and I understand that "How much?" is really important versus "How many?" but a kid has to go through both.

Inv: Yes. The more prevalent question is "How many?" We forget to ask relationship kinds of questions like "How much?" I think that was Susan's main point. We should start doing that really early for kids, not wait until middle school.

The conversation then turned to what these questions would mean to a primary school student and how the answer to "How much?" could be "one out of four," an answer that does not yet indicate any understanding of fractions. The remaining 90 minutes of the seminar focused on using "How much?" and "How many?" in growth and change situations to lead students to focus on multiplicative growth rather than additive growth when the multiplicative view is appropriate.

This seminar, toward the end of the first year, set the stage for some of the discussions in the second year. The teachers now understood the difference between additive and multiplicative situations and when students were reasoning additively and multiplicatively. They appeared to understand why they should focus on multiplicative situations in their instruction. For example, the following October one teacher spoke of her plans for the year, and said that although she would leave out many traditional topics in order to teach fundamental ones well, she would include multiplicative situations, because "we talked about multiplicative reasoning as being a real fundamental [foundation for] building other kinds of thinking—fractions, and then extending to fractions, ratio, proportion, percent."

EFFECTS OF SEMINARS ON INSTRUCTION

There are basically two ways to evaluate the effects of these seminars on classroom instruction. One way is through observations of the teachers, over the 2-year period. We do report on our observations in the following chapters. Another way is to listen to the teachers themselves describe the types of changes taking place in their instruction. The following excerpt is just such a description. This excerpt is from the final seminar of Year 1, during which the teachers discussed the effects of the seminars on their own teaching.

> I would like to share something because that's been something I've been dealing with in the classroom. . . . One of the things that we were talking about the other day was percent. What does percent mean? And so we discussed it, and they knew that it was a concept of a whole that everyone referred to as a 100%, and then you could have different percents of different kinds of things, from a classroom to a pie to whatever—we talked about those kinds of relationships. And so after we talked about that and tried to make meaning out of percent, I asked them, "Is percent a fraction?" And they said, "Yes." And so I gave them a problem of six eighths. And I said, "What percent is that—of the class?" And so they had to solve it. No algorithms, nothing. One kid converted to ¾, related that to three quarters, and came up with 75%. And they had like three different strategies for solving the problem. I guess I've never really had any confidence that if you start at one point that kids will eventually arrive at the algorithm. And this showed me that they do. And then, not only it showed me, but it showed me how . . . superficial my understanding of problems had been prior to this, how superficially I had been teaching them, even though I try to get out manipulatives and different things. It was the questioning and the discussing and the writing about it that really brought the kids to the understanding. As long as I was just showing them pictures and having them move stuff around, that wasn't getting it. It was the discussion. And so I learned a real valuable lesson with that about the way kids think. . . . And another thing that was really surprising to me is I have a wide range in my classroom from certified gifted kids to Chapter 1, whatever you want to call them— kids that are scoring below the 10th percentile on standardized tests—and one of my kids that was at the 7th or 8th percentile was able to explain. Now he used his calculator to figure out the math parts of it. But he knew what numbers, how to come up with things mathematically, and could explain it in a way that the other kids

could understand. Whereas some of the kids that were stuck on the algorithm or were used to doing real well, high achievers, had a little bit more difficulty in explaining it. I think that for me it brought me to "Teacher expectations is everything; it's everything." Because if my expectations are tied into—and I'm real concerned about the tests, because, you know, we're under court order, for heaven's sakes, to improve our test scores, so I can't just say, "Well, I'm just going to experiment." I have to always have that in the back of my mind. But as long as my orientation was to that, I was blocked from really seeing the value in the children learning how to think and reason. And then the other thing that I realized in conjunction with that is—because we keep saying, "Math's gotta make sense." One of the first speakers we had said something like that we give children the impression that math doesn't have to make sense. And I've thought about that ever since that first meeting. And so I keep telling them, "It's got to make sense." So *I* have to make sense of it.

The teachers themselves, during the seminars, sometimes spontaneously commented on the seminars: what they felt they were learning and how they felt they were benefiting. We present only a few examples here. In the spring of the first year, one teacher said

I was thinking driving over here and thinking how different this year has been, and I hope it's because of the experiences with the [project] and all the things that have been going on in my life, but it's interesting because I've never, ever, ever gotten to this point in fractions where I am now by the end of the year with the classes that I've had before—the experiences that I've had with these kids, they're just flying; they're very understanding of what's going on, and it's made everything after that a breeze, just a breeze.

Another time, a teacher reflected on what she had learned about division of fractions:

I think, like when we discussed it, that division of fractions was always a hairy area for most people because you were just taught the algorithm. And when you do see what it means, it makes so much more sense. When kids come up to you and ask you, "Why, when you do division of fractions, does the number get bigger?" which most kids will do, you're equipped with the devices to show that student why. And I think that it's so much more valuable than just saying "Because it is." And a lot of teachers do that.

All of the teachers had been involved in various teacher-enhancement projects, and more than once they compared what they had learned in those projects to what they were learning in the seminars:

> I think that the ___ Project is all fine and wonderful and I think that the ___ Project is all fine and wonderful, but they didn't make any sense to me until I got into this group—what the purposes of those two projects were. I think I'm one of the fortunate ones.

Not all of their comments related to their teaching—other aspects of their lives changed as well, as the teacher in this final excerpt shared with us:

> My daughter's in the fourth-grade GATE [gifted] cluster. Her teacher is highly regarded in the school as a teacher who pushes the kids to perform. The kids get good test scores. [Yet her daughter had no idea about how to do her homework on addition of fractions.] I told her, "We can't do this in one night. It's gonna take a little bit longer. I need to help you to understand some ideas." I wrote a note to the teacher explaining that my daughter didn't do her homework because she really didn't have an understanding of the fraction concepts, and I would like to be able to work with her over the weekend and she would turn in this assignment later. The teacher told her, "I don't buy that. I spent 10 minutes explaining that." I wrote a really nasty note back to the teacher that as a teacher and having worked in a project the last 2 years where we really looked at teaching and what it meant to understand all this, that I felt that my daughter really did not understand fraction concepts and that I thought it was inappropriate for her to say that my assessment of the situation was not correct and to tell [my daughter] this. But my daughter wants to do what the teacher tells her. She wants to have 100% on her paper. For the teacher to tell her, "I don't buy that, and your mother's a jerk," really disturbed her. So I was very upset about that. . . . But I think that if I had not gone through this project, if I had not looked at these things, that I wouldn't have challenged the teacher on that. I would have just sat down with my daughter and showed her how to manipulate the fractions and find a common denominator and add them and then divide them and take the steps and write them down. . . . I'm sure she's not the only fourth grader in that room that doesn't have a clue as to what's going on.

CONCLUSION

It would be wrong of us to claim that the teachers had never before encountered many of the concepts discussed here. We know in fact of instances in which some of the teachers had previously received instruction on the meaning of division of fractions, yet claimed not to have thought about division of fractions before. Why did the seminars have an impact greater than other experiences? We suspect that the reason is that previous instruction was just that—a brief lecture or a mandate to carry out some examples with manipulatives. The teachers had not been given the opportunities to grapple with the ideas until they were understood. Another reason might be that, in a sense, the teachers "controlled the agenda" for the seminars, except when we had an invited speaker. That is, the teachers could persist in mulling over, worrying a concept until it was understood. And often they did— turning and considering a problem from every possible vantage point. Finally, these teachers seemed not to have previously been in an environment in which they were *expected* to understand. Now they were. By the middle of the first year, they realized that this *was* the expectation—to stay with something until they—and we—were satisfied that it was understood. This realization seemed to empower them to learn and to not be satisfied until the mathematics was clear, until it "made sense" to them.

Chapter 5

LINDA: COMING TO APPRECIATE THE ROLE OF MATHEMATICS IN PROFESSIONAL DEVELOPMENT

In our case study of Linda, we show the effects on one teacher of our focus on developing the mathematical content knowledge of the teacher. When Linda came to our project, she was already engaged in a process of changing her approach to mathematics teaching, and she saw this project as an opportunity to continue the change process. Her previous experience in professional-development projects, however, had not led her to develop a deeper understanding of the mathematics she was teaching. One of the issues we will address in this case study is the difficulty Linda experienced when content knowledge was placed at the forefront of this project. During the first year she was not comfortable with this emphasis, and it took a full year before she began to under-stand and accept the fundamental differences between the focus of this project and the foci of other mathematics professional-development projects with which she had been involved. During the second year she began to notice and appreciate the role her own mathematics-content understanding had on her teaching, and with this understanding came a new-found view of herself as a teacher. She came to value the place that a focus on mathematics has in professional development and, in fact, became critical of inservice programs that failed to help teachers to grow mathematically.

We also describe how Linda's developing understanding of the mathematics she was teaching influenced her instruction. As Linda developed new mathematical connections, she began to include mathematical topics she had not covered in previous years, and she attempted to teach more conceptually. But at the same time that her developing understanding of some mathematical topics enabled her to make changes, her as yet incomplete understanding of these same mathematical topics prevented her from making other instructional changes she had come to value.

INTRODUCING LINDA

Linda is a sixth-grade teacher in a rural elementary school in which she had been teaching for 3 years at the time this study began in August 1992. This was her first teaching assignment. Many of the students at her school come from low socioeconomic households; many are Native American or are from Mexico. Linda had been a lead teacher at the school since 1990, just one year after finishing her teaching credential. Her school shared its principal with another school, and Linda assumed the role of acting principal when the principal was gone.

After earning an associate arts degree some years earlier, Linda took time off to raise two children. She returned to school to begin working on a liberal studies degree when she was in her midthirties. She worked as an instructional aide for 7 years, including the time she worked on obtaining her teaching credential. Her coursework included two mathematics courses for elementary school teachers, one mathematics methods course, and several computer programming courses. In fact, she had completed enough units in computer courses to earn a supplementary credential to teach mathematics at the junior high school level, even though the highest mathematics course she completed was college algebra. Although this credential would enable her to take a position in a junior high school, she explained, "I do not have a strong enough background to do some of the stuff [at that level]." During her initial interview in May 1992, she described how she thought about the two mathematics courses for elementary school teachers she had been required to take:

> When I went to school 7 years ago, a lot of the stuff we did in math for elementary school teachers—'cause I had to take both of those classes—it was like, "Well, I can come up with the answers, but what difference does it make if I really understand it?" Because I can tell kids. I can do it on the board, and they can copy what I'm doing. That's what I did.

On a later occasion she again talked about the two courses:

> I said to myself, "I can solve all these problems," and I just whipped through them without ever thinking why I was doing what I was doing. I was getting Bs; I was happy with that. I had too

much else going on in my life. I thought, "I want to teach Kindergarten anyway, so I'm never going to need to know how to divide. And fractions, yeah, we can cut pizzas and brownies in half and split 30 beans into two piles of 15. That's all I'm gonna need to know." So I just whipped through and never put any thought into it.

At the time of the initial interview, Linda had just completed a year-long involvement in an inservice project designed to help teachers rethink how they taught mathematics, and she was about to begin another inservice project during the summer. She spoke enthusiastically about the effect of the inservice project she had just completed:

This year is a wonderful year for me because I was part of the ____ last year through the county. It just, it turned me around, and I did not go in expecting that experience. I went in to have something to do for the summer, and I [started off] thinking, "This is not the way to teach math." I thought you taught math with two pages in your book a day and worksheets for homework. And that was math. And after being there for about a week—I think it took them about a week to convince me that this is good—and once I bought into it, I really bought in.

And bought in she did. Linda explained, "We didn't use our textbook at all last year. I used the teacher's guide, sort of, a few times, to make sure that I was covering all of the concepts that are in our district curriculum." Instead, Linda relied on the use of what she called "mathematical investigations" and a variety of problems drawn from different sources. Linda had used the Fraction Replacement Unit (a unit developed with state funding and approval to be used in Grade 5 to replace the chapters on fractions) even though she had not attended the usual inservice on how to use it. She explained, "Someone gave me a copy of it, and I'm going from there. So, I'm kind of stumbling through a little bit." She spoke of one 6-week unit that she taught twice, once to her own students and again to another sixth-grade class:

I have a whole unit that I taught that was called "Gulliver's Travels." I taught that to two classes this year. I loved it. The kids loved it. It was totally successful. I added a lot of things to it—area, perimeter, ratio—which they kind of cover in Gulliver's, but not enough. . . . I learned a lot in teaching that.

Linda explained how occasionally she would give the students a warm-up problem and then spend the entire 40-minute math session discussing the problem. She described how during the past year she had worked on having her students explain their thinking:

I've worked real hard this year on getting them not only to give me the right answer, but to tell how they got that answer. It's the most important thing to me. And I don't stress that they had to come up with the right answer. If they could explain how they got the answer, that was fine. Like the group that gave me the wrong answer to the problem [during the lesson you observed me teach today], and I put it on the board; then as we went through it as a group, they could see their own mistakes. I don't have to sit there and point out their mistakes to them.

Linda incorporated "a lot of questioning, individual questioning, because when they're working in cooperative groups, I can go around." She also explained that she convinced her principal to buy two sets of Explorer calculators, which her students used regularly.

Linda did fairly well on the content knowledge test she took at the outset of the project. Even so, she spoke about what she perceived to be weaknesses in her mathematical background, and she clearly believed that these weaknesses hindered her ability to teach mathematics. During our initial interview in May 1992, Linda responded to the question "How important is it that teachers have a deep understanding of the mathematics they teach?"

I have decided it's extremely important. It's really difficult that if I'm. . . . If I'm just going to get up to teach the algorithm to division of fractions, I can do it. You know, "flip and multiply." . . . And I understand that division of fractions is an inverse of multiplication, and that's why you do it. And I can get up there and say that until I'm blue in the face. But if I don't really understand what division of fractions means, I'll have a hard time conveying it to my kids. And I feel real strongly about that. If they ask me a question—because some of them probably are smarter than me, okay—if they ask me a question that I can't answer, I'm a failure in their eyes and in mine.

During the inservice project she had been in, participants spent time working in groups of three developing instructional units that they then taught to children associated with the project. Linda explained

We had to solve the same problems that the kids were going to solve. We had to work through them. I was sort of frustrated sometimes because one of the people in my group was really outstanding; she should be teaching high school. She was a junior high teacher—middle school. And I didn't have enough math background to do a lot of the activities that we were teaching—

tangent, ratio, et cetera. Our unit that we taught was on measuring, and there were a lot of the things that we did that. . . . I can do the mechanics. I could make the little thing where you look through the straw and you have the string. I could do that, and I could come up with the right answer, but I didn't know why or how I was doing that. She would explain it to me, but I didn't always quite get that. [But still] it was wonderful.

Linda claimed that in the year prior to her involvement in our project she had changed not only how she taught mathematics but also her goals for teaching mathematics:

It used to be that I could just teach the algorithm and give them 50 problems to do using that algorithm, and if they could use that algorithm when they were done, I felt successful. And I don't feel that way anymore.

She wanted math to be fun for her students, but she also wanted them to understand. But again, she acknowledged the role that her own understanding played in the process:

If I don't understand, I have a real difficult time teaching a concept. I mean up to now, I've probably used the book. The other 2 years I used the book, and you know, they give you a little bit on the side that gives the knowledge you need to teach that lesson, and I would read that, and I could get up and teach the lesson. Some of the kids got it and some of the kids didn't. Most of the kids did, and we fought it through and never finished the book.

During the 2 years Linda was associated with our project (1992–1993 and 1993–1994) the bulk of her curriculum revolved around a program she was piloting, based on a large middle school curriculum-development project. She had learned about the program during the summer of 1992 and had agreed to pilot it. This program provided some materials that Linda used in her class.

Our initial observation of Linda occurred in May of 1992, before our project began. The school in which Linda was teaching had just reopened at a newly constructed site in January of that year. It was air conditioned, full of light and space, and proudly maintained. Linda's room was well organized. Students' artwork and writing were posted on the walls, along with rules of conduct. Student desks were arranged in small groups of three or four, and the square-shaped room enabled every student to be fairly close to the front of the room, to Linda's desk, and to fellow students. Linda appeared comfortable in the classroom, and her students were comfortable with her. She was poised, confident, and friendly, and although she was willing to joke with students, she was clearly in control of the classroom at all times.

During our observations in Linda's classroom, we never saw a lesson being taught from the textbook. We found Linda's description of her teaching to be accurate: She often devoted much of the class period to solving problems; she encouraged her students to share their solutions; and her students frequently worked together in small groups.

YEAR 1: VALUING CHANGING INSTRUCTION

Although the primary focus of the seminars was the mathematical content of the middle school, most seminars also included some discussion of instructional issues. Generally, Linda spoke only about instructional issues, all of which were related to difficulties she experienced when she attempted to make changes in her mathematics teaching. She described difficulties she faced working with parents and students. During one of the first seminars she told us that she had to convince parents that problem-solving homework assignments (consisting of one or two problems from one of the replacement units) were indeed mathematics. Linda explained that the parents expected more traditional-looking assignments involving many exercises. She also talked about the difficulties she encountered trying to teach students to think conceptually about mathematics they had earlier learned procedurally. During a February seminar discussion on fraction multiplication, for example, one teacher suggested that if only he could get his students to think of "$\frac{1}{4} \times$" as "one fourth of" instead of "one fourth times," then he could really help his students. Linda responded

> You didn't have any kids in your class who had fractions the last 3 years and came in and said, "I know how to do it"? How do you get them to let go of the algorithm somebody else has already beat into their heads?

Because Linda shared her experiences freely with the group, we did not at first notice that she tended to be quieter during mathematical discussions. In fact, Linda did not make a single comment during a highly mathematical 3-hour discussion led by Guershon Harel in March 1993. Although she professed wanting to teach her students conceptually, she herself often approached problems procedurally and was at first attracted to "gimmicks" that she thought her students would like.[1]

---

1. For example, the "I hate math" algorithm of Tom's (described in chapter 4).

An Early Observation

The lessons we observed Linda teach during the first year generally involved her use of the curricular materials she had agreed to pilot. She would give her students problems to solve, either alone or in small groups, and then would provide students opportunities to share their reasoning. We will describe one such lesson, which we observed in September of the first year of the project.

The lesson was about coordinate graphing. Prior to the lesson, Linda's students had visited the neighboring classroom and played Battleship, a game played in pairs in which one student places five ships of various lengths (ranging from 2 to 5 units) on a grid, and the other student must try to find and "sink" the ships by identifying points the ships occupy on the playing surface. Each point is designated by a letter and number; so, for example, a small ship of length 2-units might be located at D4 and E4. After the students returned to their own classroom, Linda discussed the game they had played and generalized the activity to the more conventionally accepted x–y coordinate axes. Recognizing that her students seemed to understand how to graph points, Linda pushed ahead into the next lesson, which involved graphing the lengths of students' names on an x–y axis, with the lengths of their first names along the x-axis and the lengths of their last names along the y-axis. Linda asked her students, "What happens if someone has the same number of letters in the first and last name?" She graphed a couple such names, and the students saw that these points determine a diagonal line. This lesson ended with the students receiving graph paper and a list of names to graph. The lesson, like most of the lessons we saw Linda teach, included students working together in small groups followed by class discussions. The tasks she used came directly from the curriculum project.

The First Sign That the Seminars Influenced Linda's Teaching

During each postobservation interview, we asked Linda whether her involvement in the project had affected her teaching. For our first four visits she replied negatively. For example, in December she replied, "No, because I have not yet gotten to fractions." (We were focusing on fractions during seminars that fall.) During our fifth visit, in March, she reported for the first time that her lesson had been influenced by the project. During this lesson, Linda introduced decimals using decimal strips that were adapted from Tom Kieren's November seminar. Here is a portion of the postobservation discussion:

> Inv: You were telling me in the lounge about doing the fraction strips this year, [and how your thinking was] different from what you thought last year, so can you tell me about that again?

Linda: After doing paper folding with our [project] group, I could see how important it was. . . . I just felt that it was really important. And as I'm teaching the fraction replacement unit this year, I noticed there's one section that is "Making Fraction Strips," and last time I taught [the unit] I skipped it because I didn't think that was important at all. I totally just said, "Ah, this is a waste; you don't want to spend a week doing that." And now I see that it is *extremely* important to the kids.

Linda had designed this lesson on her own, on the basis of ideas she had encountered in the seminars. She spoke about linking fractions and decimals:

I've never taught decimals and fractions together before either—because I didn't think they went together; I didn't think they related to each other. . . . I never put the two together before, so I'm sure the kids haven't.

Linda's lesson had been affected by her new understanding of the content. Whereas in the past she did not value lessons that attempted to link decimals and fractions, she now viewed such lessons as important. Just as her new understanding of the content affected what she chose to teach, her lack of a deep understanding of the content affected the extent to which she could carry out the lesson. We provide examples from this lesson.

During the lesson, Linda's students practiced writing decimals, and they experienced difficulty writing the decimal for one tenth, which different students represented by 1.0, 1.10, .1, and 10.1. The following segment is a portion of a discussion of how to represent four tenths. (In all classroom sessions, the teacher's name is italicized in order to distinguish it from student names.)

Linda: What if I was talking about this number [.4] and I put a 1 in front of the 4. [Writes 1.4 on board] What does that [1] stand for?
Carrie: One whole.
Linda: Okay, good. It tells you that there is one whole. What if I put a 1 and a 0 in front of it? [Writes 10.4]
Valerie: Ten wholes.
Linda: Ten wholes. How about if I put 100? [Writes 100.4]
Students: One hundred wholes.
Linda: What if I put that? [Writes .01] Point zero one—what if I had that? Am I still talking about one tenth?

Some students believe that this .01 is still one tenth. Others disagree.

Linda: Miguel says that I'm talking about hundredths.

Student: Hundreds.

Linda: Hundredths.

Jim: What's the difference?

Linda: Can someone help Jim? He doesn't know the difference between *hundreds* and *hundredths*.

Von: Neither do I.

Linda: Okay. Brittany.

Brittany: Isn't *hundreds* like 100, 200, or 300, and *hundredths*, like you have one piece?

Linda: Good. What they're saying is that if we're talking about 100, like over here, we're talking about 100 pieces. But if we're talking about 100 pieces and I'm only talking about *one* of those 100 pieces, I'm talking about hun*dredth*. Do you remember talking about this ever before?

Some students remember talking about it last year; others do not.

Linda's explanation does not make explicit what the unit is. In the first case, when referring to 100 pieces, the whole or unit is one of those pieces. In the second case, when referring to one of those 100 pieces as one hundredth, then what is implicit (and likely not considered in the minds of the students) is that the whole or unit is all 100 of those pieces.

The inherent difficulty in keeping track of the unit became an issue later in the lesson when the students were reading 102.4. A portion of this discussion follows:

Linda: Let's have some practice reading some decimals. [Writes 102.4] Alfinio.

Alfinio: One hundred and two wholes and four tenths.

Linda: If you say "100 *and* two wholes," that kind of gets confusing. Is there an easier way to say it so we'll all understand?

Jackie: One hundred two and four tenths.

Linda: One hundred two and four tenths. Saying it that way is clearer and easier to understand. Carrie?

Carrie: Is it sort of like "one hundred and two remainder four," sort of four leftover from the whole?

Linda: Yeah, that's a good thought. Carrie is reminding us that the four tenths does not equal a whole. What does it equal?

Bobbie: Four tenths.

Linda: What is four tenths?

Jo: Four out of 10.

Linda: Okay, hold up four tenths of your strips in front of you. Okay, yeah, you could hold up 4 out of 10 of your fingers. Okay, put your strips down and put your hands down. Let's try another one.

At the end of this segment of the lesson Linda asked each student to hold up 4 of his or her 10 fingers. In order for a student to conceptualize these 4 fingers as four tenths, he or she would have to again recognize that the unit or whole is comprised of the 10 fingers. Otherwise, the students may simply see 4 of 10 fingers as "4 out of 10," focusing on two whole number quantities instead of thinking about the multiplicative relationship between those two quantities that creates the four tenths.

The role of the unit continued to be an elusive one for Linda. In April we observed a lesson devoted to solving the following problem:

> The sixth-grade class made a gigantic square pizza for the class party for the day after the final exam. They made it a week before the party so they could have time to study for the exams. To keep the pizza fresh they put it in the school freezer for a week. Unfortunately, a pizza pirate was in the area. On the first night the pizza pirate came in and ate half of the pizza. On the second night he ate half of what was left. Each night he came in and continued to eat half of what was left. When the sixth-grade class went to get their pizza, what fraction of the pizza was left? Write a summary of how your group found a solution to the problem. Draw any diagrams that are helpful in showing your thinking.

There were many positive features to the discussion of this problem. During the lesson Linda encouraged students to answer her questions freely and spontaneously and required them to explain and justify. She never criticized or discouraged a student. She never told students they were wrong. But the focus did not seem to be on the way the unit changed while the multiplying unfolded. Instead it focused on procedures for doubling (the denominator), with emphasis given to the patterns.

Coming to Understand Division of Fractions

During a postobservation interview in December, Linda spoke with great enthusiasm about an experience she had recently had helping an instructional aide understand division of fractions, something that Linda had come to understand as a result of her participation in the project.

Linda: [Paraphrased] I was helping an older woman study for a test she has to take to be certified as a teacher's aide. It has some fraction and decimal items on the test. [We assume they were computations from what Linda said.] We were talking about division of fractions. She could not remember which number to invert. I then told her that it was the second number that was inverted in the standard invert and multiply algorithm.

Then I got out fraction circles and said, Okay, if we divided ½ by ⅓, it's 1 and some more: It's ½ of another. So it's 3⁄2. The woman got the concept, and I thought, "I'm teaching it for understanding for the first time—I actually showed someone the meaning!"

Three days later, during the postobservation interview, Linda was still excited about the experience and repeated her story to another researcher who was observing her class that day. After retelling the story, she talked about the role of estimation and her use of the measurement model for division:

Linda: I said, "You have to realize that a third is smaller than a half, and so there's gotta be more than one of them." She said, "Why?" That was the question I had, myself, not long ago.

Inv: You didn't think of "How many of these [⅓s] are in here [½]?" as your model for division?

Linda: Never. No. In multiplication I would think "¼ *of* ½." I don't know when I started that. So I sort of knew it, but it wasn't as strongly in my mind as it is now. It's so much easier to think of it now. I thought of division as sharing, I think. But I would never see it; it was an algorithm, truthfully. In a word problem, I would think of it as sharing. But in fractions, I just thought of it as an algorithm. The numbers didn't have to make sense: I would check myself by multiplying them. If that worked, it must be the right answer.

Linda had extended her view of division to include more than partitive (or sharing) division. Her understanding of the measurement (or repeated subtraction) model of division, together with her ability to measure halves in terms of thirds, enabled her to make sense of division of fractions in a way she had never before understood.

This new understanding was fragile, as can be seen in this excerpt from a seminar that occurred 2 months later. The seminar leader, Pat Thompson, and another teacher had been discussing how to use this picture to think about $1 \div 3⁄5$:

Linda: I look at the whole square as the whole. Then I looked at ⅗ as the shaded part. And I said, "How many shaded parts are there in the whole?" And I could see that there was one. Then there was the two extras, and I realized each one of those is a fifth.

Shey: So that's two thirds of the 1 [three fifths].
Linda: So there was one, and I saw it as 1 and ⅖.

Linda understood that there was 1 entire three fifth in the whole, and she also recognized that there were two fifths left over. What was not clear to her was that the remaining two fifths represented two thirds of the three fifths. In other words, she was viewing the two fifths left over as a remainder, not a quotient.

In an earlier transcript, an incorrect idea about remainders was expressed by one of the students. Although delving into this misconception at that time would have been distracting from the topic at hand, it could have been referred to at a later time to discuss a complex idea. In a conversation about the meaning of 102.4, there was this exchange:

Carrie: Is it sort of like "one hundred and two remainder four," sort of four leftover from the whole?
Linda: Yeah, that's a good thought. Carrie is reminding us that the four tenths does not equal a whole. What does it equal?

Notice the difficulty students might experience trying to conceptualize the 4 as a remainder. Generally, in division, the remainder is that portion of the dividend that remains unpartitioned. For example, when dividing 32 cookies among five children, an answer of 6 remainder 2 is very different from an answer of 6.4. In the first case, the 6 refers to the cookies each child receives and the 2 refers to the unpartitioned cookies remaining; whereas in the second case both the 6 and the .4 refer to the cookies each student receives. It is not clear that Linda herself distinguishes between these two views sufficiently to highlight this distinction for her students.

Learning to Question Students

Our last observation of the school year took place in May, the day after Linda had attended the project seminar presented by Pat Thompson,[2] who had focused on posing questions designed to encourage students to think deeply about fractions. (Recall the $1 \div \frac{3}{5}$ example earlier.) During our postobservation interview, Linda spoke of the effect that seminar had had on her when she reflected about her own teaching. This transcript highlights Linda's new understanding of the role of questioning in developing conceptual knowledge and her realization that the questioning during seminars led to this understanding.

Inv: Was any part of the lesson influenced by the project?

---

2. See P. Thompson, 1995.

Linda: Yeah. A lot. A lot of my . . . I mean . . . my thinking. Last night talking about [the fact that] kids know more than we think they know, and I saw myself . . . . I'll ask questions down to a point, and then I start giving clues. And I even saw myself doing it today, and I don't. . . . It's gonna be hard to just. . . . Like you said, you kept asking me "Why, why, why?" I would ask "Why, why?" and then as soon as I got a little bit of a puzzled look, I'd give them that clue, you know, and I see now that that wasn't really helping them. Maybe it was, but, no . . . it wasn't really helping them. They needed. . . . If I had asked "Why?" or maybe if I had thought a little bit more about the questions I was going to ask, I could have gotten in more than I did. Not that I think my expectations are low. I'm just not sure, maybe, where my expectations are.

Inv: What do you think—when Pat questions a student—what do you think he's after?

Linda: (Deep sigh) To see what they're thinking? To help them think. I think his questions are gonna help the kid direct their thinking in the right direction. That's what I hope I was doing, but I think I'm—I think I'm doing it, but I think I'm doing it up too high. I should let them go deeper before I start directing them.

Inv: Or at that point where you see that look on their face, does it change your focus from their thinking to . . . ?

Linda: Absolutely. [It changes my focus] to me feeding them. As soon as I see that look, I don't push them. That's when I start feeding them—not feeding them the information but feeding them more leading questions.

Inv: It sounds like you interpret that look as "Help." How do you think Pat might interpret it?

Linda: Uh, God. I'm thinking. I think he would say, "It means I'm thinking. I haven't thought. My brain's going." To me it meant—maybe not after last night, 'cause I really think that made a difference—"Help, I give up," is the way I was looking at it. And he was saying, "Just help me get on the right track." Maybe that's how he thinks of it. I'm not sure. . . . I think the more I practice it, I think the stronger I'll get. In fact, the math coordinator at the county office was talking about how many people are now asking for a class on how to ask questions. "What do I ask next if I ask 'Why?' and I don't get an answer? What do I do next?" And I think we all need that. I'm getting it from experience; I'm hearing the questions [the investigators] ask during our sessions. (Laughs) Some of the questions Pat asked last night—and it was such a simple next step—and I think the only way, unless someone comes in and gives you a script, which they can't, is by experience: by hearing other people asking us those questions and by us asking the kids those questions. So that's how I think that the project's helping, immensely! Because people are saying, "Hey, where am I going to learn how to ask questions?" Well, if you don't hear them asked, how are you going to learn?

End-of-Year Reflections

At the end of the first year the teachers were asked to reflect on the previous year in the project. Linda said that she enjoyed participating in the project and particularly enjoyed the seminars: "Our bimonthly seminars were most valuable to me—more so than classroom visits. . . . I look so forward to our discussions that I fly down the freeway at 70 miles per hour with a smile on my face." Linda thought that she had learned a lot during the year, and she spoke enthusiastically about how her new understanding resulted in her spending more time on selected topics:

> I spent longer on fractions this year than I did in the 2 previous years put together. This was in part due to the unit I was piloting but more to the additional knowledge I brought to the topic. I always made big assumptions about prior student knowledge that I didn't this year. I now see the importance of a strong base. Students can't manipulate fractions if they don't know that fractions are a part of a whole or [are unable to make] correct comparisons of fractions or [don't understand] equivalency. When they had these concepts, later lessons were easier to grasp for them and to teach for me.

She also spoke about her new focus on what students are learning, rather than on what she is teaching:

> I'm still confused about myself as a teacher. Don't get me wrong; this is good. Many of our discussions have made me take a different look at myself. I am seeing teaching from the learners' point of view for the first time. I've taught many classes and never wondered before, "What are the learners learning?" I always thought, "What am I teaching?" There's a big difference. I always knew that students learn differently, but I never thought about this aspect before. I worried about whether they were getting the concepts, but I never thought with respect to what it felt like to be the learner. You've made me think, and I'm changing, thanks to you.

We commented earlier on how quiet Linda often was during the mathematical discussions. Linda appeared to have a great deal of self-confidence and was at ease with her students and with us. Yet it took most of the year before she began to fully participate in the seminar discussions.

> I'm always telling my students it is okay to take risks during our discussions, but I rarely did it myself [during the seminars]. As I got more comfortable with the group, I felt that I could take risks. . . . I think I must have felt intimidated by our guest speakers. I'm not sure why. I understood what they were sharing with us, yet I had difficulty verbalizing questions I wanted to ask them.

Linda's attempts to make changes in her instruction began before we knew her and continued throughout that first year. But she often came up against her own superficial understanding of the mathematics she was trying to teach. She did not always know which direction to push a classroom conversation, and when she did know where she wanted to take it, she was not sure how to accomplish it. For example, she recognized that Pat Thompson was engaging students in a manner that she was not, and, although she found value in Pat's approach, she was not sure what she needed to do to similarly engage students in her own classroom.

This first year in the project was not easy for Linda when she began to look at her own teaching and her own understanding in different, more critical ways. During one postobservation interview late in the academic year, she said, "I feel that I'm not even halfway to where I wanted to be. I haven't done a lot." She began to recognize that it was not enough to present activities to students without also posing questions designed to facilitate her students' mathematical understanding. She began to question her expectations of her students. She now questioned her own mathematical understanding. Linda was struggling inside, and we found out only a year later that she was considering quitting the project after that first year (even though in her reflections she said that she looked forward to the seminars). In the upcoming year, she would continue to struggle with these issues, but she would become more accepting of where she was and of what she was going through.

YEAR 2: LINDA BEGINS TO FOCUS ON CONTENT

We began our second year with the teachers by conducting individual interviews with them. When we asked Linda what she hoped to gain this year from the project, her response reflected how her struggles during the first year had undermined her confidence in her teaching ability.

Linda: What do I hope to gain this year from the project? Just, um, the word fell out of my head—confidence! I'd like to get some more confidence. I know now that I do have a stronger base than I had before. I know a lot more, in teaching and sharing with the students, in sharing my knowledge. I mean, now that I have more, I want to be sure that I get it out there.

Inv: So, confidence in your content knowledge?

Linda: Yeah, definitely in my content knowledge.

During the second year, Linda was again involved in piloting a new curriculum, but she felt more comfortable deviating from these materials and interjecting topics she considered to be important. In a postinterview in late September, Linda reported incorporating more proportional reasoning than she had the previous year. Notice that Linda again comments on her confidence level:

Inv: I get the feeling you're really dealing with proportional reasoning a lot sooner this year.

Linda: Right. Definitely.

Inv: What do you think is the reason for that?

Linda: First of all, what I now know that I don't think I really knew before. I wasn't comfortable working with it before at all, before I worked with you guys last year. I still don't feel as confident about that as I do a lot of other things, but I do feel a lot more confident about it. And I think now that I understand it a little bit better, I understand which way to lead, what kind of leading questions I can ask to get the kids to see the relationships.

Linda was becoming more aware of the questions she posed in her lessons. In a postobservation discussion held the week before the session above, she explained again that the last couple of sessions during the first year focused her attention on asking deeper questions that went beyond asking "Why?" or "How?" Linda seemed to understand that the ability to pose good questions was related to a teacher's understanding of the mathematics. When asked whether she would have any recommendations for a teacher preparing to teach a unit on ratio and proportion, she responded

Yeah, I would probably talk a bit about their knowledge of ratio and proportion to see whether they had an understanding whether it was—maybe even the multiplicative/additive choices, because I think a lot of teachers don't have that knowledge. I'm sure that I didn't. I mean I had it; I had the algorithm in my head, but I didn't know where it came from or what it really meant.

Throughout Year 2, Linda spoke often about the relationship between teachers' content knowledge and their instruction. During a seminar held in January of 1994, she said

> In some of the replacement units, the activities are really good; they're easy to follow, once you've taught one or two of them, but sometimes I'm not sure what the key concepts are—or that they are hitting the same key concepts that I've felt would be important.

Teaching Fractions the Second Year

In March we observed three consecutive lessons Linda taught on fractions. The first lesson introduced paper folding when students worked with constructing proper fractions. During the second and third lessons, the students made their own fraction strips and used them when they worked with ideas of equivalence. Linda did not use any paper folding again until April; she then used paper folding for 2 days to introduce fraction multiplication. We observed those lessons and describe portions of them here.

During our first observation in April, Linda told her students that they would multiply fractions that day, and she began the lesson by asking students to open their journals and write what they knew about multiplication, giving examples. Linda asked students to share their work, and all of the shared examples involved repeated addition. Linda then asked the students to fold a sheet of paper in thirds. She next instructed them to fold the paper in half "the opposite way from the way they had folded the thirds." The students then unfolded the paper and counted six segments. Linda asked, "If you fold thirds in half, you get?" and, using Tom Kieren's notation,[3] she wrote[4] on the

board $1 \overset{\frac{1}{3}}{\frown} \frac{1}{3} \overset{\frac{1}{2}}{\frown} \frac{1}{6}$. Linda got no response to her question, so she said, "We started with one whole. We folded it in three. Each piece was one third. We folded each piece in half. Now each piece is one sixth." She followed up with an additional question: "What would happen if we folded in half again?"

---

3. During his seminar presentation, Tom Kieren shared this notation that his third-grade students had developed while working with fractions (see Kieren, 1995, based on this presentation).

4. In this notation, the lower numbers represent how the paper looks and the upper numbers represent the operations. So, for example, this notation represents, "Start with one whole. Fold the one whole into thirds. The result is one third of the original whole. Then fold the thirds in half. The result is one sixth of the original whole."

The rest of the lesson continued in this manner. Linda gave students a task, then she either told them how to fold the paper or asked until a student told the class how to fold the paper. Linda then asked everyone to fold and she followed up with questions about what they had found. The problems included finding one third of the one sixth

they had above $\left[1 \overset{\frac{1}{3}}{\curvearrowright} \frac{1}{3} \quad \frac{1}{2} \overset{\frac{1}{6}}{\curvearrowright} \frac{1}{6} \quad \frac{1}{3} \overset{\frac{1}{18}}{\curvearrowright} \frac{1}{18} \right]$ and finding one third

of one third $\left[1 \overset{\frac{1}{3}}{\curvearrowright} \frac{1}{3} \quad \frac{1}{3} \overset{\frac{1}{9}}{\curvearrowright} \frac{1}{9} \right]$. The last task she gave her students, one that seemed to challenge them even more, was to determine what operations were necessary in the process represented by the following

notation: $1 \quad \overset{\frac{1}{3}}{\curvearrowright} \quad \overset{\frac{1}{12}}{\curvearrowright}$. Students had trouble distinguishing between folding a paper into fourths and folding four times, and they discussed the difference between finding one fourth of one third and finding four groups of one third.

During the postobservation discussion, Linda was asked whether what she had hoped would happen happened. She responded, "Yeah. I think it happened; I think that they started to realize . . . . I don't think they saw it as multiplication, but that was okay, because I didn't really think they would at first. And they didn't." She explained that she wanted the students to see that ¼ three times is different from ¼ one third of a time. She was asked what she planned for the next lesson. Linda said that she planned to give students multiplication problems to fold. The interviewer then asked Linda what kind of thinking she was hoping to promote, and while Linda was talking about the task, she became confused:

> Inv: I'm looking at Kieren's page 30. He says, "Fold these products; remember to keep a record." What will you be doing with this then?
>
> Linda: I'll probably put those on the board.
>
> Inv: Like ½ × ⅓; ¾ × ⅙? Are they supposed to fold those then?
>
> Linda: Yeah. They can fold them. I'm gonna give them smaller pieces of paper tomorrow because we don't need to have huge pieces.
>
> Inv: Some of the kids already know how to multiply these. Will they not fold then?
>
> Linda: I'm going to make them fold for at least a couple. I want them to fold it so they can see it. Then I think I'm going to have

some of the kids who really have folded it and then put them with people like Joe and Fred, who can't even fold a piece of paper in thirds.

Inv: So like ⅓ × ¾—what are you hoping they'll . . .? How will they fold that?

Linda: What I think we'll do is fold it in fourths and then maybe we'll color in.

Inv: Three of them?

Linda: Three of them. Three of the fourths of the thirds.

Inv: Would they start with . . . ?

Linda: Start with the thirds. Then fold it in fourths. Then in each third, they're gonna fill in three of the fourths. (Pause) Right?

The researcher realized that Linda was confused. First of all, her approach did not attend to the convention she addressed in class (⅓ × ¾ means "one third *of* three fourths"). According to this convention, the first fraction acts as an operator on the second fraction; the ⅓ *acts* on the ¾, and so we must first have a ¾ to be acted on. Furthermore, she appeared to want to shade in three fourths of each of the thirds, which would result in 9 of the 12 small rectangles being shaded. When the researcher asked for clarification, Linda, too, realized that she was confused:

Inv: Um. Let's do it because I'm confused. (Gets paper)

Linda: No. They're not gonna fill in three of each one. Wait. Fold it in thirds.

Inv: A third times three fourths.

Linda: Fold it in thirds; fold it in fourths. Then they are going to fill in three of them.

Linda's approach here is to fold the paper to create the required number of partitions, and then to fold in the opposite direction to create the required number of partitions in the other fraction. She folded the paper in thirds 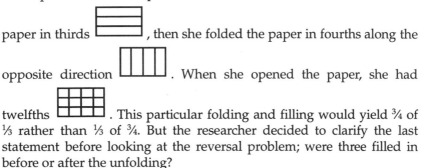, then she folded the paper in fourths along the opposite direction . When she opened the paper, she had twelfths . This particular folding and filling would yield ¾ of ⅓ rather than ⅓ of ¾. But the researcher decided to clarify the last statement before looking at the reversal problem; were three filled in before or after the unfolding?

Inv: Three of what?
Linda: Three of the 12.
Inv: (Folds) How do they know to fill in three of the twelfths?
Linda: I think we'll go over it first. Maybe they need to see it.
Inv: What if you did this?

The researcher showed Linda another approach to folding the paper. First he folded the paper into thirds. Then, instead of opening the paper up again, he kept the paper folded and pointed out that they now had one third. He then folded the one third into fourths, and marked three of the fourths, thereby having three fourths of one third. When he opened the paper, the researcher pointed out that three of the twelfths were shaded:

Linda: Okay.
Inv: Here's your third. Now this is a third. Now I want three fourths of this. This is one fourth of that third. So this is three fourths of the third. Then what portion of the whole is this?
Linda: Right. That's it. I think when I worked on it tonight I would have seen that—that that would be a lot more logical.

The researcher did not return to the reversal problem, perhaps overlooking it, which could be the reason he demonstrated three fourths of one third rather than one third of three fourths.

On the following day Linda surprised the researcher when she began the fraction lesson by demonstrating multiplication on the overhead, placing a transparency of a square with a horizontal ⅓ colored blue and another square with vertical ¼ of it colored orange.

Linda: Remember how I told you to read this [⅓ × ¼]?
Janine: One third times one fourth.
Linda: Another way.
Lew: I don't remember.
Roger: One third *of* one fourth.

Linda repeated this answer, then overlapped the two squares and asked what part of the square had both colors. Students gave answers including ⁶⁄₁₂, ¹⁄₁₂, and ⁴⁄₁₂.

Linda: I only want to know how big the piece is that is covered by both the third and the fourth strip.
Connie: The pieces with the two colors.
Linda: That's a good way to describe it.
Ruby: One twelfth.
Linda: Why?
Mike: Both colors are on one twelfth.

Walter: There are 12 pieces on the square.

Ann: Yeah. There are 12 pieces on there, and both of the colors are on only one square.

Linda: Oh. There are 12 boxes, and only 1 is covered by both.

[Students ask to have the question clarified.]

Linda: Leander, Jasmine, and Mona said that it is one twelfth. This is one third: ⬜. If the third is cut in four pieces [Linda indicates the fourths of the one third by placing the side of her hand across the third at the appropriate intervals ⬜.] . . . Let's leave it. This didn't work. We'll come back to it.

Linda did not seem to realize that the double-coloring method does not distinguish between $\frac{1}{3} \times \frac{1}{4}$ and $\frac{1}{4} \times \frac{1}{3}$; in fact, this method does not illustrate the process of taking a fractional amount of a fractional amount. However, her last statement returned to this notion, but she was indicating $\frac{1}{4}$ of $\frac{1}{3}$ rather than $\frac{1}{3}$ of $\frac{1}{4}$. She realized that most of her students were not following her, so she handed out paper to the students. She gave them the same problem, $\frac{1}{3} \times \frac{1}{4}$, and attempted to lead them through the process of folding to find a solution. A student suggested starting with $\frac{1}{3}$ (as Linda had just done) and Linda reminded the class that $\frac{1}{3} \times \frac{1}{4}$ means $\frac{1}{3}$ of $\frac{1}{4}$, so they must start with $\frac{1}{4}$. She then asked students to show her $\frac{1}{4}$, which students did in different ways: ⬛ or ⬜ or ⬛. Linda next directed her students not to unfold the paper, but to fold the $\frac{1}{4}$ into thirds. After they had done this folding, she told them to open up their paper and draw in the lines. She asked the students whether everyone had the same shape, to which the students responded, "No." Then she asked them whether they had the same area, to which students responded, "Yes." She seemed to assume that the students would realize that the small rectangle, of whatever shape, was one twelfth, and was the solution for $\frac{1}{3} \times \frac{1}{4}$.

Linda next asked the students to show her $\frac{1}{2}$ of $\frac{1}{4}$ followed by $\frac{1}{3}$ of $\frac{1}{2}$. The final problem she posed was for the students to find $\frac{1}{2}$ of $\frac{2}{3}$. Most of the students seemed to feel that they understood, and they folded paper and marked squares. Linda noted that some students were very confused, and she invited those who wanted extra help to a table. She talked them through the problem by folding thirds and showing two of them to indicate $\frac{2}{3}$, and then they folded the $\frac{2}{3}$ in half in the opposite direction, creating sixths. When she opened her paper, she explained that she was left with $\frac{2}{6}$. One student at the table did not fold the $\frac{2}{3}$ in the opposite direction, but instead recognized that half of $\frac{2}{3}$ would be $\frac{1}{3}$. Linda tried to "trick" the students by asking, "One third? You couldn't have done it the same way if he came out with $\frac{2}{6}$ and you came out with

⅓." A student pointed out that ⅓ and ⅔ are "the same," and the lesson ended.

During the postobservation interview, Linda said that the lesson went well at the end. She thought the students felt confident enough to solve the half of two thirds by themselves, and she thought that about half of the eight students who came to the table for extra help did not need any. The interviewer commented, "I saw the wheels turning in your brain as you were trying to decide the problem—or had you decided that ahead?" Linda's response characterized her general approach to lesson planning and teaching: "No. I just picked it. The whole lesson I just sort of did. I knew what I wanted to get done, and I hadn't planned anything ahead. I usually do it that way unless I'm working with a worksheet or an investigation or something that's set out for me. Otherwise I like to just go with it and go where the kids want to go." This lack of attention to the selection of prototype problems and working out beforehand the example problems was typical of Linda's planning, and when she had a solid grasp of the mathematics, this type of teaching was usually successful. However, when her own understanding was not yet robust, she tended to confuse the students. Still, students were getting a better introduction to multiplication of fractions than they had had in the past, and paper folding seemed to have much to do with it. It appeared that Linda was learning along with the students and that she realized that in her demonstration she was confusing her students because she herself was confused. By stopping the demonstration and beginning the folding, she was in effect starting the lesson over.

The problem of introducing a new notation before its need had been established is also a pitfall for teachers trying to make changes before they have thought through all the issues. In Kieren's class the children had invented the notation they used because they recognized a need to write down what they were doing in a way others could understand during their class discussions. Linda introduced the notation before the students realized a need for it.

Linda's view of what she hoped to accomplish with these lessons was influenced by her involvement in the project, as can be seen in the following excerpt:

Inv: You're doing this folding even though they know how to multiply procedurally; you're doing this folding so that they will understand. When you finish, if you've done your job well, what will they understand?

Linda: Um. The idea that we're not just moving numbers—that each number represents a quantity, some quantity. And we're taking some part of some quantity. One half is not "one over two." One half is a quantity that is equal to one half of the whole. And I want to find out what one fourth of that is. And one fourth is a quantity. Even though ¼ does represent one out of four pieces, I don't want them to think of it that way. I want them to think of one fourth as the quantity—how many. . . . I want to see one fourth of that one half. That was another thing when I was reading over my notes from last year—it talked about that one half is a quantity. I never thought of it that way before. I thought of it as a part of the whole. I didn't think of one half as being a quantity by itself.

Each new way of teaching a particular topic has its constraints and pitfalls. We see in this lesson a first attempt at adopting a way of teaching that had been successfully used by others to teach with understanding. We suspect that Linda herself is coming to a deeper understanding while she picks her way through the lesson, recognizing when she leads her students astray, abandoning one approach and trying others.

SUMMARY

During the first year of this project, Linda was a teacher who by all appearances was doing everything right. Linda was in command of the class. She was poised, confident, and in control, whether the students were working individually, in cooperative groups, or as an entire class. She joked with her students, and they liked her, but they also respected her. Her competence as a teacher was recognized by administrators, who asked her to be the assistant principal of the school. She had little difficulty creating opportunities for her children to think. She was confident in her ability to teach. She was using innovative curricula and strategies, including allowing her students to work in small groups, keep journals, and explain their thinking.

Linda wholeheartedly accepted the rhetoric of the reform movement in school mathematics. Anything traditional was considered suspect. She was moving away from the textbook, from worksheets, from teaching algorithms, from "telling" students how to do mathematics—from most things traditional. She was frustrated with parents who did not agree with her approach, and she spoke often about the struggles she was having with her students' reliance on meaningless procedures. During the first year Linda was running away from something more than she was running toward something. She had given up much of what she had come to think of as mathematics teaching, but she did not always have anything appropriate with which to replace it. She had difficulty being critical about anything that she understood to be a part of the reform movement. She was not in a position to dig below the surface, and there were no colleagues at her site who might help her do this digging.

During our seminar discussions of the first year, Linda was always willing to talk about her struggles to implement reform, but she was hesitant to engage in discussions about mathematics. When we finished the first year, Linda began to change her view of herself and her teaching. She recognized that it was not enough to give students projects without knowing what mathematical concepts she hoped they would learn. She wanted to pose deeper questions, but she recognized how difficult it was to do so. She lost a lot of confidence in herself, and for a while she considered quitting the project.

The biggest change we saw in Linda over the course of this project was in her priorities. During the first year, she seemed as if she attended the seminars in order to discuss teaching. The mathematical content was secondary. By the second year, Linda's comments about and interactions during the seminars made it clear that she viewed the opportunity to consider the mathematical ideas as the most important contribution the seminars provided her. She had become impatient with teacher development or inservices that did not focus on the mathematical ideas. During the last seminar of the project, held in May 1994, Linda commented that most elementary teachers were weak in mathematics: "A lot of teachers don't want to even teach upper grades because they don't understand the math they're teaching. That's scary." She considered some of the reasons for this problem while reflecting on her own teacher preparation, "I think it has to do with what we're taught as student teachers. . . . I didn't get a real deep understanding."

Linda's own instruction during the project was influenced by what she was learning. By the second year she was teaching topics she had skipped before, either because she now understood them better or because she had come to recognize their importance in the curriculum— sometimes both. She incorporated teaching ideas she picked up in the seminars, and she was willing to try them out in her classroom. She sometimes stumbled, due primarily to her lack of deep understanding of the mathematical concepts she was teaching and a willingness to "wing it" rather than thinking through her examples before class began. During the second year, she did not feel as constrained to follow the curriculum she was piloting. It was no longer new to her, and she was now committed to developing in her students particular types of rational number knowledge and reasoning that she had come to value during the seminars.

During the last seminar, Linda talked about a new project with which she had become involved. Her belief that the mathematics should be at the forefront of teacher-enhancement projects came through clearly:

> Linda: The new math project has begun training the teacher leaders, and I was selected as one of the teacher leaders. We had our first meeting. One of the things we talked about is as we are training other site leaders, we will be having to teach them what the math is and how to do the math a lot of times. It hit me that that's what I've been working on for 2 years with this group: Where is the math? What is the math? Do I understand it well enough so that I can go back and really truly teach it to the students, not just throw it at them: "Here it is, sort of; I'm not sure. Do it this way because I know this way will work"? So what we're going to be trying to do is working with teachers to train them.
>
> Inv: If you hadn't been involved in this project and you had gone to that meeting where they talked about teaching the math, how would you have been hearing what they were saying?
>
> Linda: I would have said, "Oh, I already know that," because I thought I did.
>
> Inv: So the first step is actually one where a person has to come to understand what she doesn't understand?
>
> Linda: Absolutely.

Chapter 6

SHEY: TEACHING MATHEMATICS TO CHILDREN OF DIVERSITY

In this chapter we describe Shey, a fifth-grade inner-city-school teacher, and the instructional effects of his coming to hold a more conceptually oriented view of mathematics. We describe how this changing view of mathematics led him to raise his expectations of his students, resulting in Shey's assigning more challenging tasks and expecting his students to provide more conceptual explanations for their reasoning. We also describe a difficulty that emerged when he raised his expectations, a difficulty that we suspect many teachers will experience when they assume more conceptually oriented approaches to the teaching of mathematics. Shey had trouble anticipating his students' understanding, resulting in difficulty selecting conceptually accessible tasks for his students. Associated with this difficulty was that some of the discussions he held with his students did not seem to converge toward a central idea.

Shey enjoys mathematics and has taken sufficient mathematics classes to obtain a supplemental degree for teaching junior high school mathematics. However, he did not always enjoy mathematics. In the late 1970s Shey came from Ireland, where he remembers having loved mathematics until the sixth grade, at which time something upsetting happened to him. Shey had completed one of the first assignments he received from his sixth-grade mathematics teacher requiring him to draw scalene, isosceles, and equilateral triangles, and because he had completed his homework on the bus, his drawings had not been done well. His teacher decided to make an example of Shey, and, in front of all of the students, his teacher, using a "black strap," gave him 12 lashings on his hand. From that point through the end of high school,

Shey "hated math, hated it and loathed it." After coming to America, he found he liked math again, and he completed enough mathematics courses to obtain his supplemental degree. His memories of being humiliated in front of his peers led him to believe not only that teachers should not intimidate their students the way his sixth-grade teacher had done to him, but also that teachers should make mathematics learning enjoyable for students.

The year-round urban school in which Shey taught had 1,250 students, mainly African Americans, Southeast Asians, Somalians, and Hispanics from Mexico and from Central and South America. The students at his school scored in the 9th percentile on the district mathematics test. There was frequent movement of students in and out of Shey's class, and at any given time there were four to seven students who spoke little or no English. Shey taught a self-contained fifth-grade class, and he enjoyed teaching mathematics. At the start of the project he said, "I like math because I do think I understand it—not all of it—but I understand." He had been involved in two inservice mathematics projects, the first a 1-week summer inservice in 1989, which he described as "fantastic," and a second that met one day each month over the course of 2 years. His involvement in these projects seemed to affect how he thought about himself as a teacher, and when describing his role, he referred to himself as a facilitator. He thought there was too much emphasis in schools on paper-and-pencil mathematics.

HOW THE PROJECT INFLUENCED SHEY

The seminar transcripts and interviews provide evidence that all of the teachers learned mathematics in the project. But for Shey, the main influence the project seemed to have was in the way his view of mathematics was affected. Early in the project the teachers administered an assessment of rational number understanding to their students, and while discussing the results, the teachers noted how much difficulty their students had comparing fractions. The following excerpt shows that at the outset of the project, Shey's focus was on learning a procedure for comparing fractions:

> Inv: What would you like for your students to be able to think when they look at $\frac{5}{7}$ and $\frac{5}{9}$?
>
> Shey: I would like for them to say, "Oh, 63 is a common denominator." (Laughs)
>
> Tom: I don't think I would like the common denominator.
>
> Cynthia: I wouldn't want to see a common denominator.
>
> Inv: Would you, Shey? Would you like that?

Shey: Yeah, I would. Ultimately I would. I would like them to know. Ultimately I would like for them to be able to find the common denominator.

By November of the second year, Shey had clearly changed his thinking about what is important for students to know about fractions. During a seminar at this time we discussed the possibility of meeting as a group during a school day with the understanding that the project could support hiring substitute teachers. Shey was very much against the idea because, as he explained, the last time he had left his students with a substitute the substitute had taught his students how to find least common denominators, and Shey found that after that his students were no longer interested in trying to make sense of the mathematics. Shey explained that he had been suffering ever since.

During the last seminar in May of the second year, the issue of what is important for students to know about fractions came up again. The following excerpt shows how Shey's view had changed from the view he held at the beginning of the project:

Shey: One question I've had—like our textbook has a problem like $\frac{5}{8} + \frac{7}{9}$. Would you prefer a child to be able to get the common denominator and do all this reducing and all the rest to come up with an answer, and not really know what they're doing, or would we prefer the kid to be able to say, "This $\frac{7}{9}$ is about 1; this $\frac{5}{8}$ is about a half. So the answer's. . . ." And really know that in fifth grade. Which would you prefer?

Linda: I would want them to know what they were dealing with. To be able to see that the—I don't remember the numbers—what they're dealing with—what it actually is, the picture, to be able to picture it, to be able to see it at fifth grade. Later on I hope that they'd be able to. . . .

Shey: In the Holt math book there are three pages of those kinds of problems. A lot of the stuff, I think, is too advanced. . . .

Linda: Too symbolic.

Shey: Yeah. If we can give them this basic knowledge that they will say, "Hey, I understand about fractions. I understand if I've got three halves, I've got one and a half. If I've got two thirds, I've got. . . ." So the Holt math book, to me, a lot of the stuff they put in there is a way. . . . But some kids like it, too, though; they like getting these common denominators and all that. But I would like kids to know the guidelines—not the guidelines. What was the word we used?

Cynthia: Benchmarks.

Shey: I really think that's so important.

In January of the second year, after a lesson he taught on decimals, Shey talked about how the project had affected his view of mathematics. Even though decimals had not been the focus of any of the seminars, Shey's changing view of mathematics influenced his thinking about decimals. Evidently, the view of mathematics that Shey had come to hold during the project affected the way he thought about all the mathematics he taught:

Inv: Was any part of this lesson influenced by this project?

Shey: I would say that the vast majority of it was.

Inv: But we didn't do decimals.

Shey: Yeah, but, just the whole discussions that we've been having on number sense and how valuable it is for the students, when they're doing things like this, to have a real understanding of what they're doing. I really do feel that the project has. . . . Plus it's influenced my way of asking questions, even when I'm teaching something that we haven't talked about.

Another example of how Shey's view of mathematics evolved involves proportional reasoning. Early in the project the teachers completed an assessment of their rational number understanding, which included the following problem:

Marissa bought 0.43 pounds of wheat flour for which she paid $0.86. How many pounds of flour could she buy for $1.00?

The following is a brief seminar discussion that took place about this problem:

Inv: Did anyone estimate?

Shey: I put zero. I assumed you could not buy a half pound of flour.

Linda: I felt stupid. I set up the proportion then saw the relationship.

Cynthia: I felt stupid when I got the answer.

Shey: We're not doing what we teach our students to do.

Shey's second comment was a portent of things to come. During subsequent seminars, Shey began doing what it was he wanted his students to do: willingly engage in activities designed to promote mathematical reasoning. In time, he grew to greatly appreciate the seminar sessions. He enjoyed being challenged, and he was willing to put himself in the position of a learner. For example, during a session toward the end of the first year, one of the researchers introduced the following problem (adapted from Susan Lamon's seminar presentation):

Jo has 2 snakes, String Bean and Slim. Right now, String Bean is 4 feet long and Slim is 5 feet long. Jo knows that 2 years from now both snakes will be fully grown. At her full length, String Bean will be 7 feet long, while Slim's length when he is fully grown will be 8 feet long. Over the next 2 years, will both snakes grow the same amount?

The discussion about this problem focused around the difference between viewing the problem *absolutely*, in which case one would note that each snake's length increased by 3 feet, and *relatively*, in which case one would be more likely to note that the smaller snake increased by a greater proportion of its length than the larger snake. The teachers considered this problem to be too difficult for their students, and one of the teachers suggested a different problem. However, Shey was not prepared to leave the original problem, and during the break he approached one of the researchers with the picture below.

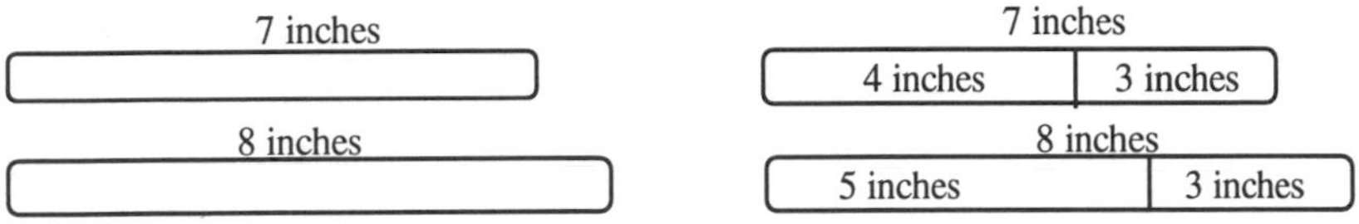

Shey noted that he could think of the first snake as increasing from 4 inches by 3 inches, and the second as increasing from 5 inches by 3 inches, but when he wrote the fractions ¾ and ⅗, he could not figure out what those fractions meant. That is, he did not know what ¾ was a fraction of. After the break he raised his question with the rest of the group, and a fascinating 45-minute discussion took place during which it became clear that Shey's question had stumped everyone. The following is a portion of the discussion that took place among the teachers when they tried to conceptualize what ⅝ was a fraction of:

Darota: Five eighths means that the snake in the past was that much smaller than it is now.
Inv: Do you all agree?
Cynthia: Umhmm. That's how big it was 3 years ago.
Inv: You don't agree?
Mike: It's not that much smaller. It's that much of what it is now.
Tom: Yeah. It's ⅜ smaller. It's ⅜ smaller.
Darota: No. Five eighths smaller than it is now.
Cynthia, Tom, and Shey: No.
Tom: It's ⅜ smaller.
Darota: Okay, wait. Wait a minute. Five eighths says. . . .
Mike: It is currently ⅝ of what it was in the past. Oh wait.
Darota: Five eighths larger.
Mike: No. Five eighths of what it is now.
Shey: It started off as five eighths of what it is now.
Cynthia: Right.

Shey had seen that making sense of the fractions in this context was nontrivial, and he raised the question in the group. This example highlights how Shey's view of mathematics had become more conceptual. Even though he realized this problem was too difficult for his students, Shey still wanted to make sense of the problem in the context. In the next section, we provide examples of how this view of mathematics learning as conceptual rather than procedural influenced his instruction.

HOW SHEY'S VIEW OF MATHEMATICS INFLUENCED HIS INSTRUCTION

Early in the project Shey gave his students a problem he had thought about in a seminar. In the problem, the numbers of brown eggs in two cartons were compared. The smaller carton contained a dozen eggs of which 4 were brown, and the larger carton contained 1½ dozen eggs of which 8 were brown. This problem, designed to address the difference between comparing the number of brown eggs absolutely (4 brown vs. 8 brown), additively (8 more white eggs than brown eggs in the smaller carton vs. 10 more white eggs than brown eggs in the larger carton), and multiplicatively (⅓ brown in the smaller carton vs. ⁴⁄₉ brown in the larger carton), elicited a variety of responses from his students. When one student called attention to the fact that ⅓ of the eggs in the small container were brown whereas ⁸⁄₁₈ of the eggs in the large container were brown, Shey steered the conversation toward calculational procedures:

> Shey: Eight eighteenths. Nice numbers. Eight eighteenths. Can we do anything with those eight eighteenths? Quinn?
>
> Quinn: Divide them?
>
> Shey: By what?
>
> Quinn: By two.
>
> Shey: Okay, divide them by two. [Students say four ninths.] Is there any possible way we can compare these two numbers? Yes?
>
> Sarah: Times the bottom.
>
> Shey: I don't know what you mean. Times the bottom by what or do what?
>
> Lin: I don't know.
>
> Shey: Okay.
>
> Doug: But I know something to do about times.
>
> Shey: Okay, you know something to do about times. What could we do? See, we're comparing here ⅓ and ⁴⁄₉.
>
> Varela: Three fourths?

Shey: Three fourths? Where do we get ¾?

Jesus: The 12.

Shey: Dallas?

Dallas: Times 3 times 3 which is 9 and 3 times 1 is 3.

Shey: So you would change this—to multiply? Okay, why are you able to apply a correction by 3 over 3? Phi, why are you able to multiply a fraction by 3 over 3?

Phi: Because the denominator is. . . .

Shey: I know, but my question to you is why can we multiply a fraction by 3 over 3? Bo?

Bo: Because it's 1.

Shey: Because 3 over 3 equals 1, and if you multiply a number by 1, Bo, what happens?

Jean: It equals the same. . . .

Shey: It equals the same number, so we're not changing this, but we are . . . ? So we found out that ⅔ of the top one is brown and ⅘ of the bottom one is brown. Which has more brown, Pat?

Pat: The four ninths.

Shey: Four ninths. But you can kind of see that looking at it.

This excerpt reflects the direction of some of Shey's classroom conversations early in the project—toward a discussion of procedures and away from a discussion of the underlying reasoning that gave rise to the procedures.

Two months later, after participating in seminars during which Shey thought more deeply about proportional reasoning, Shey again addressed proportional reasoning with his students. This time, rather than pursue calculational procedures, he provided alternate problems until he hit upon one that his students found conceptually accessible. He began the lesson by providing a variant of the worm problem referred to earlier, but with easier numbers. He provided the diagram below and asked, "Which of these two worms do you think grew the most?"

Size in

A   ▢▢ 2"   July 1992   Slimo
    ▢▢▢▢▢▢▢▢ 8"   May 1993

B   ▢▢▢▢▢▢ 6"   July 1992   Squisho
    ▢▢▢▢▢▢▢▢▢▢▢▢ 12"   May 1993

After the class discussed the problem, a student hit upon the multiplicative relationship, which Shey pursued by asking the class for elaboration:

> *Shey*: So what does that mean? (Pause) Can anyone help Nicole? She just said something that might be a little different [from what has previously been suggested]. She says that this one [B], if you multiply this by 2, you will get 12. She's saying this one [A], if you multiply it [2] by what?
>
> Doug: Four.
>
> *Shey*: Four—you get 8.
>
> Sarah: Well, where do you all of a sudden get 4 at?
>
> *Shey*: Take the 2. She's saying you multiply by 4; you get 8. What she's saying here is if you take the 6. . . .
>
> Jean: Yeah, but where did she get the 4 on the top?
>
> *Shey*: Nicole, where did you get the 4?
>
> Nicole: Well, there are eight pieces there, so if you divide that into fours, you could just take half of it and multiply by the top one.
>
> *Shey*: Come up and show us what you're talking about because I don't understand.

Nicole did come up to explain, but her explanation was about what she did, not what she had thought about. Recognizing this fact, Shey did not pursue Nicole's calculations, but instead pushed her to explain her reasoning. When he realized that this was not going anywhere, he posed another problem that had been used in the seminars:

> *Shey*: Raise your hand if you like money. . . . [Shey chooses Nicole as banker.] Nicole's a banker, and I'm going to invest money with her. I'm gonna give her some money; she's gonna keep it for me, and I'm gonna make some money. So Mr. D is going to give Nicole 2 bucks. And at the end of the year, Nicole is going to give me back $8. Phi—who doesn't like to part with his money, but Nicole talks him into a good deal—Phi's going to give Nicole 6 bucks, and at the end of the year, on the very same day, Dallas, Nicole is going to give him $12 back. Who do you think would get the better deal out of this, or would we both get the same?

Students responded that they both got the same deal, and after a brief discussion, Shey called for a vote, with the students overwhelmingly (and maybe unanimously) voting that the two were the same. At this point Shey, who had predicted during a seminar that his students would be able to reason about this problem successfully, turned to a researcher who was observing the lesson and said, "I was totally wrong about this." But Shey neither turned the discussion into one focusing on calculations, nor did he give up altogether. Instead, he revised the problem on the spot, selecting numbers designed to emphasize the multiplicative relationships:

> *Shey*:   Okay, here we go again. Mr. D is going to invest one dollar. I'm going to invest one dollar with Nicole. Nicole is going to give me $20 back. Phi is going to invest $60. And he's gonna get $79 back. I invest 1 and I get 20. Phi gives her 60 bucks and he ends up with 79 bucks. Who makes the most money? Phi, who makes the most money? [He writes numbers on the overhead beside the worm-problem information.]

Students presented arguments for their conclusion that both investors would earn the same amount. Shey posed the question again, with slight modifications: "So, do we make the same? Would you rather, if you were investing money, and you wanted to make money, Leticia, would you rather invest $1 and get 20 bucks or would you rather invest $60 and get 79 bucks?" The students struggled with this question until one student seemed to look at the problem differently:

> Henry: I'd put a dollar because if I put a dollar in there, I'd get 19 back; if I keep on putting more dollars in there, it'll go past 69. And if you just put $60, you just wasted $60, and all you had to do was just put a dollar, and you could have had 20 and all that would come up to $80 that you could have kept in your pocket, instead of wasting a 60-dollar bill.

Shey continued to question Henry, but his explanation did not become any clearer. In the meantime, Eddie raised his hand, and Shey asked Henry, now at the board, if he would like some assistance.

> *Shey*:   You want to help him, Eddie? Henry, do you want Eddie's help?
> Henry: Yes.
> *Shey*:   Okay, Eddie. [Eddie goes to the board.]
> Henry: I wouldn't want to waste 60 bucks.
> Eddie: It's the same way, but look, you could just invest $1 and get 20; keep 19 [and reinvest $1] and keep on coming back.
> Henry: All that money that you're saving up is more than. . . .
> *Shey*:   [Feigning lack of understanding] I can't see it. It's the same.
> [Students are eager to explain.]
> Eddie: I would get this one [$1 → $20] because if you had this [$60], you could make this into 60 ones, then you could invest it [$1 at a time], and it would be like 60 times 20.

Notice that Shey's interjection, "I can't see it. It's the same," was designed to push the explanation even further. It worked. Shey and Eddie continued to discuss the problem, with students asking questions and sharing their views. Many students continued to maintain that there was no difference until Shey invited another student to share his thinking:

> Johnny: Sixty dollars [invested] separately at one dollar, you'll get one thousand two hundred dollars. But if you invest $60 in all [in the $60 → $79], you get $79 instead.

Shey invited Johnny to join Henry and Eddie at the board, and Johnny, through questions posed by Shey, explained his reasoning. Students seemed to be swayed by Johnny's logic, and when Shey took another vote later in the lesson, almost everyone voted that they would prefer to invest $1 for a $20 return.

This lesson continued for another 40 minutes, during which time Shey returned to the worm problem and to the modified worm problem (which used the numbers from the worm problem but used the investment scenario). Many students who had seemed convinced by Johnny's argument reverted to saying that the two situations [6 →12 and 2 → 8] were the same. By this time, however, there was a group of students who seemed to be convinced that it was not enough to look at the problems additively. These students were at least on the road toward thinking multiplicatively. The lesson ended, but during lunch, Shey told the researcher that he wanted to return to mathematics after lunch. Although the researcher did not stay to observe, he spoke with Shey that night; Shey reported that he had spent the afternoon on this topic and had found it fascinating. Shey explained that his students seemed to "get it," and when he gave them the original worm problem [4 → 7 and 5 → 8], one student recognized that for the first worm, "every 1 [inch] grew to 1.75, but for the second, every 1 [inch] grew to 1.6." Shey said he had not thought about it that way. He also mentioned that he went home that afternoon and read a chapter about proportional reasoning from a book we had given each teacher in the project.

One year into the project we again interviewed all of the teachers. During this interview Shey talked about some of what he thought he had gained from the project:

> I think that without the project, I think that I probably would have done things the old—well, no, I never really taught like that. I always wanted my kids to think, but I'm spending a lot more time at it, I think, on more powerful mathematical thinking than I was before. Do you see what it is that I'm saying? The project has

helped me with questions; I'm asking the kids better questions that I never thought to ask them before. And when a kid doesn't know something now, I don't just tell them what it is. I'll ask them another question that may be easier than the question prior, to get them started in that line of thinking, and then maybe when they get into that way of thinking, then maybe they'll get the next question. And I'm finding that it works quite a lot of the time. And then the kids are amazed that they got the answer that they thought was impossible.

Shey's comments were accurate. He was devoting more time to mathematical thinking; he was asking richer questions, and he avoided lecturing to his students. One-and-a-half months after the interview, during the second year of our project and after teaching a new group of fifth graders for a couple of months, Shey posed a proportional reasoning problem similar to the bank problem he had used the previous year:

	Investment	In 3 months
Kelly's Bank	$20	$40
Michael's Bank	$10	$30

Shey: You have $60 to invest. Will you invest it in Kelly's bank, Michael's bank, or does it not matter in which bank you invest your money?
Jessica (and a few others): Kelly's bank; you get $20 more.
Ashea: Kelly's bank. (Reason unclear)
Clarence (paraphrased): Michael's bank. In Michael's bank you get more. If you put two $10 in Michael's bank, you get $60, but in Kelly's, you get only $40.
Shey: Could you make a table?

Clarence came to the board and, with assistance, created a table showing that in Kelly's bank $60 could be represented as three groups of $20, with each of those $20 growing to $40, for a total of $120. In Michael's bank, the $60 could be represented as six $10, with each of those $10 growing to $30, for a total of $180. A remarkable thing about this portion of the lesson was that Clarence had just recently entered Shey's class, and the only thing Shey knew about Clarence at that time was that Clarence had transferred in from a special education class.

Shey's focus on conceptual understanding was evident both during his instruction and when he talked about his instruction. In January of the second year, after teaching a unit on fraction multiplication, he talked about his students' difficulties:

> The main problem still I feel is what the unit is. They seem to have a hard time shifting to different units. They seem to have this preset conception that this [one thing] is what it could be, and they don't seem to stand back and think about it.

Shey also seemed aware of the difficulties individual students were experiencing:

> Those students who do not really grasp the sense of the unit, like Khantally when he draws all these flats and longs, I'm gonna have to work with them. I think there are about 7 or 8 of them, and I'm gonna have to work with them separately or have other students work with them in groups because they don't understand that.

A DIFFICULTY: ANTICIPATING AND BUILDING ON HIS STUDENTS' THINKING

The difficulty of the content of the elementary mathematics curriculum is often underestimated by teachers who have come to view mathematics as a set of procedures to follow. When they begin to view the curriculum conceptually, many of these teachers recognize that not only is the curriculum more difficult than they had realized, but also that they themselves have not had opportunities to learn the mathematics they are expected to teach. When they develop more powerful ways to reason about this mathematics, the teachers' excitement for mathematics increases, and some of these teachers, like Shey, want to share these experiences with their students. When Shey's view of mathematics became more conceptual, his expectations of his students increased. Shey assigned more challenging tasks and expected his students to provide more conceptual explanations for their reasoning. These changes, however, were not without their difficulties. Because he was assigning more challenging tasks and was expecting his students to make sense of the ideas in a more conceptual manner, he was often surprised by how little his students understood. When his students would get stuck, Shey often did not know how he might help his students proceed, and because he was not using a textbook or any extended curricula, he had few places to turn. Shey's difficulty was complicated by the fact that his own mathematics education had been more procedural than conceptual, so he often found that he first had to rethink the mathematical ideas he wanted his students to learn.

During a warm-up activity, Shey wrote $\frac{16}{17} + \frac{9}{10}$ on the board and asked his students to estimate the sum. During the subsequent discussion, one student explained that she added $9 + 7$ to get 16, and then concluded that the answer was $\frac{7}{7}$. Another student said the answer was ½. Another student added numerators and denominators to get $^{25}/_{27}$, which he then estimated to be 1½. Another student said, "$^{16}/_{17}$ is close to zero and $^{9}/_{10}$ is close to zero, so the answer is ½." Another student said he did not know, and still another estimated to get 1⅓. When he walked around the room, Shey was shocked at what he saw and heard, and he turned to a researcher who was observing the lesson and said, "This is blowing my mind."

In October of the second year, Shey taught a unit on fractions. In one lesson, the students were working with fractions using pattern blocks, including yellow hexagons, red trapezoids (2 of which cover one hexagon), blue rhombi (3 of which cover one hexagon), and green triangles (6 of which cover one hexagon). Following is a portion of the lesson:

Shey: Show me how to do 1 multiplied by one half.
Jonathan: You have one whole; then you add one half, so 1½.
Shey: If I asked you half of 1, what would it be?
Jonathan: A half? One fourth.
Shey: Show me how.
Tony: You need to reduce.
Shey: What?
Tony: The blue block.
Jonathan: [At the overhead, he puts triangles on the hexagon.] I'll cover half. [He puts three triangles on half of the hexagon.] 3¼.
Shey: So if you have one dollar, and half [halve it]—you get $3.25. Who agrees? [No one expresses agreement.]

Tony goes to the overhead and places two rhombi on the hexagon. He says that it does not work. Ashea disagrees with Tony, but she does not know why. David also disagrees.

David: 'Cause 1 times ½ is 1½.
Shey: Good job.

Shey wrote on the overhead: $1 \times ½ = 1½$.

Karen: (Disagrees) Anything times 1 is the same number. One times one fourth is one fourth. Take a triangle; now times 1 . . .
Letitia: One times one half is 1½. (Most students agree.)
Shey: [He holds up one hexagon.] Show me half of one whole.

Shey wrote on the overhead:

½ of 1

½ × 1

Most students show the answer to be 1½. Tony, however, shows the answer to be one half. Shey asks Tony to explain.

Tony: When you multiply times 1, you get the same number.
Shey: [To the class] Hold up a hexagon. Just block off half. Janie, what is half of 1?
Janie: A half.
Shey: I need everyone in listening position: 1, 2, 3. Thank you, Latoya. This is the question I am asking: What is one half of one whole? It is one half.

At this point Shey goes on to another question:

Shey: Can you tell me what one third of one whole equals? Hold up your answer. [Students hold up the rhombus.] I see lots of blues. Can you explain that to me?
Vanessa: One whole times a third equals one whole and one third.
Shey: You were holding up one third. [Vanessa has to leave class for some reason.]
Shey: Can anyone explain why one third of one whole is one third?
Letitia: Block off one half of one third and you get two thirds. [She blocks off one third of a whole.] So one third is wrong.
Carly: [Putting a rhombus on a hexagon] It takes three of these [rhombi] for 1 [hexagon], so one rhombus is one third of 1, so one third of 1 is one third.
Shey: Are these the same?

$$\tfrac{1}{3} \times 1$$

$$1 \times \tfrac{1}{3}$$

David: They have the same answer. Both are two thirds. One third equals two thirds.
Shey: [Holding up a rhombus, which is ⅓] Multiply by 1.
(David holds up one third.)
Shey: Is it one third or two thirds?
David: One third; two thirds.
Shey: What is 4 × 1? 8 × 1? 2,561 × 1? What is one third multiplied by 1? [David answers correctly for each.]
David: If you multiply one third by 1, you always get the same.
Shey: What is one third of 1?
David: One third.
Shey: You told me it was two thirds. I think it's two thirds. Raise your hand if you think one third of 1 is one third. [No one raises a hand.] Is everybody dead?

The students were clearly confused during this lesson. During the first portion, when Tony finally said, "When you multiply times 1, you get the same number," Shey decided it was time to move on. He did not know how to steer the conversation in a direction that might help the majority of his students who did not understand, and he told us during the postobservation interview how surprised he had been that his students had so much trouble with this question.

What is one to make of this lesson? Perhaps we might consider Shey's options. Many of the tasks Shey used were new for him, and he had little experience with how his students might think about the content. He did not know what questions to pose in order to help his students work through their confusions. Sometimes the students, with Shey as leader, would work their way through to some meaningful resolution, but sometimes they would not. In those situations in which they would not, Shey could have told his students how he wanted them to think about a task, but he resisted. Perhaps there are dues a teacher like Shey must pay for teaching mathematics the way he has chosen. Those dues may include the fact that he is not always "in command" of every discussion. He cannot always "steer" the ship, and consequently, there are discussions that appear to fall flat conceptually. But Shey was willing to live with that. In fact, for Shey, these occasions provided opportunities for him to learn a great deal about how his students thought about the mathematics. These situations taught him a lot that he could build on in subsequent lessons with his students. For Shey, a lesson was not something that always fit into a 45- or 60-minute time frame, but might go on for hours in 1 day, or continue for several consecutive days. As much as Shey disliked leaving his students confused, he could live with their confusion because he believed that lecturing them as to how they ought to be thinking would be pointless. This is not to say that he would handle a similar situation in the same manner the next time it occurred. Shey was learning along with his students, and we have seen him handle students' confusion on one occasion very differently from a previous occasion, before he had had a chance to consider alternatives. But given that he would not play the role of the mathematical authority who would bail his students out of any conceptual confusion, Shey was left with two choices: He could sustain the conversation by continuing to call on students and by altering the tasks and questions, or he could punt. We saw him do both.

On the day following the lesson described above, Shey tried another approach to multiplication of fractions, but again he was shocked at what he learned. This lesson involved pattern blocks.

Shey: Don't take the pattern blocks out until you are told to do so. What is one half of 4?

[Shey goes around the room calling on students.]
Luanna: Six.
Roseanna: Seven.
Ashea: [Inaudible]
Shante: One third.
Dan: Four.
David: Three and one half.
Kevin: One.
Janie: One fourth.
Tony: Five.
Michael: Two and a half.
Todd: Three and one half.
Khantally: Five and a half.
Rachel: Four.
Jermaine: *Of* means *times*.
Shey: Michael, what is $4 \times \frac{1}{2}$?
David: Same thing. Three and a half.
Tony: Five.
Jessica: Two. If you had four halves, it would equal up to two wholes.
[Shey puts four halves together with pattern blocks, making two hexagons.]
Shey: What about half of 4? That's not 2, is it?
Janie: It's one half. You reduce.

Shey asked four students to go to the front of the room and then he asked that half of the students go back to their seats. Two students immediately walked away. Shey then asked what half of four is, and no one responded. Shey was shocked that no one could say that half of 4 is 2, and he asked that the video camera be turned off. He turned to the observer and said he was amazed; he asked what he should do. The observer asked if the students had worked with discrete sets before, but Shey did not seem to see any relevance in that question. He continued to exclaim that he was shocked that his students did not know that half of 4 is 2. Shey repeated the experiment involving four people in the front of the room, with the same results. Some students this time said, "Two were left." Others said "one half," and still others said "two fourths."

Later in the lesson, Shey was working with a group of three girls, and he asked them to show half of 6. The girls placed six hexagons out, and then they reached for some red trapezoids, each of which represents half of a hexagon. Each time the girls reached for the trapezoids, Shey stopped them, put the six hexagons back in front of them, and repeated the question. This sequence of events was repeated for a couple of minutes until class ended.

A few weeks later, Shey, with two researchers, watched the videotape of this incident. One of the two researchers had observed the original lesson; the other had watched the videotape. Shey and the second researcher discussed the tape:

> Shey: If you [the researcher] asked a fifth grader who had been doing addition and subtraction of fractions and talking about fractions for 2 or 3 weeks what half of 4 is, how many students would you expect in the class to be able to do it?
>
> Inv: It depends on what kind of models you were associating with fractions.
>
> Shey: It would. But even without giving kids fractions. . . .
>
> Inv: What I'm saying is that maybe *before* your work on fractions, they may have given you the answer 2. But then if in your work on fractions, say you were using mostly area models and no set models—I don't know what you were doing—and they hadn't heard that fraction term in a while associated with a set model. . . . Or in your classroom, they're lining these ideas up in a certain way and they may have been trying to . . . .
>
> Shey: I never thought of that. You know because we have kindergartners who come into school who can read and write a little bit and by the end of kindergarten they don't know their. . . . Maybe that's what's happening with my kids. They knew what half of 4 was before we started fractions.
>
> Inv: I don't know, but it depends on their recent experiences with fractions in that particular setting in that classroom. I don't know. It's interesting.
>
> Shey: The other interesting thing was that none of them could say what one half of 4 is.
>
> Inv: What did you attribute it to?
>
> Shey: I don't know. I was baffled. I was just too totally shocked. So then I told them to stop. Then I put four kids up in the front of the classroom, and I told half of them to leave.
>
> Inv: And two immediately walked away.
>
> Shey: Two immediately walked away. Then I had the rest of the class raise their hand and tell me how many were left. Kids would put up their hand [and say], "A half." There were two kids standing there! [One student said,] "A quarter." I just couldn't believe it!

Our discussion continued with Shey, and it became clear that he had not considered that the girls at the end of class were thinking of half of one whole instead of half of six wholes. Shey had not unpacked the difference between viewing fractions from an area model and from a set model. He could move back and forth between these different models of fractions so easily that he had not considered the kinds of problems these tasks might cause for students. Furthermore, because this was the first time he had approached fractions in this manner with fifth graders, he had no experience with their thinking.

It is tempting here to conclude that Shey had created his own difficulties—if only he had listened more carefully to his students, these problems could have been painlessly overcome. We disagree. Shey had not experienced this curriculum with students before, and he had not developed a deep understanding either of the different types of models for fractions or of how his students might think about these models. To expect Shey to do all of that on the fly seems to be too much to expect of teachers. We contend that what Shey was expecting of himself is too much to expect of any middle-grades teacher—that is, to create a curriculum, teach it, and assess it. But for an inner-city middle-grades teacher with a class of students as diverse as Shey's, this combination of tasks is seemingly impossible. However, given that Shey did not have access to any available curriculum that might support his more conceptually oriented view of mathematics, he was left in the position of either compromising by using the textbook or accepting the difficulties inherent in creating his own lessons. He chose the latter. And in the long run we believe that Shey's students were better off because of that choice.

We have described the dilemma Shey experienced associated with the difficulty of anticipating or building on his students' thinking. An associated difficulty involved a tension Shey felt between fostering diversity and having convergence of ideas as a goal. In order to increase student participation during class discussions, Shey always encouraged his students to share their thoughts during discussions, and although he often directed students to consider a thought that seemed to make sense, he seldom discussed with the students a contribution that made little sense. All ideas were accepted equally, often resulting in contradictory ideas being introduced but neither resolved nor even acknowledged as contradictory. As a result, occasionally lessons seemed to fall "flat," leaving observers and students alike wondering what they were supposed to learn.

During a conversation in October of the second year, Shey explained his approach:

> I find that a lot of times with the kids—they see something or they
> think they see something, but they can't explain. What I try to do is

try to get back to them again when they've thought about it a little more. A lot of times when they're on center stage, they get frustrated, so I try to get back to them.

In a postobservation interview, one of the researchers raised the tension he felt:

Inv: A lot of times you get explanations—that's pushing it to call them explanations—you get words from kids that don't seem to make much sense to me, and I assume to you either, and you sort of have an interesting way of dealing with that. Is that an intentional decision you've made about how you're going to deal with those things?

Shey: Well, I knew that Jermaine, when he went up there, he just wanted to be in front of the camera. He's a pretty smart little boy, but I could see that when he started talking about 3 weeks and $100, he just wanted to be there for the sake of talking. He likes to get up in the front of a classroom, even if there's not a camera there.

Inv: So you didn't want to push it.

Shey: No. And sometimes when I see that he's—there have been a few times—I think it's even on tape—where he's gone up there, but I think this time he was so far off that it just wasn't worth pursuing. Maybe I was wrong.

Inv: I didn't ask that question to push you in a different direction because you get it a lot. A lot of times you get kids saying things that don't make much sense, and I'm not sure it would be worth your time to pursue them. It's a tough call.

Shey: Yeah. It's just a judgment. You just have to say, "Is he saying anything that's worthwhile, or is he just here to . . . ?"

The difficulty Shey experienced converging all discussions toward meaningful mathematical goals is one with which even the most experienced teachers find themselves struggling. Daniel Chazan (Chazan & Ball, 1995) described a high school lesson he had taught during which the students were provided four scenarios, each of which involved an employer giving $5,000 in bonuses to 10 employees. He wanted the students to understand that an average bonus depends on the total amount of money available and the number of people, regardless of how the money is distributed. The students were doing fine discussing the first three scenarios, and then he introduced a fourth scenario in which the bonuses ranged from $0 to $1000. The students got into a discussion as to whether or not a bonus of $0 is really a bonus. Chazan wrote

> I was enjoying the discussion and appreciating students' engage-
> ment, when I began to grow uneasy. I wondered about where the
> class would go with the disagreement over the zero. . . . My
> concern stemmed from a desire to have students appreciate what
> they had accomplished so far and to go farther. From past
> experience, I knew that students in this class tend to become
> frustrated with unresolved disagreements and would either turn to
> me and ask me to tell them who was right and who was wrong or
> would try to intimidate everyone into agreeing with them. I
> suspected that in order to feel that the discussion was worthwhile,
> they would need to feel that their ideas had developed or that they
> had come to some kind of conclusion or closure—or at least see
> their way towards some resolution. (Chazan & Ball, 1995, p. 6)

Chazan's dilemma revolved around two seemingly conflicting goals. On one hand, he wanted students to consider the meaning of *average*. On the other hand, he "wanted students to develop confidence in their ability to reason their way to mathematical decisions" (p. 7). For him to take sides in the disagreement and to state how he was thinking about a raise of $0 would have undermined his attempts to instill confidence in his students about their abilities to reason through disagreements, whereas to do nothing might undermine the entire lesson. Chazan and Ball (1995) stated that episodes like this one were common for them.

One of the most amazing observations we made about Shey was that even though he experienced these complications, he continued to introduce tasks that his students found to be difficult. He was willing to provide his students with difficult questions, and during one seminar, when another teacher suggested that students need to experience some success by beginning with simpler tasks, Shey responded, "See, I don't want my kids to be successful, 'cause I wasn't successful when I did it the first time. I had to struggle through it, so I think my kids need to struggle through it." In our observations, we saw that he was able to sustain a high level of student enthusiasm toward the mathematics. Even when working on a difficult problem, Shey's students generally stayed with the tasks at hand, and Shey continued to challenge them. For example, during an introductory fraction lesson with pattern blocks, Shey was posing questions such as "If two hexagons equal one whole, what is one half?" or "If two hexagons equal one whole, what is one third?" Most of his students were struggling with these questions, although some students were solving them. The observer decided that he would probably not have proceeded to pose more difficult questions here, but Shey continued. He asked, "If three hexagons equals one whole, what is one third?" A student responded correctly and gave a nice explanation. Shey pushed for a generalization by asking if the students saw a pattern, and another student explained that each part is two times as big (for two hexagons) as it would be for one hexagon. Then, in a question that appeared to the observer to be significantly more difficult, Shey asked, "If seven hexagons equals one whole, what is one third?" His students thought about this for a moment, and then Alberto answered 2⅓. Shey asked for an explanation, and Alberto explained, "Six of the hexagons can be divided into 2, 2, 2; so 2 is one third of those [six] and one third of the seventh makes 2⅓." Alberto's thoughtful response was possible because Shey challenged his students.

During the second year of the project, Shey described how he hoped to maintain high expectations of his students even though he felt that his students were weaker than the students he had taught the previous year. Speaking about this situation he said, "This year I would like to be able to do what I did last year, and I'm really trying to because I feel that I'm not going to lower my expectations for these kids. But I feel that it is going to be much more of a challenge for them, much more."

An interesting and important outcome of the changes Shey made in his teaching involved how he felt about the job he was doing. The following conversation took place at the end of his first year. We end our discussion of Shey with this conversation, because it captures the commitment he felt to teaching and the difficulties he experienced when he tried to meet the high expectations he set for himself:

Inv: Let me guess. Your expectations were not met. What you wanted the students to accomplish they were not. . . .

Shey: They were—when I look back on it, I realize that they did do a good job. But, there were nights when I would go home and go, "Oh my God, I brought them too far; I'm going to have to go back; I'm going to have to take them back."

Inv: What do you mean by that?

Shey: That they weren't ready for it yet. Yeah, and that happened on several—like four or five cases—where I'd run into something, and my thinking on it was that they should be able to do it; in actuality, they weren't ready for it yet.

Inv: I'd like to come back to what you said [earlier] about sometimes you felt you weren't a good teacher . . . and you felt that way more last year than you had in previous years. . . . Do you think you were a worse teacher last year than you were in previous years?

Shey: No, no. I don't think that I was.

Inv: Do you think, while you were going through it, did you feel like you were a worse teacher?

Shey: Yes.

Inv: You did?

Shey: Yes, uh huh.

Inv: So, you thought you were accomplishing something in previous years that you weren't accomplishing last year?

Shey: No, no.

Inv: Well help me understand. The reason I'm asking is because how teachers feel when they are going through this process is very important for being able to help them to go through a process.

Shey: Well, I feel like last year I was striving for more, with my kids, than before, partly because of this project. And, then, when they weren't achieving as much as I expected from them, I was feeling that I was letting them down and that my teaching wasn't what it should be. And the reason I think that this happened was because I wanted them to achieve so much more than I had before. Do you understand?

Chapter 7

DAROTA: IDEALS COLLIDE
WITH REALITY

Darota is an extremely intelligent, articulate, African American female teacher of inner-city, Grade 6 students whose standardized test scores are well below average. The school is under a court mandate to raise those scores. Clearly these factors more profoundly affected the instruction taking place in Darota's classroom than did her participation in this project, and these factors encompass dilemmas to which the project only added. In this case study we explore some of these dilemmas as they countered the work we and Darota undertook in this project to effect instructional change. But we do this only after introducing Darota and describing changes we observed in her thinking and in her teaching actions during the 2 years of this project.

INTRODUCING DAROTA

Darota began college as an engineering major who ran into "big trouble in third-semester calculus." She decided that she would prefer to become a teacher. She served as an instructional aide for 5 years at an inner-city school before receiving her credential, then returned to a teaching position at the same school. She had been teaching at this school for 4 years when she began work on this project, and she remained there for the duration of the project.

Darota was committed to providing her students with a way to escape their present lives of poverty and gang influence. During the project seminars she often spoke eloquently and passionately about the importance of better education for her students and volunteered examples of ways she felt the project was helping her to provide such an

115

education. She wanted to teach in a way that would help her students achieve a better life through an education in which they were thinking, participating, and making sense of the mathematics they desperately needed to learn. Her eloquence was such that her fellow teachers in the project were often moved, as after this impassioned monologue from early in the first year:

> Darota: But you have to teach that [a sense of community]. That's why we have kids in gangs that have no regard for human life, for anyone's life, because they have not been taught that. Way back families taught that. . . . You don't go out and play all day. There's more to life than that. . . . And you need to learn these courses, but ultimately it's for a greater good. And I think that we fragment things and departmentalize things and we get into learning for learning's sake and art for art's sake and all of these abstract kind of things, and society's going to hell as a result. And we are breeding generations of kids that have no sense of responsibility to the world, to their elderly parents, to anyone.
>
> Shey: Darota, I would just like to say, "That was wonderful." (Applauds) Why don't you join me? (Others applaud.)
>
> Darota: I get real passionate about these things.

Her fervor regarding the importance of a good education for her students was again evident when she spoke of the world in which they live:

> Darota: Whereas in the past, that [weak education] was sort of okay—you could kind of make it. Now the rate that the world is changing is phenomenal compared to how it was 20 years ago, 50 years ago. So that whereas it was okay to kind of bongle [sic] through before, it's critical now. Life or death. Survival or not survival. Anarchy or some kind of organized political system. There's no room to continue to perpetuate miseducation. It's just too critical now!

She often spoke about learning styles, because she felt that her students' learning styles were different from those of many students, and that this fact needed to be acknowledged and instruction designed to accommodate these differences. In April of the first year she said

> I think there are many conceptual learners who turn off and drop out—right-brained children who learn in a conceptual, global way. At my school, many of those kids don't try to go on to higher mathematics because it doesn't make sense to them.

She found district inservice generally lacking in efforts to focus on sense-making in mathematics and felt that instead, "They're giving you activities; they're giving you things, maybe, that can extend thinking *accidentally.* . . . It's not purposeful."

Although these strong feelings about teaching may have been present from the beginning, they were not at first in evidence. Darota described herself as a very traditional teacher in the beginning, slowly evolving into a teacher who first focused on the needs of her students and only then on the curriculum:

> I just kind of let go this year. I could see this progression from the first year where I just looked at the page. I didn't read the stuff in the margins [teacher notes]; I didn't have time for that. I just had to look at the page and try to figure out "What are these kids supposed to be doing?" The second year I kind of glanced at the things in the margins, but I still stayed pretty much with the book, and then I was anxious [that] another teacher was on chapter 7 and I was on unit 4. The third year I started to blend what I wanted to do with the book. Then this year I finally said, "I'm just gonna start here." I had an overall plan of the year of what I wanted to cover, and it was pretty much the content of the book, but I was gonna approach it much differently. So I started with geometry, and what happened was we just got into it. What I planned on doing for 3 or 4 weeks, I ended up doing for 9 weeks, thinking, "Please don't let the Resource Teacher come in." I just decided to go for depth rather than just coverage. I found that we had a lot of opportunities for computation, a lot of opportunities to talk about place value and all kinds of things that I was supposed to have been covering since August anyway.

The preceding paragraphs set a stage for helping the reader understand much of what is yet to come. We begin our exploration of possible project effects on Darota's thinking and teaching by first considering her participation in the seminars—what she contributed and what she gained, and changes as she described them. Our classroom observations, described in the penultimate section of this case study, did not however provide much evidence of change. In the final section we explore other aspects (the dilemmas) of Darota's professional and personal life in an effort to explain inconsistencies between what we heard in the seminars and what we saw in the classroom.

IMPACT OF SEMINARS

In assessing the impact of this project on Darota's instruction, we first consider her own descriptions of the effects of the project on her teaching. For the most part, these descriptions dealt with unplanned, serendipitous lessons that she felt were successful and strongly influenced by her participation in the project. One such lesson, on her students' understanding of percent, was described earlier (in chapter 4). On another occasion she described how, when trying to provide the students with a task to keep them busy and give her time to complete some required paperwork, she instead became engaged in an extended lesson involving proportional reasoning:

> I have a problem I did with my class that I want to share. I was doing this place value unit, and then we had report cards and parent conferences and discipline and some other stuff came in and interrupted that. So during one of those days that I needed the kids to be doing something, I was searching for stuff to pass out, and I found this sheet on estimation. And I really didn't look at it closely. I passed it out. Then after I passed it out, I looked at the paper, and there was a whole series of questions where the kids were supposed to estimate their answer and then find out what the actual answer was. The first one was "Estimate the number of students in your class." The second was "Estimate the number of right-handed students in your class." So after I read that, I said, "I can't just give them this. We need to talk about estimation. We need to talk about when it's appropriate, why you use it, et cetera." I needed to give them some purpose for doing this estimation.

With the class, Darota discussed strategies for estimation (a topic we had discussed in an earlier seminar). She created a context (ordering scissors) for needing an estimate in the second problem, then extended it so the students would need to estimate the number of left-handed students in the entire school, bringing in the ideas of ratio and proportion. Darota explained

> We didn't necessarily call it that, but we were trying to come up with the relationship of right handed to left handed. The next day we analyzed the problem using clustering. . . . The first thing we clustered was "What do we need to know to solve the problem?" . . . The next idea we clustered was The Plan for solving the problem. They went through the steps. One of the steps of the plan was "Analyze the information we had." On one side they put what went in, and on the other side they put what came out. The last was The Conclusions that came up. But it was interesting. With just that one situation we did a lot of things. We talked about taking a random sample, extrapolating to the whole. We talked about ratio

and keeping things in a proportion. We talked about estimation and it having a purpose. It was interesting.

On yet another occasion, Darota discussed her increasing aware-ness of the importance of sense-making in mathematics:

And then the other thing that I realized . . . is "Math's gotta make sense." One of the first speakers we had said that we give children the impression that math doesn't have to make sense. And I've thought about that ever since that first meeting. And so I keep telling them, "It's got to make sense." So *I* have to make sense of it.

She went on to describe how when working on warm-up word problems, many students did not understand or associate any meaning with the concept of speed. She took time to pursue that.

And we really get in and put those simple problems into a real-life situation, and then ask, "What do those numbers represent?" And that's where I'm finding that all this time, they don't have a clue. . . . You know, like things they take for granted like miles per hour. . . . I asked them, "What does miles per hour mean?" And so they said, "Well, you know. It's the speed." So finally through talking about it and through not accepting. . . . I set the standard of "It's okay not to have the answer, but it's not okay not to think about it, and it's not okay to not try to find a way to come up with the answer"—and not so much the answer to the problem but the answer to my question. And so finally we got to "Well, miles per hour is a relationship of time and distance." And that, for me, was a real sophisticated concept that just grew out of a simple question, "What does that mean?" and trying to just make sense of it. So that one problem that was real simple turned into a real rich teaching experience, and we never got to the rest of them. . . . I don't know; it's like this is the first time this ever happened to me, so I'm real excited about it.

The students, too, seemed to be excited by this approach to mathematics, according to Darota:

The whole day no one ever said, "We're tired of math; we're still doing math." And then the next day they said, "Well, can't we do math the way we did it yesterday?" And that was real interesting to me because at first—I mean it's painful for them to think. (Laughter) It really is. And a lot of them are real lazy and real accustomed to not thinking, not thinking at all. And then I put pressure on them 'cause we all just stay and wait for them to think. . . . I'm real pleased with how they're starting to think. And now they're starting to almost feel comfortable thinking.

Darota told us that in this project she had found something that was missing in her other experiences:

> Before, in the methods course, they were always saying "Teach for understanding," but they didn't really tell you how to do that. They gave you some activities; they pointed you in the right direction, and they tried to get us to think about what you wanted children to learn—which was probably better than a lot of people had—but what this project has helped me do that that did not do was to look at the way that children think: How are they thinking about the problem? What kinds of questions can I ask them in order to ascertain what they're thinking or how they're thinking? Then once I hear that, how do I evaluate that in terms of information that I'm presenting to them or activities that I'm involving them with? How do I assess that and use that to further develop a concept? . . . It's made a big difference. . . . It's just led to a whole new approach to questioning.

She felt, too, that she could better understand her students' difficulties and ask appropriate questions after her own experiences solving problems during the seminars:

> When we did problems on the board and activities, I thought, as I was thinking through the process in my learning style and the way that I did it and how I had to come to grips with understanding it or finding a solution to the problem, then that made it easier for me to see where the kids were. If they were just sitting there staring at the paper, I could ask them questions and get a feeling of what it was they didn't understand or where they were stuck. Whereas before I might have just gone over and just shown them what to do. And that doesn't necessarily make them understand.

After several seminars focusing on fractions, Darota became very interested in incorporating the many ideas and activities to which she had been exposed into a comprehensive unit plan.

She was convinced that her students knew next to nothing about fractions, as was confirmed by the Fraction Understanding Test that had been given early in the year to all project students. She hoped to use what she learned about her students from their performance on this test to design instruction:

> I want to know what they know, and then I want to determine what I want to try to teach them and get more into understanding

of certain ideas. And I'm gonna limit them [the ideas to be covered]. I'm not gonna put a whole bunch of them, because one of the important ones I would say is the benchmark things, being able to estimate fractions. To me that's a really central one. I would like them to understand that fractions are part of a whole, and the thing with [the more equal-sized pieces into which the whole is divided] the smaller the piece—I think that's real important. And that you can have fractions that are greater than a whole and also that decimals are fractions. If I could do that, I think that would be a whole lot—a whole lot to teach, and that would probably take me 8 weeks.

Darota was enthusiastic about the idea of integrating the new and old activities around the critical ideas about fractions she had come to consider through a seminar presented by Nancy Mack and seminar discussion of those ideas. But she was not sure at what point to begin.

Do I start with multiplication? Do I start with addition? Where should I start? I think it will be helpful to look at the critical ideas and maybe put them in some kind of sequential order. . . . Basically I want them to be able to perform four operations on fractions, and I want them to have a concrete understanding of what a fraction is. Those are like my broad goals. But how do I choose activities to accomplish them? What do I need to know in order to decide which ones are going to be more valuable than others? . . . After hearing the various presentations we have had on fractions, I became aware that the way I've taught fractions is haphazard.

The various components of her unit plan emerged from several discussions during January and February of the first year. Then in March, with input from the other teachers and from the researchers, Darota designed a fractions unit plan. She tried to incorporate all of our work on fractions into the plan. For example, when another teacher shared her experience using Fraction Dragons, an activity presented to the group by Tom Kieren, Darota immediately related that experience to her own plan for a fraction unit:

Linda: We'll use 10ths dragons for decimals, then bring these familiar [fraction] ones back out.

Darota: This would be a good opening activity for starting the unit on fractions, to talk about fractions in general, establish relationships, give them a concrete understanding of part. . . .

With input from the group, she developed the following diagram at the chalkboard:

Theme Outline (After Completion)

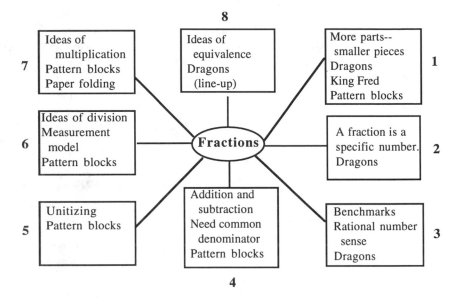

During the development of this outline, the discussion ranged over many topics. Critical ideas associated with fractions was one theme of interest to Darota:

> Nancy Mack's critical ideas only go through addition and subtraction, but there are critical ideas related to multiplication and division of fractions. If you could help find what those might be, then I could put those in a box, too, because those are things that I want to do also. I was thinking about the "½ of," how could you express that as a critical idea—what multiplication means. . . .

There was also considerable discussion about the role of the unit and the necessary ability to unitize in order to multiply. Models useful for teaching multiplication and division of fractions were noted. The importance of fraction benchmarks and their role in estimating was discussed. Different activities and models, particularly those introduced by seminar speakers, were considered in terms of their potential roles in the unit plan.

Darota continued working on the unit plan that evening, and later she said that she spent the night working on it. She was pleased with her plan and felt that, for the first time, she had a grasp of teaching fractions. She saw this unit as a means to meet district expectations.

Ultimately my goal is, through this unit, that they be able to do work from the book. Not that that's the ultimate or anything, but I know that the expectations of the administration, the test, and the district is that kids are going to be able to work with fractions expressed as numbers and multiply them, divide them, add them, that kind of thing. But I want them to have more than that. I want them to have meaning for those operations. That's really what the challenge is. I'm looking at this to be a 6-week unit.

WHAT OUR OBSERVATIONS SHOWED

Given Darota's intense interest in creating a unit plan, it is not surprising that when asked about high points in the first year of the project during an interview at the beginning of Year 2, she would state first, "My fraction unit. That was definitely a high point for me." In a December discussion of student fraction-test-results (from this project), Darota talked about how her goals had changed:

Usually I just assume that they know very little, and then I try to teach them what's in the book or what I think is gonna be on the test. Now that I don't look at things that way anymore, I want to know what they know, and then I want to determine what I want to try to teach them, and get more into understanding of certain ideas.

Yet in spite of her often expressed interest in creating such a plan and her effort in designing it, she was able to execute only a small part of the unit. We observed all three of the lessons she taught from the unit. The first lesson was introductory; students were asked to brainstorm about what they knew about fractions. In the second lesson, during a fantasy story (from Nancy Mack) used to introduce part-of-a-whole fraction meaning, Darota's students seemed more engaged than at any other time we observed in her classroom, but the content focus of this lesson was on the language arts aspects rather than on the mathematics content inherent in the story. During the only other lesson taught from the unit plan, we noted that the emphasis seemed to be more on the students' following detailed instructions on folding and coloring their dragons than on the mathematics. Darota explained why only three of the lessons included in this extensive unit plan were taught:

The problem that I had was I was not able to get through it because when we started fractions, it was not at a good time. It was at the time when the principal was saying, "The test; the test." So I couldn't relax and do what I wanted to do and spend the time.

> Then we went off track (classes in her year-around school were "off track" for 3 weeks for every 9 in class), and then we came back and had the test. I felt that of the activities that we did and the time that we spent talking about it and the things we made, I felt that, yes, they had a much better understanding based on those experiences. But I felt that it was nowhere what it could have been had I been able to go through and spend 7 or 8 weeks on it.

Apparently she did not feel that the unit sufficiently addressed the fraction items students would encounter on the standardized tests, even though she twice had made specific reference to having planned the unit with bridging the gap to the symbolic, textbook work in mind. How she prepared students for the fraction parts of the tests is unknown. This conflict between Darota's ideal of having her students interact meaningfully and in depth with the mathematics content and the reality of needing to prepare them to answer fractions questions on a standardized test is one that permeated much of Darota's mathematics instruction. The fact that the school was under court order to raise standardized test scores seemed never far from Darota's consciousness; she mentioned it often.

Given that the unit plan about which she was so enthusiastic was implemented to such a minor extent, it is perhaps not surprising we were unable to find many direct effects of this project on Darota's instruction. In fact, we were unable to find any effects during the four observations that took place during the second year. (Several others were scheduled, but Darota was not at school on those days, and the observations had to be canceled.) Darota claimed that to learn math is to be able to apply it in real-life situations, to use it for problem solving; "otherwise it is just memorizing stuff." However, in the lessons observed, real-world context was often specifically noted by the observer for its absence. In spite of her stated determination to see that her students thoroughly learned some mathematics—rational numbers in particular—during that year, and her disdain for the way others might teach fractions, she did not undertake any instruction on fractions during the entire school year. The lessons on decimal place value that she planned to begin within a few weeks after the September interview were actually begun at the end of February. There was little evidence of instructional preparation during the second year. In each of the last three lessons we observed, lesson planning appeared to begin at the time of day scheduled for the lesson, and the scheduled lesson began over an hour after the scheduled time. For whatever reasons, there appeared to be an almost total breakdown in instruction during the second year of the project.

DEALING WITH REALITIES

In Darota's case, more so than for any of the other teachers, context played a major role in mediating the effect of this project on instruction. The problems and dilemmas Darota faced were extreme, and our impression was that she became overwhelmed by them. We discuss these problems here under four categories: the school situation, the need to act as a role model, forces from outside the classroom, and signs of burnout.

The school in which Darota taught could serve as a setting for a film on urban schools and what makes it difficult for teachers to teach in them. The classes are large—Darota's enrollment hovered at about 33. Classroom and school management problems are overwhelming. Darota described an incident during which she had removed all the students from her classroom and had them wait outside while one student threw a destructive tantrum. On another occasion Darota was over an hour late for a seminar (at the beginning of Year 2) because she had been dealing with the horror of a drive-by shooting in which a student was killed at the school. She was late because she had been trying to convince the principal of the need for special counseling for the students.

A constant reality at this school was the court order to improve test scores. Darota often referred to this reality when talking about her instruction. In this excerpt she spoke of the way she hoped this project would mesh with her others in meeting the needs of her students and in meeting her responsibilities within a school under court scrutiny:

> The African American males make up most of my class and [most of] the group I teach in the after-school program, and they are, for the most part, very kinesthetic learners. I'm also dealing with a language situation where the language that the children use at home does not necessarily match the language of the school. And so, making connections between very abstract concepts like fractions gets real interesting, to say the least. . . . I really have to rely heavily on bringing in the children's background knowledge and including that in whatever I do in the classroom. So, I'm concerned about making the transition to the numbers because our school is one of the schools that is part of a lawsuit for the integration program. And as part of the monitoring of this civil lawsuit, the test scores at our school have to improve, as well as some other things. So there is always that. You never can get around that.

Dealing with the pressure to raise standardized test scores and at the same time wanting to focus on mathematics as exploration and sense-making presented a serious dilemma for Darota. There was never time for both.

> I think some of the barriers are time constraints, my own—I don't know what you want to call these but—kind of preconceptions about math and expectations by administration. I think all of those kind of work together as a barrier sometimes. Because sometimes I'm real torn between wanting the kids to really just go up into an exploration kind of math activity and being aware that X amount of weeks have passed and I need to have covered this, that, and the other thing so that I can get it all in before the test.

Darota's desire to raise test scores and prepare her students for seventh grade was balanced by the reality of her students' very poor preparation for sixth-grade mathematics. This lack of mathematics background was particularly pervasive in her students during the second year of the project. During a discussion of her students' results on the rational number pretest, Darota discussed the even greater than usual challenge she faced with her class of that year and their weak preparation in all math content areas:

Darota: I wish you had a test for even some more fundamental things like place value, multiplication, division—the same type of test, with questions—because what that test did for me was it helped me get at the understanding that the kids need to have. And then it was real enlightening, but it was also depressing, to find out how little they understood. . . . What am I gonna *do*? These kids are going to junior high school! This is the class of 2000. If they don't even know what a fraction is—I mean just some kind of idea, . . . where do I begin?

Inv: I think you have to begin at the beginning and pretend that they know absolutely nothing about fractions and try to. . . .

Darota: But they *don't* know anything about fractions! That's the *truth*! . . . With this class being as challenging as it is, I want to know, are there things that I can do? I'm gonna have to cope with it one way or the other. I don't want to just cope. I want to change the situation around. Maybe I will not have these kids all up to seventh-grade expectations by the end of the year, but I want to bring them somewhere from where they are. I need to see at least a couple years' growth in two areas. And as much as I want to do a real enriching social studies program, I really want to see them grow in reading and language and math, at least 2 years' growth. Because quite a few are at third- and fourth-grade level. If I can at least get them in some things up to sixth grade, I'll feel good about that. And I don't care about how they test. I just want to have a feeling that they're not doomed to failure when they go to junior high.

Besides being poorly prepared mathematically, students were poorly prepared for learning, particularly during the second year. One can hear Darota's frustration caused by the lack of readiness to learn on the part of her students:

Inv: It seems like for a lot of the kids there was very little time [during the periods we observed last year] that they were really engaged, watching, listening, trying. And you end up spending a lot of time, like you count down from 20 a lot [for class management].

Darota: I do that *all* the time. I spend most of my day doing things just to get them focused or get them back on task, or move them from one place to another, or get them to take out their books.

Inv: It bothered me because I don't know what to do, but I thought, "Gosh, a lot of these kids are just not getting it at all."

Darota: See. You can imagine why I was so frustrated.

Inv: There was so little mathematical thinking going on in the course of a period.

Darota: No thinking. Multiply that by seven subjects. They don't even pay attention in PE. Their PE teacher brings them back. . . . They stop my lesson. They blurt out. They do that *all day long*. I feel like Felix the Cat, with my bag of tricks. I have to be constantly thinking, "What can I do now?" I've cut all my things down to 15-minute blocks. Fifteen minutes is hard when you've got sixth-grade curriculum. You cannot do it in 15 minutes.

Another time during the second year she said the following about teaching mathematics to her class:

With this class, this year, it's kind of frustrating them, so I have to do it in small increments, and start with really easy things so that they can explain it and be successful. And I'm gradually moving to more complex ideas. But I've had to slow way, way down, because a lot of basic knowledge they don't have, and they have not mastered a lot of really fundamental skills. So that makes it difficult, but at the same time, it's also showing me that you don't have to wait until they've mastered those things before you can start looking at other things. But it helps when they have *some* knowledge. So I'm still trying to go ahead with math the way I want to teach it, and then I have my aide working with kids one-on-one on some real basic things, like place value and number facts and sentence structure.

Darota often found herself resorting to teaching behaviors she deplored, either to deal with class-management issues or to give herself time for paperwork. An interview at the beginning of the second year produced a further example of the intrusion of reality into the ideal of having students meaningfully engaged:

> I could keep them on task all day long if I gave them papers, which is what they're used to. That's what I want to see is ways to engage them in things that are meaningful. They will do handwriting papers, spelling papers, . . . What gets chaotic is trying to get them to go to another level. If I gave worksheets or stuff that's real trivial, they like that because that's what they're used to.

These and similar comments Darota made during the second year showed a growing frustration with her students, their backgrounds, their attitudes, and her inability to make inroads with them in mathematics or any other subject. Within this context, perhaps it is not so surprising that she did not teach her fraction unit. She felt that she had to focus on whole number operations; it seemed she simply never got to rational numbers that year. She claimed that the onus of raising test scores had little effect on her the second year, but it is clear that these tests were on her mind. In the final seminar she said

> What I did this year with the ASAT test was—because I almost drove myself crazy last year trying to balance teaching like I really wanted to teach and then having them cover this by the time of the test—so this year I just said, "Forget it," because . . . the test scores were just so erratic, and what I concluded from that was that they didn't mean anything anyway. So this year I just didn't even think about the test, but when we came back to school after break, we had 2 weeks before the test, so what I did was I kind of covered some things generally that were on the test. And then every night 2 days before we were gonna test that particular area, I sent home the practice test in that area, and then we went over the problems together, rather than trying to bombard them with everything, we just took—okay, the computation part—then we worked on computation 2 days before the test. And applications—we worked on that. I don't know if they're going to do better or worse.

Darota's life as a teacher was further complicated by the lack of administrative support. She was unable to obtain materials she felt necessary for her classroom instruction. She claimed that she obtained an overhead projector only after making a scene and demanding one. She wanted manipulatives for her mathematics class but could not obtain them through her school. What manipulatives she had she had received as a participant in another project. She was angry that counseling was not automatically available to her students when a student they knew was killed in a drive-by shooting. She felt that she could not in good conscience send students, even those causing total disruption in her classroom, out of the room to be dealt with in the office because the offending students would simply be isolated in a room for the rest of the day, with no counseling and no access to instruction. She said that for many of her students this isolation had been a common experience in the earlier grades and was a major contributor to their being so ill prepared for the content in Grade 6.

Darota's classes might be interrupted at any time. During one observation, after several public address interruptions concerning a parent's concerns during which Darota explained that that was not a good time for her to leave her classroom, Darota was instructed to come to the office to meet with the parent, and a vice principal was sent to the class to "babysit." She spoke of other examples that suggest that a regular schedule is difficult to maintain in her classroom:

> The DARE (Drug Abuse Resistance Education) officer is trying to make up 20 classes that he missed. We've had 5 days straight of DARE, 2 hours long. Graduation is Thursday. I knew the DARE officer was coming back today, so I was trying to rush and get done. I'm desperately trying to get to decimals [as I had promised to do before you visit again].

Darota felt additional pressure as an African American teacher. She wanted to be a role model for her students. And she wanted to teach her students manners and social skills so that they could be successful.

> The other difficult thing about my situation is that culturally I have to be a role model. It's an added responsibility. It extends beyond "Just get your work done." What I feel my kids need to learn most in the classroom is to behave and speak appropriately according to the situation. And they really don't do that. They don't have good manners. Maybe other teachers aren't concerned about that. I'm concerned about kids having good manners. They don't have a sense of what are appropriate comments, things that are socially acceptable.

Because of her abilities and because of needs of many projects to demonstrate diverse participation, Darota's time and talent are in great demand. One dilemma for Darota is whether to participate in all of these projects and activities, each seeming to offer a piece of a solution to the overwhelming difficulties in her inner-city classroom, appealing to her deeply felt desire to prepare her very underprepared students for junior high and high school. Over the period of years we knew Darota (both before and during this project), we knew that she was involved in an after-school mathematics-enrichment project for primary grades, in another mathematics enhancement project for teachers, in a project for developing gifted potential, and in a program on teaching to learning styles. She attended a mathematics conference each year, served as a consultant for a mathematics textbook company, served on a school-evaluation team, and elected to substitute teach during her 3-week intersessions. In selecting Darota for this project, we were primarily concerned about the time commitment in light of her involvement in so many other activities beyond her teaching. But when we voiced this concern during the preselection interview, Darota replied, "I don't have problems with the time with things that I think are worthwhile and with things that I think are going to support and enhance what I'm already doing." She said that she thought that this project would help her "by giving me a focus, something that I—by concentrating on—I think would sharpen my skills and make me more aware of what I'm doing with my teaching." In spite of her intentions, each project demanded a piece of her life, exacerbating her problems of finding time to plan and prepare for teaching while dealing with the numerous problems of her life as a single parent of three, including a teenage son.

Darota had difficulty finding time in her life for the planning required in teaching effectively. During our observations, Darota often did her planning on her feet. She once sent students to photocopy worksheets needed during a lesson that was already late in starting. According to Darota's own descriptions, some of her most successful lessons were serendipitous. Here she describes an effort to catch up so that the long-delayed lessons to be observed by project researchers could begin. She told the researchers that she would be beginning a decimal unit in September; however, it was late February before she actually got to the lessons. Even then, Darota was rushing to get to the lessons in question:

> I knew I had to get through Lesson 4 in order to start the decimal thing, so I had run off Worksheet 4, and so my first group that I met with, I didn't go through the lesson. We just went through the worksheet. I didn't even read the worksheet. I had just handed it out because I thought it was just kind of a review. And then I noticed at the top that the unit—what represented the ones—had changed. So I had to stop.

This discovery led to a class discussion, and once more Darota's real goal was thwarted while she engaged in a lesson she described as involving rich discussion.

During the second year, Darota seemed to lose some of her enthusiasm. There were signs of burnout. Comments such as these were more frequent: "It was Friday; I was real tired. I needed to go on to . . . , but I just couldn't bring myself to do it today." . . . "Today's goal was to have a stress-free day."

Darota recognized the burnout. This quote from early in the second year did not bode well for the remainder of the year.

> I don't know what to do. My plan was that in the 9 weeks I had really thought about doing fractions actually, only because I figured if I didn't, I wasn't going to get to them. But at the same time, I found that the kids have so little understanding of place value that I wanted to spend maybe the first 2 weeks on place value. I don't want to confuse them, because they're already confused, and they haven't really learned any—not everyone—but for the most part, they have not learned any one thing in depth. So I wanted to pick something and just really. . . . I don't care if I teach that for the rest of the year. I just want them to learn *something* from beginning to end, or as much as you can at that age. So, I'm still thinking about it. I did not want to think *school*, because I was so burned out when we went off track.

At the end of the first year Darota told us that she was unsure whether or not she would be able to participate in the second year of this project; she had applied for a position in the district's Race and Human Relations division. Although she did not get this position, she expressed the hope that in the future she would be in staff development.

> I know that I'm not going to be able to do this forever. After a certain point, you don't have the patience to deal will all of the things that you have to do. It's too demanding. At a certain point in my life, I don't want to have that demanding a career. [And later] I want to design my own job. I want to spend part of my time working with students and the rest of my time working with adults and help them in terms of working with students, and share with them what I've learned and experiences. But I also want to have a connection so that I can continue to grow and experience because I feel that there's still so much more that I want to learn, that I want to do.

CONCLUSION

In describing the effects of projects intended to improve education for inner-city children, Stake et al. (1994) noted that an unintended consequence was the burden these projects placed on the teachers:

Some critics of the schools believe that the problem is one of professionals "goofing off." "Teachers arrive just before 8:00 and head for home minutes after 2:30." One Chicago executive said, "Thousands are just going through the motions out there." Those critics are wrong. There are many things unsatisfactory about elementary education in Chicago, but the professional corps was working hard. The demeanor was serious; the effort was engaged. One of the reasons the schools are so bad is that few others are willing to face such a task. Few are able to work as hard in such adverse conditions as the classroom teachers of Chicago. (p. 109)

Although the same may be said for any large city's inner-city schools, the parallel here is drawn between teachers in the schools of Chicago and the case of one teacher in San Diego's inner-city schools, Darota. The comments on and descriptions of Darota's conflicting ideals and reality are never meant to suggest a lack of sincerity of dedication and effort or a lack of ability on her part. Her difficulties are especially acute precisely because of her sincere desire to improve the lives and futures of the students she teaches under adverse conditions similar to those referred to by Stake. Her efforts to take advantage of each opportunity that might promise to help her reach these goals could have prompted her to state, as one of the Chicago teachers did, "Such a burden. . . . Each [program] comes with a gift, but each extracts a price. . . ." At a minimum the price extracted by this project was meant to be the time involved in attending the seminars, the in-class administration of pre and post fraction understanding tests, being observed and debriefed in postobservations interviews. Even this commitment was too great a price in Darota's hectic life. She was often late for seminars; she often was unprepared for observations or was not even in school on the day we had scheduled and gone to the school for observations; she seldom had time for the postobservation interviews; she did not administer the posttest to her students either year of the project.

And yet, Darota is a teacher who cares about teaching, cares about herself and her own growth, cares about her students and their futures in lives outside of gangs and drugs and all that drags them down when they are not schooled and not socialized. We do not know what the future holds for Darota. But her ideals and the realities with which she lives are in conflict now, and some resolution must take place before Darota can help her students, or herself. The details of mathematics knowledge and teaching take a backseat in this conflict. Darota's case serves as a metaphor for the ideals of what we all want for the children who are this country's future and for the problems of the inner-city schools today.

Chapter 8

TOM: MATHEMATICS AS CONCEPTS
VERSUS MATHEMATICS AS PROCEDURES:
FINDING A BALANCE

It is easy for a teacher to pick up on the rhetoric of change, to believe that change is necessary, but difficult to recognize how much or how little one's own teaching actually changes. In this story we follow Tom over 2 years during which he attempts to make fundamental changes in his teaching behaviors. We consider the constraints he feels, whether real or imagined. We particularly focus on the difficulty Tom has in helping his students reason about mathematics. Tom began the project with the attitude that students need easy-to-remember rules for carrying our arithmetic procedures. He came to understand that this view was in conflict with his belief that mathematics should make sense, and we can trace his attempts to reconcile this conflict. But his focus on rules was firmly entrenched and had led to success in the sense that his standardized test scores were high and he was regarded as a good mathematics teacher by his administrators and by parents. This focus was based on a teacher-telling mode of instruction, and this instructional practice, too, was much more difficult to change than Tom first realized—this teaching behavior was so ingrained that often Tom did not recognize it. Tom did change over the time we worked with him— his goals changed, and his beliefs about student learning changed. Yet his frequent lack of recognition that old behaviors continued to mark his instruction made change slow in coming.

In terms of coursework, Tom's mathematics background was probably stronger than that of the other teachers in the group. He had completed precalculus some 20 years previously and had just a few years before this project completed the requirements for a supplementary authorization to teach mathematics, which allowed him to teach mathematics through ninth grade. He had never had a methods course in teaching mathematics. He had, however, been involved in two summer projects focusing on mathematics. In one he had become familiar with the rhetoric of change and with the *California Framework* and the NCTM *Standards* (1991). The other project had focused on assessment, and he had come away with the conviction that traditional testing was not effective: "I'm cutting down on the scantron. I'm incorporating a lot more open-ended questions, thought processes."

As a student and in the Air Force, Tom had always done well in mathematics. On the basis of his test performance at the beginning of the project, we concluded that he had a good understanding of the mathematics of fractions and proportions, although his performance on the pedagogical-understanding portion of the test was not as good. Tom frequently claimed not to have a strong mathematics background, and he seemed to feel that a calculus course would provide him with the mathematics he should have as a middle-school teacher. He spoke of trying to learn calculus on his own, and, on finding that a difficult task, enrolled in a calculus course for a period of time while he was with this project. In fact, his feeling that he lacked a "formal education in math" was the reason he gave for wanting to participate in our project.

Tom began this project with a strong focus on teaching procedures and skills, and little attention was given to conceptual understanding of the procedures he taught. When asked, at the beginning of the project, how he balanced conceptual development with skill development in his class, he responded

> At my [sixth-grade] level we are still working on basic skills. I mean, when I think about conceptual, the first thing that I think about is probably variables and algebra and stuff, so I still basically deal with skills. And the way that I do that is I put up problems of the day. And there's five problems and it's a way for me to check to see if they maintain their basic skills. Now halfway through the year, I'll probably start more of the conceptual, but I still maintain the basic skills, so as to keep in line when they get their tests at the end of the year through the district or in the CAP [California Assessment Program]; they don't really test for conceptual skills, they test for basic skills, so, it makes the district look good if the kids score high. So I got to keep that going.

As an indication of Tom's focus on procedures, we relate the following incident, which occurred during our first seminar and is described in chapter 4. The teachers had read an excerpt from a research article in which a teacher explained division of fractions in a very traditional way, and a student asked why you "change over" (invert and multiply). We asked our teachers how they would respond to the student.

Tom: Maybe I'm way off the wall, but I don't teach kids to flip numbers upside down. I tell them what a reciprocal is. I say, "The reciprocal [is] the two numbers you multiply and it comes out to 1." So we review multiplying fractions. . . . Then I put up a problem with division. I say, "This is going to be easy for you to remember: I hate math; I hate math; I still hate math. Just two Xs. Just follow the lines. Multiply the numbers, and you're gonna come up with the answer."

Linda: Do you want to show us?

Tom: Yeah. But I have to do the review of the multiplication, so they know that there's a big difference. So [demonstrates multiplication on board].

$$\frac{1}{2} \times \frac{2}{3} = \frac{2}{6}$$

I review. I say, "Yeah, it's easy. Just go straight across." And I don't even bother cross-reducing at sixth grade because, heaven forbid, they'll forget it. It's just too complicated. I'll tell the kids, I'll scoot over, and I'll say, "Okay, those of you that are really smart, here's a faster way that you don't have to reduce it later." So I do that. Then I say, "You know, a lot of people will tell you to turn this [second fraction], turn it upside down, but it's gonna confuse the heck out of you because when you see it on a piece of paper you're gonna say, 'Which one do I turn over?'" I could say, "Some of you can remember it if you say, 'Flip it good; flip the right one good.'" Or I could say, "Follow these lines and multiply, and you got your answer. Just go 'I hate math (Line 1); I hate math (Line 2). Boy! Do I really hate math (Lines 3 and 4)!'"

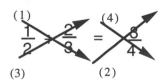

Inv: But what if a student says, "But why is that division?"

Tom: Well, I say, "Well, look, we multiply. What's the opposite of multiply? Divide. . . . You know, if this is multiply, we have to do something different. So what's the only way different? You can't multiply these two numbers. You have to multiply the other numbers." So I kinda explain, I say, you know, "opposites." I tell them, "You know, this reciprocal thing is ridiculous because you're gonna get confused." . . .

Inv: I still don't see why that's division.

Tom: It's because it's the opposite. If you explain to them when you multiply fractions, you go straight across, to divide you have to do something. . . .

Cynthia: Well, why do you go straight across when you multiply?

Tom: It's easy that way. So when you teach them to multiply, you say, "Okay, it's easy to go straight across, because you got this nice line."

Our observations in Tom's classes at the beginning of the project indicated that he followed the "mandated" curriculum loosely; he paid little attention to the textbook and developed his own curriculum as he went along. In the class we observed in November, his goal was to teach estimation skills with a focus on understanding. Although his intentions were good, he slipped into giving students a procedure for estimating for the type of problem under consideration, without students understanding or buying into the procedure.

Tom's lesson on this day included a segment on solving equations of the form $17 - n = 3.5$. He wrote on the board

$$17 - n = 3 \text{ Answer here is } 14$$
$$17 - n = 4 \text{ Answer here is } 13$$

Using these two equations, Tom tried to help students see that the answer must be between 13 and 14, but without saying much about why this should be. In response to an error he observed in a student's work, he wrote "$17 - 20.5 = 3.5$." He then asked students what they thought about this equation. One student said that the result would be negative, and Tom responded, "Right—but we haven't talked about negatives yet in here." Nothing more was said about negatives. He then asked, "How many did it like this: 'Something minus something equals 3.5, so if I add these two (circles the $n = 3.5$ portion of the equation), I should get 17?'" No one responded. Finally, a student said that he did it by "adding a zero and subtracting: $17.0 - 3.5$." Tom then wrote on the board

$$\begin{array}{r} 17 \\ -\ 3.5 \\ \hline n \end{array} \qquad \begin{array}{r} 17 \\ -\ n \\ \hline 3.5 \end{array}$$

He asked, "Are these the same?" Some students said yes, others said no, but when asked why, none could articulate any reasons. Tom then wrote $17 - n = 3.5$ and asked, "Does it matter if we switch these two [n and 3.5]? Aren't I just saying that these two numbers [n and 3.5], if I add them together, will equal 17?" He then gave the problem $28 - 8.75 = \Box$, allowed time to work the problem, gave the answer without discussion, then assigned homework problems similar to these problems.

After the lesson, he seemed baffled: "Why can't they see that $17 - n = 3.5$ is the same as $17 - 3.5 = n$?" This question was typical of other incidents we observed: Why can his students not do what he has *shown* them to do?

Tom's understanding of the role of conceptual development began to change during the seminars, as can be noted in these later seminar excerpts related to teaching multiplication and division of fractions. In the first instance, the teachers were discussing multiplication of fractions; in particular, how to show that ¾ of ½ is ⅜.

> In the old days, I would spend 30 seconds saying, "Multiply the numbers and get your answer." But for me to see that they have the concept of fractions down, I would need to go through and say, "When we talk about fractions, we're talking about one unit and parts of that one unit. Everybody agree that this is one unit? How do I know it's a half?" I would go through the whole thing. "So we figured out a half. Now we want to figure out what three fourths of that half is, so how would we do it? We would chop this into fourths and only talk about three of them." You always have to reference back to the unit.

But his own understanding of multiplication of fractions was fragile, as shown by a later excerpt:

Tom: What's really confusing is if you try to explain this in pizza: How can you have a three fourths of a pizza, divide it in half, and get 1½ pizzas?

Shey: Because you're not giving a whole pizza. You're giving halves of pizzas—1½ halves.

Inv: When you divide in half, you're really dividing by 2.

Tom: So is this how Jesus fed the multitudes? . . . But I will spend more time on fractions because I could see how this would more imprint on their mind *fractions*, rather than "Guys, in 30 seconds I'm gonna show you how to multiply fractions—straight across, no problem."

At about this time, when one of the researchers brought up his "I hate math" method, Tom professed that he had given up that method for teaching division of fractions:

No, no. I gave that away. I threw that out the window. For division
I'll cut the fractions out in different colors. I'll ask how many halves
are in one fourth. We won't get an exact answer. It has to be less
than 1, so it can't be 2. Those of you who are yelling out 2 or 4 or
8—forget it; you're wrong. It's got to be less. We'll chop it up. How
many halves go into a fourth? A half. This is my second edition [of
a fraction manipulative I created]. I put numbers on the first set [of
the fraction manipulatives], and they just looked at the numbers.
Now they have to count. I think that is the proper way to teach
fractions.

Tom's attempt to move away from procedural mathematics was
not easy for him, but he began to find rewards in trying to teach
conceptually:

Tom: It's hard to let go of algorithms.
Inv: Who's having trouble letting go?
Tom: I was. Because the last 3 or 4 years it's been easy. Just tell them
       how to do it. This past week, I have to wait, and I would put up
       these slides and we figured them out. Then I would ask, "Does
       anybody see a pattern to this?" And the kid that's zero said, "It
       looks like if you multiply the top numbers and the bottom
       numbers, you get the same one. But I don't think it works for
       every one." So we tried it out. He stayed with me. He noticed the
       pattern. I said, "I wonder if that's the same pattern?" They looked
       at the homework and a lot said, "Ah." So we called it Sam's rule.
       Hey, we'll just do it Sam's way. It was hard because there's dead
       silence, and then this kid speaks up.

Yet to Tom, letting go of the *algorithms* often meant letting go of the
standard algorithms for the four operations. He often introduced new
algorithms for solving problems, as in this excerpt from a class in the
spring when he introduced the method for estimating sums and
differences for mixed numbers: "Drop the fractions." He introduced this
lesson by saying

Tom: Here we go. Ready. Tonight's homework on subtraction might
       have something like this:

$$33\tfrac{3}{7}$$
$$- 18\tfrac{4}{5}$$

Now, there's a couple of these things that I want you to figure out.
The easiest way is to do what? Just cover up the_____?
Kristine: Fractions.
Tom: Fractions. Is that true?

Paula: Yeah.

Tom: So we should get this drunk equals sign, *about* [≈] and it's what? Fifteen, right?

Coltrane: Yeah.

Tom: Now what if we decided to round these numbers to 34 and 19?

Chrys: It would be 33 since. . . .

Tom: What if we decided since there's a fraction, I'm just going to round up. It doesn't matter if it's one tenth, one hundredth; I'm just going to round up to the next number. What do you think the estimate's gonna be?

Gary: Fifteen.

Tom: The same. 'Cause all you really did was add 1 to both of these, right?

Trevor: Yes.

Tom: Let me ask you this. If I had said, "Give me an estimate of this," and somebody said 15, somebody said 15½, and somebody said 14, and somebody said 16, are they kind of close?

Gisela: Yeah.

Tom: Yeah. But this half [in 15½] kind of bothers me because it looks like they're doing something else. They're trying to get an exact answer. So an estimate is just a rough idea, okay?

Tom moved to a distant school district the following year and so no longer attended seminars. However, we continued to occasionally observe his classes and mark his progress through his lessons and postinterviews. Before we observed his class in December of Year 2, Tom discussed his previous day's lesson. He showed us a copied sheet of the homework for the day we visited. This sheet was called RETEACH and was on comparing and ordering fractions. It began with a box marked REMEMBER, and in the box was the cross-product rule for comparing two fractions. It was followed by nine pairs of fractions to compare; three triples of fractions to order, and two questions (e.g., Which holds the greater amount, 13 fourth-cup containers or 7 half-cup containers?). Tom said that he had told the students to use the rule given on the comparisons, but that to order three fractions, it was better to get the calculator out and change the fractions to decimals, then order them. He appeared pleased with this page. When asked if he had suggested that some of the comparisons could be done using benchmarks, which he was teaching at that very time (e.g., comparing the two fractions to ½ or noting the distance from 1, as for ⅚ and ⅞), it was clear that the idea of using benchmarks on the homework problems had not occurred to him. He immediately recognized, however, that this connection was an important one; he remarked that he had blown it again, or something to that effect. He seemed to be referring to the previous year, when other teachers in the group would point out to him that he was at times just teaching a procedure, with no emphasis on understanding the procedure. During the previous year he had never appeared to be "hurt" by this criticism, but several times on this day he had said that he had really changed. . . . he would not teach just procedures any more. And he sincerely was trying. Late in the day he said

> It's tough for me because I know that even before I came in [to the project] I thought I had a pretty successful math program. But I had a pretty successful math *computational* program. And I would "drill and kill" them to death and hope that maybe the concept came later on. But now I'm finding out that—I'm sure I said it before—but if I hound on the concepts and hound on them enough so that they understand the concept, the computation will come. It might not come today, it might not you know. But it will come eventually. I found out that it's more long lasting—the conceptual ideas, like "Which is smaller and which is bigger?"—when they visualize it and stuff and see how it looks.

The last time we observed Tom and interviewed him was the following year, more than 2 years after the beginning of the project. He was teaching only seventh-grade mathematics. He had become a teacher leader in a large state project and spent much of his time visiting and helping other teachers. He seemed very comfortable in this role and was trying out new curriculum materials. In the postinterview that day, he said that he now looked for conceptual understanding through the type of questioning he used.

> So my questioning techniques have changed dramatically. Instead of saying, "Why aren't you taking the bottom number and multiplying it by the side number and adding the . . . ?" I usually end up saying, "Well, why did you do it the way you did it, and can you draw a picture of what you're doing? Can you explain it in a picture?"

After observing all of his classes during that day, however, our impression was that although he asked some good questions, he answered many of them himself, rarely listening to students' responses and building on them.

CONCLUSION

Tom was involved in our seminars for only 1 year. During that time, while he himself was coming to understand the conceptual underpinnings of the mathematics of sixth and seventh grades, he began to let go of his highly procedural manner of teaching mathematics. This letting go was difficult for him, however, because this mode of instruction had served him well in the past, in terms of high test scores. In addition, he was a well-liked, relaxed, and charismatic teacher who was seen by others as a successful teacher before, during, and after this project. He was an outgoing, pragmatic individual, and he needed to be convinced, with evidence rather than theory, that what he was doing could use some updating:

> What was really beneficial for me, was to [see that] even though I went through the changes, the scores remained high anyways. So they couldn't say, "The reform is not good because the scores dropped." No, my scores stayed the same; in fact they went up a little bit more in the conceptual—[the scores are] split up into computational and conceptual. Well, the computational was fine because that was the drill and kill; I'd cut down on that, and I increased the conceptual, so the scores went up. I didn't completely get rid of the computational. I never really thought that I was doing it the wrong way. I just felt like I was given more tools to work with, and then finally I realized, "Wow, these are better tools. I don't need the hammer; I can use this adjustable wrench instead."

At times we were disappointed to find in Tom a lack of awareness that he continued to teach procedurally, even though this practice was certainly less pronounced at the end of the project than at the beginning. It appeared that when Tom himself came to understand the mathematics in a more conceptual manner, he was able to make some changes in the way he taught the mathematics. Could it be, then, that Tom still lacked some fundamental understanding of the mathematics he was teaching? On the basis of his reflections on what he had gained from this project at the end of the first year, one could assume this might be the case. Whereas others responded in terms of their deepened understanding of the mathematics, Tom responded by saying

> One thing was that . . . we were from so many parts of the county, but we took upon ourselves to sacrifice and come down here and stuff, but I was really, I guess, impressed by the fact that with only five people in the project, then having seen and interacted with people like Nancy Mack and Tom Kieren and Guershon Harel. I mean, those are people like "Wow." . . . I think the story was how we all jelled together because we had a common purpose, which was that "we wanted to know more."

But Tom does not consider the change process to be over. In his new position as a teacher leader, working with other middle school teachers, he recognizes that he, too, is in the middle of a change process:

> We talk about the different struggles. . . . But I kind of grin because here I am—I've got a title now, but I still think that I'm going through the changes. It's like, "Yes, it's a long-term process. I've been at this for 4 years, this change, and I don't see the light at the end of the tunnel." I see that I need to change more and more. . . . Change is a long-term process; I'm going through the change; yes, I'm continuing to change.

Chapter 9

CYNTHIA: THE PAIN OF CHANGE

Of all the teachers described in these case studies, Cynthia seemed to us to have undergone the most changes and to have experienced most deeply the anguish that sometimes attends personal change. Like the other teachers in the project, Cynthia had been involved in previous mathematics teacher–inservice projects, and she was committed to helping her students develop a deeper understanding of mathematics. Yet she seemed intimidated by the mathematical discussions we held during the first year's seminars, and she participated far less than any of the other teachers during these seminars. At the end of the first year she considered dropping out of the project because her engagement in the project was leading her to have painful doubts about her own effectiveness as a teacher.

Things turned around dramatically for Cynthia during the second year. She spoke out more than other teachers during the seminars, and she made significant changes in her instruction. In this case study we examine the changes Cynthia made in her views of the nature of mathematics and of mathematics instruction, in her understanding of the mathematics of the curriculum she taught, and in her understanding of her students' understanding. We examine the effects of these changes on her teaching, and we speculate about the role that personal examination, doubt, and even pain played in this change process.

BACKGROUND

At the time of her interview before beginning the project, Cynthia was finishing her ninth year of teaching. During those 9 years, she had taught kindergarten, Grades 3, 4, 5, and 6 and had run a mathematics lab at an elementary school. When selected for the project, she was teaching fifth grade, and she continued teaching this grade throughout our project.

Cynthia reported during the initial interview that as a mathematics student she was deeply affected by an experience she had while taking high school geometry. Prior to that time she had always struggled with mathematics, and she was struggling with geometry until her father stepped in and tutored her for 3 weeks, 3 hours each evening.

> I struggled with math, and then all of a sudden—it was when I was working on geometry with my dad, and the light went on, and it was just like everything seemed to fall in together. I started seeing patterns in everything.

After that point she loved mathematics and subsequently took all the mathematics in high school that she could, including calculus. She then completed requirements for a bachelor's degree in clothing design, during which time she took statistics and another calculus class. During her preparation to become an elementary teacher, she took a computer mathematics course in LOGO and an elementary mathematics methods course. After graduating from college, she worked as a designer of wedding dresses for 5 years before switching careers to teaching.

While involved with this project, Cynthia taught in a school located in a large urban area in Southern California. The population of the school was ethnically mixed, and most of the students were from middle socioeconomic levels. Many of their parents were well educated and took an active role in their children's educations. The parents, with support from the principal, held high expectations of their children and of their children's teachers. For the parents, an important measure of the quality of education was the district's standardized achievement test. During an interview early in the first year of the project, Cynthia said that she felt a great deal of tension between teaching for conceptual development and preparing students for this achievement test.

We asked Cynthia during that interview what she thought it meant to learn mathematics. Her response reflected a growing commitment to helping her students develop a deeper understanding of mathematics:

> I think that it's not just to learn how to plug in the numbers, that it's understanding what they're doing and why they're doing it so that they know when it's important—when a certain application should be applied in a certain problem that they're going to be experiencing, and just a good strong basis of understanding what it is, instead of more of the drill and learning by rote.

Cynthia explained that she had been making changes in the way she taught, in part as a result of her involvement in a local mathematics project and in part as a result of her use of curriculum replacement units. She explained, "The [local mathematics] project, I would say, is the most influential because we just deal with hands-on and having kids experience for themselves what is going on." When asked about a teacher's role, Cynthia's image of what she would like it to be differed from her image of her role at the time:

> I think that theoretically it's to be someone who should just give direction and let the children explore. That's what I would like to be in the future. I know that I can't all of a sudden change into that, but . . . I am having a hard time letting go of the control or saying that I don't need to be in control of this.

Cynthia attributed part of her difficulty with "letting go" to her feelings of responsibility for student performance on the standardized achievement test.

Cynthia told us that she was ecstatic when she was selected to take part in this project because she wanted "to be the best that I can, especially [in] the areas [of mathematics] where I found that I was having problems as a child." Cynthia specifically mentioned two topics that she thought she could teach better if she had more time to explore them:

> Fractions and long division I think are my two main concerns. Sometimes I think that we're asking children to understand things that they're not quite ready to understand, and we're not giving them enough of the actual visual. . . . I don't think my children really understand what a fraction is—that it's part of a whole, and they have a real hard time with understanding that.

Notice that she spoke of difficulties her students had, not ones that she had, in understanding these topics.

YEAR 1: RECOGNIZING THE CHALLENGE OF CHANGE

During a seminar in September of the first year Cynthia spoke again of the difficulty of teaching long division and fractions and of her students' difficulties in understanding these two topics. About the division algorithm she said, "They didn't have a clue. And that's when I felt, 'Who cares about the steps if they don't know what these numbers mean.'" In speaking of their understanding of fractions, she described an article she had read about making connections in understanding fractions:

I found that the article really applied to what I was feeling last year in dealing with the children—giving them lots of manipulatives— and then not knowing how to bridge that gap to "Here's the fractions; now you have to understand what these numbers are. We're not playing anymore," type of thing, and they couldn't [understand the symbols], so I was very frustrated.

The First Observation: A Different Twist on the Teaching of Procedures

Our first observation in Cynthia's classroom occurred in October. We found her classroom to be attractive and neat. There were two mathematics bulletin boards and she aesthetically displayed students' work. The population of 30 students was ethnically mixed and included 4 African Americans, 9 Hispanics, and 2 Asians. Students sat four to a rectangular table. Our first impressions were that the classroom was orderly, the students were comfortable, and Cynthia was very much in control.

That first mathematics lesson lasted about an hour. Cynthia began by giving the students a logic puzzle that all the students appeared to understand and enjoy. After 10 minutes she wrote three problems on the board and asked the students to copy them into their portfolios. She gave instructions: "Write down anything you would like to say about these problems."

$$
\begin{array}{rrr}
1782 & 2682 & \$3672.15 \\
-\,1193 & -\,310 & +\,823.28 \\
\hline
611 & 2992 & \$449.543 \\
\end{array}
$$

After 15 minutes, during which Cynthia walked around the room assisting students, she opened the discussion by asking for their thoughts. Several students responded. One said, "This is an odd thing . . . because you wanted us to be the teacher," and a second student agreed. A third student said, "You wanted us to look deeply at the problem," and still a fourth added, "I thought, 'What is she doing? She put up the answer.' Then I saw it was wrong."

The students then discussed each problem in turn, pointing out the errors. For example, one student reasoned that the student solving the first problem forgot to borrow. Another student pointed out that 2 minus 3 is a negative number, and Cynthia asked him to explain his solution at the overhead projector. The student did so using a number line, but the explanation was not clear to some of the others. The use of the number line led to a brief discussion, concluding that there is "no largest number."

Cynthia asked the students why they thought she had given these problems. Students suggested that she wanted them to avoid those same errors, to check and correct their answers, and to learn to read signs correctly.

This first observation in Cynthia's classroom left us with a sense that she was, as she had claimed, moving away from traditional mathematics instruction. Her lesson was unusual in that it required her students to analyze incorrect solutions. She engaged her students in conversation by asking many questions and allocating time to listen to her students. She was willing to follow up on the ideas of her students. She asked them to reflect on why the problems were selected. The lesson also left us with some questions about the perspective from which Cynthia might be approaching the teaching of mathematics. The discussion revolved around dissecting the procedures used and seemed to focus solely on how to carry out the algorithm. For example, she never suggested that the students estimate to see whether the answers made sense. Although it was not reasonable to draw conclusions about Cynthia's orientation toward mathematics or mathematics teaching on the basis of one lesson, her focus on the calculational aspects of the lesson caught our attention as something to note during subsequent visits and discussions.

One of the key issues teachers encounter when they attempt to teach mathematics conceptually is their own sometimes weak understanding of the mathematics. A second issue for teachers is their degree of understanding of their students' understanding of the mathematics. At the beginning, Cynthia seemed less aware of the role of the former than of the latter in her instruction. She made several comments in seminars subsequent to this observation indicating that she assessed her students on a regular basis. She also seemed aware of the difficulty in being certain of what students understand. During a seminar in October, a fellow teacher, while talking about his students' fraction understanding, said, "If they can figure out the correct answer and know what they're doing, I really don't care [about anything else]," to which Cynthia responded, "How do you know that they know what they're doing?" She often spoke in detail about difficulties her students had and some of the reasons for these difficulties. For example, during a seminar in December, she described how language difficulties affected some of her students' mathematics test scores. After she read an examination to her Vietnamese student, his score increased from 60% to 90%. She spoke about the information she gained by having her students write story problems: "I think that you get a lot of insight, especially when you are doing division problems and you see whether they understand what that remainder is all about." She spoke of difficulties her students encountered when she situated a problem in the context of the 1992 Olympic games: "My kids were getting confused [about the running times] because none of them were track stars. They were basketball players, so they thought the higher your score, the better you are." During the December 1992 seminar we discussed results of the students' performance on a rational number assessment. Of all of the teachers, Cynthia seemed to be least surprised by her students' poor performance, perhaps because of her ongoing assessment:

> I'm not surprised. It's what I've been—through the math project and through being here and the math conferences—it's what I've been hearing is that the kids are not getting enough concrete knowledge—especially of fractions—of what's going on. I think that we've been taught to *tell* instead of having them *experience* and *discover*, and I think that that's the hard thing for us, letting go, backing off, and letting them go and discover things. And each child is at—they're at different abilities and able to grab onto something. I'm not surprised.

In addition to these examples, Cynthia made other comments during our seminars and classroom visits that indicated that she had considerable awareness of her students' mathematical understanding.

Cynthia's Attempts to Focus on Student Understanding

Our second observation of Cynthia's teaching took place in December. In this lesson Cynthia situated practice on the multiplication of decimals algorithm in a real-world context. Cynthia asked her students to create lunch menus for imaginary restaurants they would be running. The small-group conversations were lively while students worked cooperatively on this task. After the students selected their menus, Cynthia told them to imagine that they each had $6 to spend on food and reminded them to pay sales tax:

Cynthia: Does anyone know what the sales tax is?
Dan: Eight.
Ellen: Six.
Trang: Multiply times fifteen hundredths.
Tonisia: Seven.
Logan: Seven and five hundredths.
Cynthia: The sales tax is point zero seven seven five. (She writes .0775 on the overhead, saying "zero tenths, seven hundredths, seven thousandths, and five ten-thousandths.")
Steven: Huh, we don't have numbers like that. Can we round?
Cynthia: I want the exact sales tax. This means that we have 7 cents and seventy-five hundredths of a cent on every dollar.

At this point, the students seemed to be confused about what this number represented. Rather than helping her students conceptualize .0775, Cynthia guided them toward the procedure for calculating the tax.

Like the first lesson we observed Cynthia teach, this lesson actively involved the students in conversation. The majority of the lesson was devoted to the students' constructing their menus, a task they all seemed to enjoy. However, when it came time to consider the tax, Cynthia focused on procedures. It was not clear from the observation that the students had had conceptual experiences with the quantities that decimals represented, much less with a conceptual approach to multiplication of decimals.

During the postobservation interview, Cynthia explained her purpose for the lesson:

> The lesson was taught because I wanted to have them work with multiplying decimals, and that's what we've been studying this past couple of weeks. I wanted to have an exercise for them that they were enjoying and could see the reason why also they need to know how to multiply by decimals, because we use it all the time.

As much as the students seemed to enjoy the lesson, it was not clear to us that they understood decimal multiplication. We asked Cynthia about that, and she agreed:

> I think that a lot of them still rely on the mechanics of multiplying decimals, instead of actually looking at what's happening and understanding that we're talking about a part of something instead of the whole or having multiples of. . . . We've been working on it for about 2 weeks, but it takes a long time for them to really absorb it instead of relying on the mechanics of just doing it because I told them to "do it this way."

Cynthia intended to spend the next week working with decimal multiplication, but her focus seemed to be on applying decimal multiplication in context, and not on the underlying conceptual understanding of rational number multiplication.

Cynthia wanted to teach for understanding, and she was making instructional changes. During a January 1993 seminar, she spoke of a major instructional change:

> I think that a real important thing that I learned this year was the importance of letting children explore whatever they're doing— going as far as they're able to go, my not dictating but facilitating where they're going. . . . This whole last couple of years has been

more of letting go, and letting the children direct me as far as where I'm going to go next with them instead of looking at the textbook and having the textbook dictate to me.

But while she was making instructional changes, Cynthia was struggling with just how far her teaching should shift away from the traditional approach of focusing on algorithms. She said, "I just read a Marilyn Burns article about throwing the whole algorithm theory out the door. I'm not quite there. I think they still need a few ditto sheets."

When we had spent more time observing her teaching and when she shared her concerns during seminars, the sources of Cynthia's struggles became clearer. Cynthia felt accountable to parents and to her school administration. She told us that parents became "real uptight" when she deviated from the traditional curriculum. She continued to be concerned about the standardized achievement tests and felt responsible for seeing that her students were prepared.

Cynthia's attitude about her teaching was generally positive. During a seminar in January she told the group, "I'm feeling that I'm more confident with my mathematics, but I'm also feeling confident in saying, 'I don't know; let's explore it.'" She told the seminar group that making the transition from using ditto sheets and textbooks to having students actively involved was "really not that much work," and that she had other students share the teaching by having them share their thinking. She said that she loved the change.

As positive as Cynthia appeared to be about her teaching, she was at the same time critical of herself. One source of doubt developed when she began to realize that she herself did not possess a good conceptual understanding of content she was teaching. During the January seminar we discussed fraction multiplication and division. The group was in the middle of a discussion about the difference between $\frac{3}{4} \times \frac{1}{2}$ and $\frac{3}{4} \div \frac{1}{2}$ when one of the researchers noticed that Cynthia had been quiet.

Inv: Cynthia, are you comfortable or not?
Cynthia: No, I'm not. I'll be real honest. I'm not comfortable.
Inv: I don't blame you, because it's very difficult.
Cynthia: And I can see where my students wouldn't be comfortable because it's the complete opposite of whole numbers.

After more discussion, Cynthia told us that she had never thought about fraction division the way we were discussing it, and for the first time she could see the importance of distinguishing between a measurement model of division and a partitive model of division. At one point she became excited with what she was learning, but she also recognized that her understanding was too fragile to enable her to help her students:

Cynthia: This is probably the clearest thing I've seen. (Laughs) It is; it's very clear. This is something that always confused me. Here *I* am.

Inv: So you can see why your students are confused.

Cynthia: I wouldn't be able to explain it to them. [I would say to them,] "Just do it. Don't ask how; do it."

Later in the seminar Cynthia showed how fragile her new understanding was when she again confused fraction division and fraction multiplication. She expressed her feelings:

Cynthia: I feel really stupid right now. (Laughs) At least I'm starting to be more enlightened.

Inv: Why should you feel stupid?

Cynthia: Because I knew how to do the algorithm, but I didn't know why. I just did it because I knew. . . .

Inv: But that's where a lot of people are.

Even though Cynthia was rethinking what she wanted to teach, she continued to feel it was her responsibility to cover the old curriculum. During this same seminar, Cynthia and a researcher discussed the importance of teaching for conceptual and procedural knowledge. Although Cynthia generally seemed to agree with the researcher, her reluctance to give up part of the curriculum may have reflected a more traditional image of what she was trying to accomplish with her students:

Cynthia: I'm curious. Children are just beginning to be exposed to fractions at my level—[they get a little] at fourth grade, very little at third grade—but then they get thrown in these questions where they have to get common denominators for one fifth and three twenty-ones.

Inv: Why can't they just estimate the answer to that? Where are they ever going to need an exact answer to something like that?

Cynthia: Okay. Because to me, those were the ones that were the mind messer-uppers that just threw the kids off. They can do ¼ + ⁵⁄₁₂ very easily, but then you throw in those ones that are so obscure and I want to just go (makes motion of marking problems out) in the book and not to even have the kids deal with it. . . .

Inv: The rationale for including such problems was and is to check if students really know the algorithm.

Cynthia: But isn't it more important [to include more accessible questions] at the beginning levels . . . ? I'm feeling that with fractions the kids get so flipped out.

Inv: My point is they don't need to know those algorithms in the first place.

Cynthia: And I agree with that. But I mean, to me it just seems that they dump an awful lot on the kids' laps, and they expect them. . . . If you're a teacher and you're trying experiences for them to explore these, and you see that kind of a problem, and you're thinking, "I've got to make sure they know the obscurities of mathematics."

To Cynthia, the obscurities of mathematics included knowing how to apply the algorithm for adding $\frac{1}{5}$ and $\frac{3}{21}$.

In our third observation, in February, Cynthia again showed us that one of her goals was to teach for understanding. She was teaching a lesson from the *Seeing Fractions* replacement unit (Corwin, Russell, & Tierney, 1990). The unit was designed to reflect research findings on how children develop conceptual understanding of fractions and was intended to replace the traditional textbook unit on fractions at the fifth grade. Cynthia had attended an inservice workshop on teaching this unit. In the lesson we observed, students were to write two-step story problems (of a type that they had solved in earlier lessons) that would lead to adding fractions with unlike denominators. The students worked in groups and were to decide who in the group wrote the best problem; then that problem was shared with the class. The first group's problem was quite long, involving cookies (some of which were eaten by a family dog) and family members (some of whom wanted cookies and others who did not). Ultimately the problem was how four cookies could be shared fairly by seven people. A student from the group went to the overhead projector to explain her solution to this problem:

Briana: There was [sic] seven people; there was [sic] four cookies. [She drew four squares for the cookies and a row of seven circles for the people.]

First you divide all the cookies in half—and each person gets one half. [She partitioned the square cookies and wrote the symbol $\frac{1}{2}$ below each circle to indicate that each person received one-half cookie.] Then you have a half left, so you divide that into seven pieces, but really it's fourteenths.

Cynthia: Does everybody agree that it's really fourteenths?

Students: Yes.

Briana: And you give each person one fourteenth. [She partitioned the half square into seven parts then wrote the symbol $\frac{1}{14}$ below each circle to indicate that each person received one fourteenth of a cookie to go with the original one-half share received.]

You add $\frac{1}{2} + \frac{1}{14} =$ [She wrote this much of a number sentence on the overhead.] . . . and what you do is you make an example cookie. [She drew a new square to represent her "example cookie."]

First you divide it in half and then you divide it in four-teenths. [She partitioned the square into halves and then into fourteenths.]

And this half goes to here. [She shaded in one half (seven fourteenths) of the square.] Plus one fourteenth is right there. [She shaded one more fourteenth.]

And you add up 1, 2, 3, 4, 5, 6, 7, 8 fourteenths. [She counted the fourteenths and then wrote 8/14 to finish the number sentence.]

Cynthia: Did everybody come up with eight fourteenths? Did anyone come up with a different answer? Roy, what did you come up with?

Roy told the class that his answer was four sevenths. Cynthia asked if anyone else had four sevenths as the answer, and no one responded. Cynthia was excited about Roy's solution; she told him his answer was right and asked him to explain his strategy. Roy came forward, but became a little confused and said, "Seven fourteenths equals one whole." Cynthia gave Roy some acetates and asked him to continue thinking about his solution at his desk. Chad then came forward and explained that four sevenths and eight fourteenths were both correct and that there were many other answers:

Chad: Four sevenths times two over two equals eight fourteenths. Keep multiplying eight fourteenths by two by two [*sic*] equals sixteen twenty-eighths, and multiply that by two by two equals thirty-two fifty-sixths and keep going. . . .

At this point, Cynthia directed the discussion to calculating equivalent fractions. The long discussion on equivalent fractions ended with the following exchange:

Cynthia: Okay, what happens when we multiply any number by one whole, 1? Who can tell me what happens if we multiply seven eighths by 1? What are we going to get? Jennifer.

Jennifer: An equivalent fraction.

Cynthia: Okay, we'll get an equivalent fraction. An equivalent fraction, but any number multiplied by 1 is . . . ?

Students: . . . that number.

Cynthia: . . . that number, the same. Yes?

Evan: Well, all that Roy did was, he put it in simplest form. That's all he did.

Cynthia: Exactly, exactly. When you start working with fractions and start working with the algorithms, that's what they'll want you to do is to get—just doing problems, doing problems—they'll be wanting you to put it in simplest form.

The entire discussion was a nice example of students working with several fraction concepts. Cynthia followed the lesson outlined in the replacement unit and provided students opportunities to write their own problems, and then solve them. She seemed dedicated to focusing the students' attention on understanding the concepts, but she did not always know how to direct their attention. When one student wanted to prove procedurally why fractions were equivalent, Cynthia seemed pleased because it was important to her that her students "bridge the gap" between understanding and the algorithms. Cynthia considered it important for her students to draw connections between mathematical conceptual and procedural knowledge.

Many teachers, when attempting to teach conceptually, jump on the first available calculational escalator and ride it away from the land of conceptual mathematics (A. Thompson, Philipp, P. Thompson, & Boyd, 1994). Cynthia, though tempted to allow the conversation to become calculational, tried her best to sustain the discussion about the concepts. Later she reflected on the direction in which the lesson went, and again highlighted one of the recurring constraints she felt when teaching mathematics:

Cynthia: We've been dropping off from taking the book and doing the algorithms, which has been a real interesting experience.
Inv: (Laughs) Do you want to elaborate on that?
Cynthia: Well, a little bit of me is quite nervous about doing it, especially when I look at the book and see that they want to have simplified fractions, and the kids are not even aware of that. I don't even know if that's really important except for test scores, which, of course, being a teacher and having your job, that's a real important factor, making sure that everybody is accountable. But it seems like this is really kind of a nebulous way of being accountable.

Cynthia's Reactions to the Seminars

Cynthia attended the seminars regularly. However, she often struggled during discussions of mathematics, as demonstrated by her earlier cited comments on multiplication and division of fractions. When we analyzed the seminar transcripts, we found that she participated the least of those in the group. She seemed less enthusiastic than the others about the outside seminar presenters during this year, and when one of their Saturday presentations conflicted with other obligations (non-serious ones), she debated about what she should do, not recognizing that many people would travel far for the privilege of a 3-hour workshop and seminar with the speaker. In hindsight, we wonder whether the mathematical intensity of these sessions was somewhat frightening to her, perhaps at an unconscious level. Her comments during the second year supported this theory, as will be seen later in this chapter.

One indication of Cynthia's reactions to the seminars was the frequency of her comments that the mathematics we discussed in the seminars was far too difficult for her students to understand. Yet the topics we discussed were standard for fifth and sixth grades; what seemed too difficult appeared to be the nonalgorithmic approach and the probing questions that focused on deep understanding. Her comments were particularly interesting in light of the fact that over half of her class was considered gifted (a term used in this school district to classify the top 25% or so of students). She told us several times that her students were very bright, and challenging to teach, yet she felt that a conceptual approach was beyond their capabilities. None of the other teachers made similar comments.

A positive outcome of the seminars was that they provided Cynthia with opportunities to think about how she might sustain conceptual conversations with her students. She began to attend to her questioning strategies, and during the interview at the end of the first year, she explained the reasons for this practice:

> It was a snowball of things. You know in the video of watching Nancy [Mack] working with the young student and the questions that she came up with; she never walked them through anything; she just kept on asking probing questions. Nothing in particular, but I want to say that somehow Pat Thompson's [seminar] really came to me. I was sitting there saying, "I'm not quite grasping what they are getting at," and even though you were showing me these things it was like all of the sudden you realize that it's not showing the children, but letting them experience this for themselves, in a lot of different ways.

As much as Cynthia seemed to be gaining from her participation in the project, she seriously considered dropping out at the end of the first year. Because of our fundamental focus on mathematics content, our project was unlike any other teacher-enhancement project with which Cynthia had been involved, and it was therefore not what she had expected. She is perhaps overly conscientious, and so the dawning realization that she did not know the mathematics well caused her great discomfort and doubts about her ability as a teacher. This feeling of self-doubt was exacerbated by her feeling that our message was in conflict with the messages of both her principal and her students' parents, particularly in the area of testing. During our final seminar of that year she reflected on the year:

> Change can also be difficult, challenging, and stressful. . . . That is what I've felt through this project. Being able to fit this together with the [other math project] and also the way that we test our children—fitting this all together has been one of the most challenging and stressful and soul searching times. It really has been a real tough. . . . I'm getting emotional. I think it's real tough.

Fortunately for Cynthia and for us, she decided to continue for the second year.

Reflections on Year 1

Cynthia was in the process of changing her teaching practices before she began this project, and during our first year together she spoke often of the difficulties she experienced. She wanted to learn more about teaching with manipulatives. She wanted to learn how to be a better facilitator. She wanted her students to focus more on understanding. Her attempts to shift from teaching algorithms to teaching conceptual mathematics were supported by replacement units. However, her goal of teaching conceptually was often in conflict with the responsibility she felt for preparing her students for the more procedural mathematics required by the district standardized achievement test. She believed that her principal and her students' parents would prefer that she teach a traditional curriculum if this practice would result in higher test scores. Cynthia spoke often of these tensions.

Cynthia began the project expressing a desire to think about how she might help her students develop a deeper understanding of long division and fractions. She did not speak then about developing her own understanding of these areas. But as the year progressed, she began to talk more about her own mathematical understanding. By the end of the year, in a postobservation interview, she spoke of feeling much more comfortable with fraction multiplication and with division:

> One of the other things I should mention is that I knew how to do the algorithms before I came into your project. I knew how to do the algorithms. I knew what I felt was a sure-fire way of teaching it to those who are willing to be taught, but I really didn't, until after this year, I realized I really didn't understand and I wasn't able to give. . . . In the past I haven't been able to give the total under-standing of, when they multiply fractions, what is happening. It was very hard for me to really understand what you were talking

about [during the seminars]. At times I just wanted to say, "Enough is enough." But I really feel comfortable now in teaching multiplication and division of fractions.

There were internal constraints in addition to the external constraints to Cynthia's goal of teaching conceptually. One such constraint was her tendency to fall back on calculational discussions whenever she felt uncomfortable about the direction the conversation was taking. A. Thompson et al. (1994) distinguished between conceptually oriented teachers and calculationally oriented teachers. They described a conceptually oriented teacher as one who tends to "focus students' attention away from thoughtless application of procedures and toward a rich conception of situations, ideas, and relationships among ideas" (p. 86). Such teachers do this focusing by asking questions designed to support students' views of arithmetic in noncalculational contexts. For example, "[This number] is a number of what?" or "What are you trying to find when you do this calculation?" Calculationally oriented teachers are

> driven by a fundamental image of mathematics as the application of calculations and procedures for deriving numerical results. This does not mean that such a teacher focuses only on computational procedures. Rather, his view of mathematics is more inclusive but still one focused on procedures—computational or otherwise—for "getting answers." (p. 86)

The replacement units supported Cynthia when she attempted to teach more conceptually, but her own calculational orientation often caused her to direct conversations away from the relationships among ideas and toward the application of calculations.

Although there were many positive experiences for Cynthia during this year, it was often more difficult for her than we realized at the time, since it was not until the end of that year and again during the second year that she spoke about the pain and feelings of failure she was experiencing with regard to her image of herself as a good teacher.

YEAR 2: THE PAIN BEARS FRUIT

In October of the second year we observed three consecutive decimal lessons Cynthia taught. She had been dissatisfied with her textbook's treatment of decimals, and she decided to teach a unit on decimals designed by Judy Sowder and Zvia Markovits (Markovits & Sowder, 1991). Our first observation took place during the second day the unit was being taught. At the beginning of the lesson the students used base-ten blocks to build models of such numbers as 2.63. (The flat was serving as the unit.) Cynthia then reversed the task by showing students pictures of blocks and asking students to write the number represented by the blocks. After the students worked on a page of similar problems at their seats, Cynthia led the class in a discussion of how to represent four longs. A student came to the overhead and wrote *0.4*. Cynthia then asked the students to write a number for four small blocks, and a student wrote *.04*. Cynthia changed *0.4* to *0.40* and asked the number of hundredths in 0.40. After a pause she answered her own question, telling the students there were no hundredths in 0.40. She then wrote *0.400*, and asked how many hundredths, then how many thousandths, were in the number. Students responded that there were neither hundredths nor thousandths in 0.400. Cynthia acknowledged their response as correct, and the students then worked on handouts. Later in the lesson she wrote *0.400* and *.04* on the board, and she asked the students how these were similar or different. She later posed the same question using *0.40* and *0.04*. She tried to assist her students by asking them, "How many of each do you need to make one whole?" The students struggled some with this task, and soon after this lesson ended.

Cynthia's questions had directed her students toward identifying the value of each place, but not toward the important underlying place value concepts. To Cynthia, the question How many hundredths are in 0.40? was equivalent to the question What digit is located in the hundredths place of 0.40? She did not direct her students' attention toward the fact that one could simultaneously view 0.40 as 4 tenths or 40 hundredths. Later, when comparing 0.40 and 0.04, she asked, "How many of each do you need to make one whole?" Cynthia's focus was on the *number* of pieces, not on the *part of the whole*.

Although it was not clear to Cynthia how she might direct her students' attention to the role of the unit, she was aware of its importance and she questioned whether her students understood. During the postobservation interview Cynthia began by reflecting on the lesson:

> One of the things that I'm going to be real interested in finding out is how they perceive a decimal, because we've been talking about them as blocks, but are they really understanding that as a part of a whole? . . . I'm not sure they're really catching on to that, so it will be real interesting to see. . . . That's what I'm really concerned about . . . , because I see that this unit will really help out with my fractions [if the students see decimals as parts of a whole].

Cynthia talked with us at length about how she might make the unit (the 1) more explicit. She decided that, among other things, she would introduce a problem involving multiple units. At the suggestion of one of the investigators, she asked the students to consider a small cake and a large cake, with the large cake being 10 times the size of the small cake, so that one hundredth of the large cake would be the same amount of cake as one tenth of the small cake. Cynthia was reluctant to pose this question, and feared that her students might not understand.

We returned the next day and videotaped Cynthia's lesson. On this day she presented the cake problem, but only after preliminary discussion to focus her students' attention on the role of the unit. She began the lesson by asking students to compare four pairs of decimals. One pair was 5.05 and 5.50.

> Juanita: They're different. (Cynthia asked Juanita to read the numbers.) The first number, it's in the hundredths place; the second number, it's in the tenths place.
>
> *Cynthia:* Is there another way to explain it?
>
> Valerie: Five and five hundredths—you need ninety-five hundredths to make a whole. The second number you need five tenths to make a whole.
>
> *Cynthia:* I have a question related to the numbers. Could I also have five and fifty hundredths? Think. I have five and five tenths and five and five hundredths. Could I have five and fifty hundredths? Would that be the same question?
>
> Joe: Five and five tenths is the same [as five and fifty hundredths]. They are just different names.
>
> Fagiz: It doesn't matter about the zeros behind the number.

This conversation surprised us, considering that the day before Cynthia had told the students that there were no hundredths in 0.40. We wondered whether the work with the blocks helped them to realize that 5.5 and 5.50 represent the same amount. The conversation continued:

> *Cynthia:* We are representing the unit with a flat. How would we represent hundredths?
>
> Erna: With a small block.
>
> *Cynthia:* What represents tenths?
>
> Eddie: A long.
>
> *Cynthia:* How many longs for five tenths?
>
> Eddie: Five.
>
> *Cynthia:* How many small blocks would you need for 50 hundredths?
>
> Anna: Five. [Cynthia repeats the question.]
>
> Anna: Fifty.
>
> *Cynthia:* They [.5 and .50] equal the same. How are they different?
>
> Beatriz: One is in hundredths; one is in tenths.
>
> *Cynthia:* What do you see that is different?

Gavin: Five tenths is five long blocks; 50 hundredths is 50 small blocks.

Cynthia: So what is different? This demonstrates what?

Juan: There is no difference; 50 blocks equals five tenths.

Cynthia: Does anyone see any difference?

Li: You use a lot more of the hundredths, the small blocks, than the longs.

Cynthia next asked her students to compare 0.1 and 0.01. She was still assessing whether or not her students knew that a "decimal is part of a whole," a point she believed to be crucial to their understanding decimal numbers.

Carol: Zero and one tenth; zero and one hundredth. The first number, the one is in the tenths; the second number, the one is in the hundredths.

Cynthia: Is there a different way to . . . If you picture it, is there a clearer way to explain?

John: One tenth doesn't have a zero before it.

Cynthia: I'm still looking. . . . The most important thing to remember is a decimal is part of what?

Justin: Of a whole.

At this point Cynthia presented the cake problem with the goal of making the unit explicit:

Cynthia: We said these [0.1 and 0.01] are not the same. What if I had a cake like this (draws small square on board) and took one tenth of it. And then I had another cake 10 times as large (draws larger cake and shades small corner, labeling it $\frac{1}{100}$), and I took one hundredth of it. For my family I had a small cake cut in tenths. For a party I had a large cake, 10 times as large, and I take one hundredth of it. Would [one piece from each cake] be the same amount of cake?

Carolyn: Yes. It takes 10 of the small cakes to make one whole big cake.

Gordon: Yes. When you cut the small cake in tenths for 10 people, there would be the same amount of cake.

Cynthia: What about the large cake where you have 100th of a piece [sic]?

Li: Ten little cakes fit on the big cake. The tenth of the little cake would be the same as 1 one hundredth of the big cake.

Aaron: The big cake is 10 times as big as the little cake. One hundredth of the big cake would be the same size as one tenth of the small cake.

Cynthia: Good thinking. Did our unit ever change?

Students: Yes.
Cynthia: Would one tenth of a candy bar be the same as one tenth of a piece of gum?
Students: No.
Cynthia: So it depends on what?
Beatriz: The size of the whole.

Although Cynthia's goals during this lesson were similar to those of the previous day, her approach was different. In this lesson she helped her students realize that .50 could be viewed as either five tenths or fifty hundredths. She also wanted her students to understand that one tenth is one tenth *of something*, and she wanted to help her students make the unit explicit. She later said that she did not think all of the children understood the cake problem, since some seemed confused. Later in the lesson she shifted the context to money, and when a student suggested that a flat, long, and single might represent a dollar, dime, and penny respectively, Cynthia asked the entire class to reflect on that: "How did you decide that 1 dollar would equal the unit, 10 cents would equal one tenth, and 1 cent would equal one hundredth? Prove it to me. Write why you would use that as the unit."

The students worked with this task, presenting their solutions. It was of interest to us, though, that Li continued to work on the cake problem on his own, and Cynthia allowed him to do so. Later in the lesson Li asked if he could talk about the cakes again, and he presented this solution, relating the cakes to the blocks, at the overhead projector:

Li: If the big cake is equal to a flat and the small cake equals a long,

$$\frac{1}{10} \text{ of a long} = 1 \text{ small block}$$
$$\frac{1}{100} \text{ of a flat} = 1 \text{ small block}$$

One small from a flat, one hundredth, is the same size as one small from a long, one tenth.
Cynthia: What has changed?
Li: The size of one tenth, of one hundredth. The 1.
Cynthia: The size of the unit.

It is noteworthy that Cynthia decided to make changes to the way in which this lesson was laid out for the teacher. During our past observations Cynthia had diligently followed each lesson exactly as the authors had planned. She seldom openly questioned the extent to which the lessons might accomplish their stated goals, and she did not make changes to the lesson. But her attitude about texts and authors had changed. Cynthia expressed doubts as to whether her students understood that decimals involved parts of wholes, and these doubts led her to the lesson on cakes, involving a change of unit. We think that by participating in the seminars, many of which were devoted to discussing rational number reasoning, Cynthia had developed a richer image of what was important for her students to know about decimals, and this image empowered her to be more critical about the lessons.

Later that evening we met in seminar and Cynthia talked about her lesson. She continued to wonder about the efficacy of changing the unit, or the whole, so early in her instruction on decimals. During the seminar she reflected on the questions she had posed to her students:

Cynthia: You have your perception of what your kids can do. I guess what I want to know is "Am I asking the right questions?"

Inv: When you first asked the questions [about the place value], students' first responses were, "Because it's in this place . . . ," but when you pushed them further, they went further.

Cynthia: Yes. It was very difficult. That's what I was doing when you were there. I was asking, "How many would it take to make a whole?"

Teachers' success in posing conceptually oriented questions rests on their understanding of the content and of their students' thinking about that content. As Cynthia's understanding of decimals and her understanding of her students' understanding of decimals developed, she was able to pose questions that directed her students' attention toward the important underlying concepts. Her lesson on the second day we observed engaged her students at a deeper level than her lesson of the previous day because she had thought through the concepts she was trying to teach. Her own understanding was still fragile, however. That is, when she thought about the role of the unit in one context, she did not necessarily transfer that knowledge to a different context. For example, during the seminar she expressed her surprise at her students' confusion when they were asked to use decimals to represent money:

But there were a couple of them that didn't get the money, which was really shocking to me. I mean fifth grade—not dealing with money very well. You would think in fifth grade they would be able to—I mean allowances. I was shocked.

On the one hand, Cynthia's surprise that fifth-grade students were confused about money is understandable. On the other hand, we question what Cynthia was hoping her students would understand. For many students, $1.25 is thought of as 1 dollar and 25 cents, or 1 dollar, 2 dimes, and 5 pennies. To these students, the decimal point serves only to separate dollars from cents. If Cynthia wanted her students to see that .25 represents 25 hundredths of a dollar, it may not have occurred to her that without constraining the tasks she gave to her students, there would be no reason to expect them to have developed that thinking. Whereas Cynthia thought of money as a context to develop rational number reasoning, many of her students were able to answer the questions by applying whole number reasoning and so did not apply decimal number reasoning.

Cynthia completed the decimal unit, and 2 months later, during a seminar, she reflected on it and on her students' success on the standardized test:

> Cynthia: I'm done. My kids all passed the test, the AGP test [the district standardized achievement test]. I went over the things I didn't think correlated. My kids are real clear on what decimals are—that they are a part of the whole, no matter what the whole is. That was the most wonderful thing for me to have them have that realization. They all passed.

Cynthia's instruction on decimals and her instruction during other classes we observed but have not described here were more conceptually oriented than the lessons we observed during the first year. We were surprised, then, to see a lesson we observed in May of the second year. Cynthia was teaching a geometry lesson on angles. She gave an assignment directly from the textbook, and the students' questions during the lesson were about procedural aspects. She did not use any of the questioning techniques that we had watched her so successfully use during previous lessons. When we walked around the room observing students' work, it became evident that the students did not possess the level of understanding that we had observed during her fraction and decimal units. During the postobservation interview it became clear that Cynthia was not aware of her students' lack of a deeper conceptual understanding.

Yet when, as a group, we (the investigators) discussed and reflected on this lesson, we realized that we should not have expected a conceptually oriented lesson about geometry. We had not discussed geometry during the seminars. Conceptual understanding is about specific content. Cynthia did not have a good understanding of the mathematics she was teaching that day, and, moreover, she may not even have been aware that there is more to the geometry than is in the textbook lesson. If teachers have not had an opportunity to think about what constitutes conceptual teaching in a particular content, then how can they be expected to teach for conceptual understanding of that content?

Reflections on Year 2

In the first year of our project, nearly half of Cynthia's students had been identified as gifted, and she found them to be a bright and capable group. At the beginning of the second year she told us that few of her students were exceptional, and she expressed concern that she would not be able to expect nearly as much of these students as she had from her students of the previous year. However, as the year progressed, we observed that her students seemed able to sustain more conceptual discussions and were learning more mathematics than her students in the previous year. What had changed? We suspect it was Cynthia's own understanding of the content that changed, and the effect of this change was that she was able to pose good questions and to sustain the discussion that focused her students' attention on the more important mathematical concepts.

During the second year, Cynthia became more comfortable with the seminars, and as she did, she participated to a greater extent in the discussions. Our analysis of seminar data showed that during the second year she participated more fully than any other teacher. Cynthia also became convinced that the value of the seminars was in great part due to the focus on mathematics, and she became critical of mathematics teacher inservices that did not deal in depth with mathematical content. During a seminar in January 1994 she expressed this view:

> We're involved in two other projects, and I don't think they even touch the depth of what we do in here. It's overwhelming when I walk away from here, and the things that we discuss in this room. What they're doing [in the other projects] doesn't even touch close to what we're doing in here: the expansion, the whole philosophy of mathematics. [In other projects] it's more of still the manipulation, and we're not getting into the theory of mathematics and how a child does really learn and what are the concepts.

A month later, in another seminar, she critiqued the school district's workshops:

> And even to workshops—I don't think that even the workshops that are given—at least in [this school district]—I've never seen any one make me think about how the child really is thinking and what kind of questions I'm asking that will get the response that I need.

When Cynthia thought about what she had gained from the seminars, she began to feel sorry for other teachers who did not have a similar opportunity, as she expressed in February 1994:

I think it's really frustrating knowing that there's a lot of teachers coming in that haven't had experiences to talk. . . . I mean, this is a unique experience, being able to talk to mathematicians, and to be able to ask the questions that we're dealing with and to get the feedback of what you're seeing. And a lot of people, once they get that credential, they're in the classroom doing their thing year after year after year. And you can send them to every single math conference that you want to, and still they won't. . . . [They say,] "Oh, here's a brand new game that I can play with them," or "Here's a lesson that I can do—dividing up bananas. Then I can show them fractions of bananas, and we can make a fondue, and isn't that a wonderful concept for the kids." But they're not getting the idea. Do you know what I mean?

Cynthia became more critical of the teacher she used to be. During a seminar in January of the second year she asked, "How was I teaching before? How did these kids even—what did they walk out of my classroom with?" During a seminar 1 month later in February, she spoke of the frustration that she and others experience:

That person is frustrated because that's [the old way] how he was taught. He's feeling the frustration because now he needs to learn *why* to be able to answer questions that come up or to be able to ask questions that lead to some of these answers. I was never taught this way, and I was never taught in my methods class to teach this way.

During the first year Cynthia felt overwhelmed. The sources of these feelings were twofold: First, she was frustrated with the long mathematics sessions. Second, she did not know how to apply what she was learning to her teaching. During our last seminar of the project she thought back:

I have to admit when I first worked with this group, I sat there and thought, "This is overwhelming." First off, sitting down and thinking for 3 hours, strictly math, after I'd done a day of work, was just overwhelming to me. And then secondly, I thought, "I teach so many other subjects that are as important. How do I start fitting this additional stress and anxiety into my life? How do I deal with it?" . . . And looking at how you deal with children and what are you expecting out of them. And it is, it's extremely painful. It was one of the hardest things. I wanted to quit. I wanted to leave the group because it was just. . . . It was like saying everything that I was doing before wasn't right. And so it's easier to just say, "Okay, I give up."

DISCUSSION

Of all of the teachers in the project, Cynthia may have made the most substantial changes in her teaching. This finding is cause for optimism, because in many ways she was the most typical of all of the teachers. She began the project saying that she loved mathematics and was committed to making mathematics accessible to all of her students. Her view of what this commitment meant changed over the next 2 years. While she was developing a more conceptual orientation to the teaching of mathematics, she also was developing a better understanding of the mathematics itself.

The process of engaging in mathematical discussions with other teachers and with the investigators and visitors was difficult for Cynthia, and she considered quitting our project after the first year. But she decided to stay, and her levels of participation and self-confidence changed dramatically—it was as though she had emerged from a tunnel. During the second-year seminars Cynthia had more to say than any other teacher, a significant change considering that during the first year she spoke far less than anyone else.

Although Cynthia began the project with an expressed commitment to having her students make sense of mathematics, over the course of the project her deeper understanding of the mathematics she was teaching, along with her more conceptually oriented view of mathematics, helped her "let go" of much of what she had been doing in terms of tightly controlling her class. During the second year of the project she became more critical of the textbook and replacement units and questioned whether her students would be able to make sense of the mathematics as it was laid out in the materials she was using. She was willing to adapt the instructional materials if she thought that the adaptations would help her students understand the important concepts.

Coming to hold a more conceptually oriented view of mathematics was an important factor contributing to Cynthia's instructional changes because it changed her overall goals for instruction. But perhaps more important was her own increased understanding of the content. She was very successful with the decimal unit she taught. Yet when we observed her teaching content that had not been addressed during the seminars, we found that it was difficult for her to sustain conceptually oriented mathematical conversations. Her deeper understanding of the content enabled her to make instructional changes. We expect that when she takes the time to explore other mathematical topics we did not cover in our seminars, her instruction on these topics will also change.

Chapter 10

STUDENT LEARNING

One way of measuring teacher change is to measure change in students' performance. We focused on two areas of mathematics related to the seminars, areas in which we might therefore expect to see change. The first area we tested was fraction knowledge, which was a major focus of our work with the teachers. We limited this area further to focus primarily on aspects of fraction size. The types of items selected had been shown in other research (Cramer, Post, & Behr, 1989; Markovits & Sowder, 1989, 1994) to differentiate between students with and without basic fraction understanding. The second area we selected was proportional reasoning. Because less seminar and class time was spent on this topic, we did not have clear expectations for student performance. We decided, however, to test proportional reasoning primarily to see whether or not students would attempt to solve these problems in increasingly meaningful ways.

Students were tested in project teachers' classrooms at the beginning and at the end of both the first and second years the teachers were in the program. In this section we consider results from the second year of testing only. Although we were generally pleased with testing results for the first year, we felt that teachers could not be expected to make serious changes in their instruction until at least the second year of the project. During the second year, one teacher left the program because his new school was too far from the university for him to drive to seminars. Unfortunately, one of the remaining teachers did not administer the posttest at the end of the second year, because of several emergencies during the last 2 weeks of school. We therefore consider pretest-posttest results for classes of the other three teachers only.

It happened that the sixth-grade teacher had taught mathematics to one of the fifth-grade classes the previous year and had selected some of these students to be in her present sixth-grade class. We found profound differences in performances of the students she had taught for 2 years and the students who were in her class for the first time. We therefore decided to separate out the performance of these two groups in our analysis.

In addition to completing the whole-class written tests, six students from each of the four classes were interviewed at the beginning and end of the second school year. A subset of the written items were given to students during the interviews, which were held after the written tests had been administered. The interviews served to clarify and expand on responses on the written tests and to help us ascertain the reasoning processes used by the students. The teachers selected the students; they were each asked to select two of their best performing students, two average performing students, and two of their poorest performing students in mathematics.

For comparison purposes we also administered the written measures of fraction understanding and proportional reasoning to 58 seventh graders from a local middle school approximately 4 weeks into the school year. The school served primarily middle-class students; the students tested were considered "average" in that they had not been placed in prealgebra. We believed this group to be representative of average seventh graders in this geographical area and thought that comparison of posttest performance of our project students with the performance of these beginning seventh graders would provide us with another indication of the growth of understanding of our project students. None of the seventh graders tested had been in our project teachers' classrooms.

FRACTION UNDERSTANDING

Table 10.1 shows the percentage correct (and percentage change) on the pretests and posttests in the three classrooms; two fifth grade (the first from the inner city, the second from a middle-class neighborhood) and one sixth grade (from a low-SES rural area). The sixth-grade scores are separated into two groups: the group who had had mathematics instruction from a project teacher for 2 years, and the group who had had the teacher for only 1 year. The last column shows the performance of the comparison group of seventh graders on the same items.

For the first item the students were given eight pairs of numbers and asked to circle the larger in each pair or to place an equal sign between the two numbers in the pair. Performance on the posttest in the urban fifth-grade classroom approximated the performance of seventh graders; on 13 of 18 items posttest performance for the fifth graders was

TABLE 10.1

Pretest and Posttest Performance on Fraction Items in Percent Correct

Item	Grade 5 Class (Inner City) $n = {}^{25}\!/_{28}{}^{a}$	Grade 5 Class (Middle SES) $n = {}^{30}\!/_{25}$	Grade 6 Class (Rural) 2-yr. Ss[b] $n = {}^{13}\!/_{12}$	Grade 6 Class (Rural) 1-yr. Ss[b] $n = {}^{15}\!/_{18}$	Grade 7 Classes[c] (Mixed) $n = 58$
1. Circle the larger or place = between:					
a. $^7\!/_7$, 1	$^{28}\!/_{75}$ (47)[d]	$^{70}\!/_{92}$ (22)	$^{92}\!/_{92}$ (0)	$^{67}\!/_{89}$ (22)	78
b. $^5\!/_4$, 1	$^{20}\!/_{82}$ (62)	$^{43}\!/_{76}$ (33)	$^{38}\!/_{83}$ (45)	$^{40}\!/_{56}$ (16)	45
c. $^7\!/_7$, $^3\!/_7$	$^{92}\!/_{75}$ (−17)	$^{60}\!/_{88}$ (28)	$^{92}\!/_{92}$ (0)	$^{93}\!/_{50}$ (−43)	83
d. $^1\!/_6$, $^1\!/_8$	$^{12}\!/_{39}$ (27)	$^{47}\!/_{76}$ (29)	$^{85}\!/_{100}$ (15)	$^{40}\!/_{94}$ (54)	52
e. $^5\!/_7$, $^5\!/_9$	$^{16}\!/_{36}$ (20)	$^{37}\!/_{68}$ (31)	$^{85}\!/_{92}$ (7)	$^{40}\!/_{83}$ (43)	48
f. $^3\!/_4$, $^6\!/_8$	$^4\!/_{29}$ (25)	$^{10}\!/_{44}$ (34)	$^{54}\!/_{100}$ (46)	$^{13}\!/_{50}$ (37)	38
g. 0.7, $^1\!/_2$	$^{44}\!/_{57}$ (13)	$^{27}\!/_{36}$ (9)	$^8\!/_{83}$ (76)	$^{33}\!/_{28}$ (−6)	28
h. 0.5, $^5\!/_{12}$	$^0\!/_{32}$ (32)	$^{10}\!/_{48}$ (38)	$^{23}\!/_{83}$ (60)	$^7\!/_{50}$ (43)	31
2. Which is closer to $^1\!/_2$, $^5\!/_8$ or $^1\!/_5$?	$^8\!/_{39}$ (31)	$^{43}\!/_{60}$ (17)	$^{100}\!/_{92}$ (−8)	$^{40}\!/_{61}$ (21)	52
3. $^9\!/_{10} + {}^{11}\!/_{12}$ is about (choose one) 1, 2, 20, 22, 42	$^4\!/_{57}$ (53)	$^{17}\!/_{44}$ (27)	$^{31}\!/_{42}$ (11)	$^{33}\!/_{28}$ (−5)	26
4. Which would go best with					
a. A: $^5\!/_8$, $^1\!/_3$, $^7\!/_7$	$^{12}\!/_{25}$ (13)	$^{10}\!/_{36}$ (26)	$^{38}\!/_{67}$ (29)	$^{13}\!/_{11}$ (−2)	19
b. B: $^1\!/_{10}$, $^{11}\!/_{12}$, $^{13}\!/_{10}$	$^{20}\!/_{43}$ (23)	$^{33}\!/_{48}$ (15)	$^{69}\!/_{83}$ (14)	$^{33}\!/_{39}$ (6)	34
c. C: $^1\!/_4$, $^5\!/_4$, 3	$^{32}\!/_{46}$ (14)	$^{23}\!/_{52}$ (29)	$^{46}\!/_{83}$ (37)	$^{33}\!/_{22}$ (−11)	31
5. Jane said that 12 ÷ $^1\!/_2$ is 6, but Sammy said no, it is 24. Who is right?	$^{20}\!/_{46}$ (26)	$^{13}\!/_8$ (−5)	$^8\!/_{25}$ (17)	$^{20}\!/_{22}$ (2)	21
6. Hadad ate $^2\!/_3$ of a candy bar. This much is left. Make a drawing of how big the candy bar was before Hadad ate any.	$^8\!/_{18}$ (10)	$^{23}\!/_{44}$ (21)	$^{46}\!/_{83}$ (37)	$^{40}\!/_{72}$ (32)	31

For item 4, a number line is shown with points labeled A, B, C between marks 0, $\frac{1}{2}$, 1, $1\frac{1}{2}$.

Item	Grade 5 Class (Inner City) $n = {}^{25}/_{28}$[a]	Grade 5 Class (Middle SES) $n = {}^{30}/_{25}$	Grade 6 Class (Rural) 2-yr. Ss[b] $n = {}^{13}/_{12}$	Grade 6 Class (Rural) 1-yr. Ss[b] $n = {}^{15}/_{18}$	Grade 7 Classes[c] (Mixed) $n = 58$
7. $5 + \frac{1}{2} + 0.5$	⁰⁄₄₆ (46)	²⁰⁄₅₂ (32)	⁶⁹⁄₇₅ (6)	²⁷⁄₃₉ (12)	34
8. John found ¾ of a pie in the refrigerator. He sat down and ate ⅔ of the pie that was left. What fractional part of a whole pie did he eat?	¹²⁄₃₂ (20)	⁴⁷⁄₄₈ (1)	¹⁵⁄₈ (−7)	²⁰⁄₂₈ (8)	22
9. Shade in ¾ of this rectangle.	⁴⁄₃₆ (32)	⁷⁄₅₆ (49)	³⁸⁄₆₇ (29)	¹³⁄₂₂ (9)	12

a The first n is for the pretest; the second for the posttest. b 2-year students were taught fractions by the same teacher in both fifth and sixth grades; 1-year, only in sixth. c Provided for comparison purposes. d Pretest/posttest (change in percent).

the same or better than for the seventh graders. Posttest performance for the other two classrooms was considerably better than that of seventh graders.

Overall, the results on Item 1 show considerable improvement from pretest to posttest. The only remarkable drop in performance, for one fifth-grade class and the "new" sixth-grade group, came on Item 1c asking that ²⁄₇ and ³⁄₇ be compared. Note that in the sixth-grade class the scores on this item dropped although at the same time they were exceeded by scores on the item asking for a comparison between ⅙ and ⅛. We have noticed this phenomenon before with other students; it appears that while students are coming to understand how to compare fractions with different denominators and like numerators, some mistakenly apply their newly discovered "rule" to fractions with like denominators and different numerators.

Interview data on these items indicate a strong development of understanding to match these test scores. When comparing ²⁄₇ and ³⁄₇, all students except two of the low-performing ones correctly selected ³⁄₇ on the posttest and explained their reasoning adequately. Most said that when something was cut into seven pieces, three was more than two; one held up seven fingers and said that three fingers was more than two fingers; another placed sevenths on a number line and showed that $\frac{3}{7}$ was more than $\frac{2}{7}$. Those students who gave an incorrect answer on the pretest provided reasons such as "You need four here to make one but you need five here" and "$\frac{1}{3}$ is less than $\frac{1}{2}$." Some students who were correct on the pretest gave as their reasons "Because that's the rule" or "Because 2 is less than 3 but 7 is equal to 7." It appeared that by the time these students took the posttest, they could answer this item correctly if they had to explain their thinking; whereas if they were hurriedly answering items on a written test, they simply applied the (wrong) rule and did not think through their answers.

On the pretest interview item asking them to compare $\frac{5}{7}$ and $\frac{5}{9}$, students who selected $\frac{5}{9}$ as the larger said it was because 9 is larger than 7, or because "there are more pieces left: four here and two there." On the posttest all students asked said that $\frac{5}{7}$ was larger and provided an explanation based on the reasoning that 7ths are larger than 9ths when a whole is cut up. (The low-performing fifth graders were not given this item in the interview if they could not correctly compare $\frac{1}{6}$ and $\frac{1}{8}$.) When asked to compare $\frac{1}{7}$ and 0.7, only 2 sixth graders answered correctly on the pre-interview, but half the fifth graders and all sixth graders answered correctly during the postinterview and provided good reasons for their answers: "Seven tenths is closer to one half"; "almost a whole versus one of seven."

Items 2, 3, and 4 all depend on being able to use 0, $\frac{1}{2}$, and 1 as benchmarks for fractions. The fifth-grade students showed impressive improvement on these items. Sixth-grade performance for the "new" students did not show gains as impressive as at fifth grade, although performance for the "old" students generally improved. It appears that this teacher devoted time to instruction on benchmarks in Grade 5 but not in Grade 6. If this is the case, it might be because one of the seminars during the first year (when the teacher had the students as fifth graders) focused on the importance of benchmarks in work with fractions. The result was that students from the previous year were able to consolidate their knowledge, although the knowledge remained shaky for those who had not received instruction in this area.

Previous data (Markovits & Sowder, 1991) on Item 7 asking for the sum of 5, $\frac{1}{2}$, and 0.5 showed that many students at this age believe that fractions and decimal numbers cannot be added together; only 1 of 20 sixth graders could provide the sum. The dramatic increases in fifth-grade scores on this item may be due to a change in this reasoning; those students who were beginning to make sense of rational numbers did not hold this misconception. (This item was not included in interviews.) Similarly, students who had a good understanding of fractions could ignore the distracting "thirds" marks on the rectangle in Item 18 and successfully partition and shade in three fourths, even though data from another study (Cramer et al., 1989) have shown this task to be difficult for students.

The remaining fraction items (5, 6, and 8) all show general improvement, in some cases quite significant; in other cases there are slight drops that indicate a change in the performance of one or two students. There could be several reasons given for change or lack of change; performance on these items is to some extent dependent on whether instruction focused on similar items or on making drawings when solving problems.

A final item used in most pre-interviews and all postinterviews was to ask students to say everything they could about ¾—they could draw pictures, compare it to other numbers, or do whatever made sense to them. Pre-interview responses in all grades were trivial or incorrect; students drew a circle and shaded in three fourths, sometimes correctly, sometimes incorrectly, or made statements such as "¾ is bigger than 1." Postinterview responses were much improved. The top two and middle two students in each of the three classes all provided multiple ways of thinking about ¾; for example, one inner-city student said that ¾ is ⁷⁵/₁₀₀; it is close to 1; it is greater than ½; it can't be reduced; ⅔ is greater than ¾; ¾ is about ⅚, it is about ⅞, it is about ⁹/₁₀.

PROPORTIONAL REASONING

Four proportional reasoning tasks were given to the students:

1. Eel Problem. Origin: Piaget, Grize, Szeminska, and Bang (1977); Resnick and Singer (1993)

   There are three baby eels in fish tanks. Eels are long fish. The eel in fish tank A is 10 cm long. In fish tank B the eel is 20 cm long. In fish tank C the eel is 25 cm long. The number of food balls each eel gets depends on the length of the eel. Eel A gets two food balls each day.

   How many food balls should eel B get? (Show how you got your answer.)

   How many food balls should eel C get? (Show how you got your answer.)

2. Gum Problem. Origin: Bezuk (1987)

   Jean and Carla each bought the same kind of bubble gum at the same store. Jean bought 2 pieces of gum for 6¢. If Carla bought 8 pieces of gum, how much did she pay? (Show how you got your answer.)

3. Bank Problem. Origin: devised during seminars in Year 1

   At Bank A, John put in $4 and after 1 year got back $8. At Bank B, Maria put in $10 and after 1 year got back $15. If you had $7 to put in a bank, would you put it in Bank A or Bank B? Why?

(Note: In the inner-city Grade-5 class, the pretest item read that Bank A returned $12 instead of $8 for a deposit of $4. However, these numbers allowed students to obtain the correct answer by additive reasoning [Bank A returned $8 whereas Bank B returned $5], and so the numbers were changed on all other tests.)

4. Pizza Problem. Origin: adapted from Kieren (1991)

   On the left you see some girls and some pizzas. On the right you see some boys and one pizza. The girls share their pizzas fairly, and the boys share their pizza fairly. Who gets more pizza, a boy or a girl?

   (Show how you got your answer.)

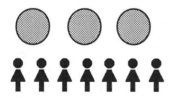

Performance results are shown in Table 10.2. Since performance on these items depends in part on the development of the ability to reason proportionally, which is age-related, it is difficult to say what effect instruction had on students. Still, Lamon (1995) has suggested that early intervention can help students bridge the transition from additive to multiplicative thinking, which is crucial to proportional reasoning. The inner-city Grade 5 teacher made special efforts to begin this intervention, and the gains from pretest to posttest in this class are particularly impressive. In the one instance in which a large gain was not made (the bank problem), the item was different on the pretest and posttest, as explained above, and so these numbers are suspect.

TABLE 10.2

Pretest and Posttest Performance on
Proportional Reasoning Items in Percent Correct

Item	Grade 5 Class (Inner City) $n = {}^{25}\!/_{28}{}^{a}$	Grade 5 Class (Middle SES) $n = {}^{30}\!/_{25}$	Grade 6 Class (Rural) 2-yr. Ss^b $n = {}^{13}\!/_{12}$	Grade 6 Class (Rural) 1-yr. Ss^b $n = {}^{15}\!/_{18}$	Grade 7 Classes^c (Mixed) $n = 58$
1. Eel Problem	${}^{8}\!/_{32}$ (24)^d	${}^{50}\!/_{52}$ (2)	${}^{69}\!/_{83}$ (14)	${}^{40}\!/_{67}$ (27)	48
2. Gum Problem	${}^{12}\!/_{43}$ (31)	${}^{43}\!/_{68}$ (25)	${}^{77}\!/_{92}$ (15)	${}^{67}\!/_{89}$ (22)	57
3. Bank Problem	${}^{24}\!/_{25}$ (1)	${}^{37}\!/_{52}$ (15)	${}^{69}\!/_{58}$ (−11)	${}^{27}\!/_{72}$ (45)	34
4. Pizza Problem	${}^{32}\!/_{71}$ (39)	${}^{50}\!/_{52}$ (2)	${}^{69}\!/_{75}$ (6)	${}^{53}\!/_{44}$ (−9)	46

^{a} The first n is for the pretest; the second for the posttest. ^{b} Two-year students were taught fractions by the same teacher in both fifth and sixth grades; one-year, only in sixth. ^{c} Provided for comparison purposes. ^{d} Pretest/posttest (change), in percents.

It is, of course, more difficult to make impressive gains when scores begin higher. The pretest performance for the first group of sixth-grade students was also quite good, particularly when compared with Grade 7 scores.

Eel Problem. Because these items required students to explain their answers, we also looked at the explanations. In many cases, particularly at fifth grade, students did not give reasons. When we considered only those sixth graders (from both groups) whose written reasons were clearly multiplicative on this item, we moved from 17% on the pretest to 50% on the posttest. Examples of multiplicative reasoning are "[B gets] 4 food balls. Because on ell [sic] A I figured out you get a food ball for every 5 cm. [C gets] 5 [food balls]. You just count by 5s and there are 5 5's in 25." Another student wrote "[B gets] 4: I doubled Eel A's diet. [C gets] 5: Every five cms you get a food ball." An example of an answer that was correct but for which the reasoning was not clearly multiplicative on both parts is "[B gets] 4: The length of them is Doubled. If that's Doubled, the food has to Be. [C gets] 5: Because if 20 cm eel gets four Balls, the 25 has to Have 5 balls of food [sic]." An example of a correct answer resulting from a combination of additive and multiplicative reasoning is "[B gets] 4 becase it tice [sic] as long so it gets two times more food ball. [C gets] 5 becase it 5 cm longer than eel B so it get one more food ball [sic]." The correct answers in Table 2 contain reasoning of these three sorts. Students had incorrect answers if they said, for example, that eel B received 4 balls and eel C received 6 balls, an answer that indicates additive reasoning alone. Other incorrect answers contained no explanation, or the reasoning was not at all clear.

Gum Problem. This item was the most traditional of the proportional reasoning tasks. Almost all correct answers were obtained by one of two methods: unitizing the ratio 2:6 and taking it 4 times to obtain 8:24 or forming the unit ratio 1:3, then taking 3 × 8. The second method gained in popularity between pretest and posttest. The other correct answers were not accompanied by work that indicated a method. No students set up a proportion. All groups tested appeared to perform significantly better on the posttest than on the pretest on this item.

Bank Problem. Results were confusing on this item, particularly in the first fifth-grade class, in which students received a slightly different version of the item on the pretest and posttest, so that student reasoning was not always clear. This is the only class that had received similar problems during instruction. It became clear during instruction that students (at least in this inner-city classroom) interpret the question of where to bank in different ways: some, for example, would choose the bank with the lowest initial deposit simply because they did not want to place too much money in a bank; the rate of return was irrelevant in these cases. This thinking could also be found in test explanations, for example: "Bank A because it is for little amounts of money and Bank B is for bigger amounts of money." In any case, this problem was the most difficult of the four in that the multiplicative nature of the situation did not seem to be as apparent to students as in the other problem situations. Even when the multiplicativeness was apparent, it was difficult because of the nonintegral ratio involved, which was either recognized but confused (e.g., "I would put in Bank A because John got double his money and Maria only got half of her money") or was not recognized as a multiplicative growth in the same manner as for Bank A (e.g., "Bank A because at bank a dubbles [*sic*] the amount, but at bank b it adds 5 dollers [*sic*]").

Pizza Problem. The only significant gain in performance was made by the inner-city fifth graders, perhaps reflecting the fact that theirs was the only instructor who devoted instructional time to proportional tasks. Although students were asked to show how they obtained their answers, most did not, in any of the classrooms, so that these percentages may not be truly indicative of understanding.

This item was also used in the interviews, but was preceded by a problem in which there were three pizzas for six girls and one pizza for three boys. Almost all students, even those in the low third, could solve this problem meaningfully in both the pre-interviews and post-interviews. The test problem, three pizzas for seven girls and one pizza for three boys, was much more difficult for them. It was not asked of the inner-city fifth graders in the pre-interview. During the postinterview, the two fifth-grade students at the high level were able to solve the problem by grouping girls into two sets of three, each set sharing a pizza, with the last girl having part of the third pizza and sharing the rest. The two middle-level students were confused: one suggested they all share the pizzas; the other seemed to be on the right track but could not imagine the cuttings that would yield pizza for seven girls. One of the students in the low third was able to solve the problem by having three girls share one pizza and two pairs each sharing one pizza. In the other fifth grade, the problem was not given to one student in the low third; four of the other five students solved it correctly in the postinterview, and the fifth tried to solve it by comparing $\frac{1}{3}$ to $\frac{3}{7}$ and thought $\frac{3}{7}$ was larger. The same five students were unable to provide reasonable explanations for their answers during the pre-interview. Sixth graders had some difficulties with this item in the pre-interview, but five of the six were successful in the postinterview; the sixth estimated that boys and girls would get about the same amount of pizza.

SUMMARY

Students' understanding of fractions improved in all classrooms. The improvement was greater than could be expected in traditional class-rooms, based on comparison with beginning seventh-grade students. Not all students improved; each pair in the low third of each class appeared to make little headway in understanding fraction concepts. But the majority of the students appeared to understand fractions at a much deeper level than is usual in fifth and sixth grades—witness the change in responses to the request to tell everything they could about $\frac{3}{4}$.

The improvement in proportional reasoning was also noticeable, but not so impressive as gains in fraction understanding. Only one of the four teachers deliberately focused instruction on proportional reasoning (and in a manner that went beyond the traditional setting up of a proportion). The gains made in this classroom appear to be the result of this focused instruction.

We conclude that the project teachers, armed with a better under-standing of the mathematical concepts appropriate for these grade levels, were able to assist their students in making substantial gains in understanding mathematics conceptually.

Chapter 11

REFLECTIONS AND CONCLUSIONS

We began this project with two related research questions. These questions reflected our beliefs about the kinds of changes we thought would occur.

1. How does teacher understanding of rational number, quantity, and proportional reasoning influence the manner in which teachers teach? That is, what changes and shifts, both subtle and overt, can be noted in the way these topics are treated by the teacher, as the teacher becomes more familiar with the mathematics involved and comes to understand better how students learn this content? After teachers have opportunities for study and reflection, how does a teacher's decision-making change? How does a better understanding of the mathematics and the ways in which students come to learn this mathematics influence teachers' views about what it means to teach mathematics?
2. As teachers' understanding of rational number, quantity, and proportional reasoning develops and as teachers become more aware of how students learn this mathematics, how is their students' learning enhanced? How does student understanding change over the course of a year?

Over the course of the 2 years, as we regularly discussed our work with the teachers in our project, the original questions became actualized into the following three questions:

As a result of work with these five middle-grades teachers in our 2-year project, during which we focused on the mathematics of rational number, proportional reasoning, and quantitative thinking,

1. What can we say about these teachers' understanding of and their beliefs about the mathematics? What changes did we find?
2. What can we say about these teachers' mathematics instruction and their beliefs about their instruction? What changes did we find?
3. As these teachers' understanding of the mathematics developed and as they became more aware of how their students learn this mathematics, how was their students' learning enhanced? How did student understanding change over the course of a year in their classrooms?

We have tried to answer these questions in the preceding chapters. In this chapter we will reflect on the first two questions from the perspective of time—time spent with the teachers, time talking about the teachers' changes, and, later, time spent thinking about the teachers while we wrote this monograph. We conclude with some general thoughts on teacher preparation and professional development.

WHAT CAN WE SAY ABOUT THESE TEACHERS' UNDERSTANDING AND BELIEFS ABOUT MATHEMATICS? WHAT CHANGES DID WE FIND?

Our teacher-selection process required that teachers be interested in changing their teaching and willing to learn more mathematics in order to undertake change. To gain a better understanding of what these teachers believed about mathematics and what they believed about the role of the mathematics teacher, we asked each one at the beginning of the project to respond to the following two views of mathematics. They were specifically asked which of the two views was closer to their own views of what mathematics is, with implications for teaching mathematics. (The two views were written based on descriptions in A. Thompson, 1992.)

The "Knowing Mathematics" View

Mathematics is a discipline characterized by accurate results and infallible procedures. It is more accurate to say that mathematics is discovered than to say it is created. Knowing mathematics means being able to apply basic concepts and being skilled in performing procedures. It follows then that a good teacher of mathematics presents concepts and procedures as clearly as possible and gives students opportunities to identify and apply concepts and to practice procedures.

The "Making Mathematics" View

Mathematics is socially constructed and involves conjectures, proofs, and refutations. The results are subject to change, and therefore their validity must be judged in relation to a social and cultural setting. It follows then that the primary aim of teaching mathematics is to engage students in the processes of doing mathematics, through activities that grow out of problem situations. The problem situations require reasoning and creative thinking, gathering and applying information, discovering, inventing, and communicating ideas, and testing those ideas through critical reflection and argumentation.

The teachers found it difficult to choose one of the two. All felt that the first no longer fit their view of mathematics: "Well, I just read the first part of the first one, and I'm already curling my toes. I would say definitely the second one." Yet when questioned further, they were not sure what the phrase "mathematics is socially constructed" meant. Some chose the second simply because they liked the references to problem solving, creative thinking, and discovering. Some were unwilling to choose just one view and wanted to pick some of each. "Knowing mathematics—I agree with the last sentence. To me, that's learning mathematics. I didn't agree though with when it says 'mathematics is a discipline characterized by accurate results and infallible procedures.'"

It was interesting to us that the teachers all felt that the first view was typical of most of the teachers with whom they worked and also had characterized their own views only a few years earlier. Certainly these teachers had begun the process of changing their beliefs about what mathematics is. Their own understanding of much of the mathematics of the middle grades made it difficult for them to follow through on the kind of teaching demanded by the second view.

While we were working through the mathematics during the seminars with the teachers, as described in earlier chapters, we were struck by the fragility of their developing knowledge. Although they felt that doors were opening to them while they were coming to understand the meanings, for example, of operations on fractions, we would later find that when these same concepts were the bases for a class we observed or for another seminar, the concepts had not yet taken hold— the teachers could easily become confused again. It took time for them to come to grips with their own struggles to understand and to realize that their own understanding would never be complete; it would continue to develop and grow. They came to realize that the mathematics they teach is not trivial; in fact, it is quite complex.

There were emotional reactions. Cynthia was angry that she had not been taught these concepts during her own schooling or in her college teacher preparation courses. She felt that it was unfair to expect her to teach what she had never had the opportunity to learn. It upset her to know that she had not even known it was possible to understand operations on fractions, for example. She, and others, found very painful the experience of facing their own weak and unconnected knowledge of a subject they taught daily. This pain was particularly marked at the end of the first year. The teachers made statements to the effect that they had for years been teaching badly without even knowing it, because it had never dawned on them, for example, that there were reasons behind steps in the algorithms they taught—that the algorithms themselves could be changed and adapted once they understood them. At the end of the second year, when the teachers reflected on the 2 years, one of the teachers said

> The painful part was not what you were doing to us. The painful part was the self-reflection, the questioning of what we've done in the past, and looking at how we're going to present this, and kind of giving up the security of the "follow the textbook." That was the painful part.

Perhaps it is necessary that a project like this one, or any professional development with goals similar to ours, be extended over a long enough period of time (2 years in this case) for teachers to begin to feel comfortable again with themselves as teachers of mathematics, accepting where they were and knowing both that the mathematics is comprehensible and that they can make sense of it. It takes time for teachers to be able to look critically at their own teaching and yet be comfortable with their attempts to improve it.

We were also struck by the teachers' lack of understanding of what their students knew and did not know. One of the most productive seminars took place in the middle of the first year, when we shared with the teachers the reports on the understanding their own students had of rational number concepts and of proportional reasoning, based on tests we had given to their students (Philipp, Armstrong, & Sowder, 1993). The teachers were often surprised by responses given by their students and had difficulty understanding why such mistakes were made. For example, large numbers of students were unable to correctly compare ½ and 0.7.

Inv: It's not only that they missed it, but look at the number that thought they were equal.
Tom: I can't understand how two things that sound totally different. . . .
Inv: Equivalent fractions sound totally different.
Inv: Yes, it's not that they sound different.
Shey: I can see they could confuse that.

Tom: That they're equal?

Shey: Yeah.

Inv: How do *you* compare these?

Shey: Well, we know they are seven tenths and one seventh, but the kids. . . .

Inv: Wait a minute. So you look at zero point seven and say "seven tenths." How do you know that seven tenths is bigger than one seventh?

Shey: Okay, one seventh is less than a half; seven tenths is bigger than a half. But the kids aren't mature enough to do that.

Inv: So first they must see zero point seven as seven tenths.

Tom: Yes, which I feel they didn't.

Inv: They need some benchmarks, and to know what one seventh is.

Shey: Yes. There's a lot involved in this.

The following year, when the pretests were again given to students and discussed, there was much less surprise at the results. Also during the second year several students had been interviewed, and the teachers were far more interested in the results of the interviews, in what students would say were their reasons for answering as they did. Simple test results no longer held as much interest for them.

When the teachers themselves experienced frustration in trying to understand mathematical concepts, they came to understand the kinds of frustration their students had. For example, during one seminar each teacher worked with a different investigator on a computer program designed to prompt thinking about rate problems, particularly problems such as "If you drive from X to Y at 60 miles per hour, and return at 40 miles per hour, at what rate would you have to drive so that you could go in both directions at the same speed in the same amount of time as the first round trip?" Shey later described his reaction to his struggle to understand why the answer was not 50 miles per hour: "Damn it! I can see why my kids in my classroom sometimes get frustrated! She was asking me the right questions, but there was something I just couldn't see, and it was driving me nuts."

In our final seminar with the teachers, we asked them if they had any thoughts about the type of professional development that would be most beneficial to teachers. They said that what this project had helped them to do was to begin to think about how students learn rather than focusing only on how they should be taught. For other teachers to come to this point, the project teachers felt that it was necessary that professional development in mathematics go far beyond a focus on activities or on how to use manipulatives. It should focus on helping the teachers understand the "theory behind the math": Teachers themselves need to build mathematical power. They expressed dissatisfaction with the inservice help that their school districts currently offered; it was too superficial, without any real learning going on. One complained, "There's no dialogue about how children learn or what's going on in their heads, what the process is that they're going through, where we need to be directing our questions." The teachers now saw themselves as learners and believed that the point of professional development should be to help them in their roles as learners as much as in their roles as teachers.

WHAT CAN WE SAY ABOUT THESE TEACHERS' MATHEMATICS INSTRUCTION AND THEIR BELIEFS ABOUT INSTRUCTION? WHAT CHANGES DID WE FIND?

The seminar discussions and the case studies of the teachers clearly indicate that instructional behaviors, and the types and degrees of changes in these behaviors both as described by the teachers and as observed by us, were idiosyncratic and heavily dependent on both the personalities of the individual teachers and the contexts within which they taught. No two of the teachers were alike. The individual personalities of the teachers were reflected in the ways in which they planned for instruction and managed their classrooms. Cynthia, for example, needed at first to feel almost total control over what was happening in her classroom, and in order to maintain that control she was meticulous and detailed in her planning, with goals laid out for what she wanted to achieve during each segment of a particular class period. During our final observations we noted that she was more open to the different types of responses she was getting from students. She still planned her classes in great detail, but she was less tied to carrying out her plans should something serendipitous occur that she felt would be an attractive side trip. Shey also had excellent classroom management skills, but appeared to manage through a kind of charisma that led his students to want to please him. He rarely if ever planned his classes in detail but rather would have one or two problems selected to begin the class, then let the students' responses guide him through the remainder of the class. The primary change we noted in his planning was that he more deliberately selected situations and problems that could lead to rich mathematical discussions. He came to understand the importance of a good choice of wording of a problem and of choosing numbers within problems with some care.

Contextual differences also played a major role in influencing the types of instruction in the classrooms, so much so that we frequently found ourselves wondering how individual teachers would change their teaching styles if they were to switch schools and classes. Our predictions were that the changes could be quite drastic when the schools were very different. For example, Linda taught in a small rural school in a low socioeconomic area populated with many Native Americans and Mexican immigrants. The new school appeared safe, clean, cheerful, and comfortable. The appearance of the school was in enormous contrast to the school in which Darota taught, an urban school in a poor and unkempt area of the city, where drug dealing and drive-by shootings were not unusual events. Many of the buildings on the school campus where Darota taught had been built as temporary classrooms but were in permanent use. We found it a depressing environment, even while recognizing that for many of the students it was probably more pleasant and safe than their home environments. Both teachers were relatively new, with less than 5 years teaching experience. Linda, who had entered teaching after her family was grown, exhibited maturity and poise and an aura of authority, of "knowing the system." Because her school's principal was shared with another school, Linda frequently found herself in the role of acting principal in her school. She interacted well with the school authorities and wielded a certain amount of power in her school. She could (at least to some degree) select her students; she had access to a variety of instructional materials; she frequently interacted with parents; she felt and acted as though she "belonged." Darota, on the other hand, had few interactions with the principal. According to her descriptions, these interactions were not always pleasant. She felt reduced to pleading with the principal in order to obtain a permanent overhead projector for her classroom. She begged for counseling for her students after a student was killed in a drive-by shooting. She (and others) were told they *had* to raise test scores. She had little say about which students were assigned to her class and, in fact, received children with the worst behavioral problems for her grade level because she did not send students to the office as frequently as did other teachers; she told us that students sent to the office were forced to sit in a room and do nothing, which she felt was a waste of learning time and an ineffective punishment. She preferred to keep the students in class and to find other means of sanctioning their bad behavior. With as many as half a dozen such students, her classes were sometimes reduced to chaos; once she took her students outside while an individual student inside threw a destructive temper tantrum. What would instruction look like if Darota were in Linda's school? If Linda were in Darota's school? We can only wonder.

Given the considerable differences in personalities and in school contexts and in the effects of these differences on instructional practices and change in those practices, we acknowledge the difficulties in making generalizations about the teachers. Yet there are some areas in which we feel that generalizations can be made, while recognizing that for each teacher the manner in which the effects of the project were realized differed in both degree and character. In the remainder of this section we summarize those areas, for the most part interrelated, in which we observed changes in the teaching practices and beliefs about teaching for these five teachers.

First, changes in instruction were obviously influenced by teachers' changing understanding of content and by their comfort levels with that content. They could not teach what they did not know. For example, during the first year, Cynthia said that she could not use many of the ideas presented by the seminar speakers because they were too difficult—her students would not understand them. Yet during the second year she was willingly using many of the ideas presented in the first year; she herself was now ready. She understood the ideas. Cynthia was absent the day Susan Lamon spoke about proportional reasoning. On the one hand, we could not help but notice that over the next 18 months of observing in Cynthia's classroom, we saw very little in the way of her helping children develop the ability to reason proportionally. On the other hand, Linda told us during the first year that she did not teach proportional reasoning because she did not feel comfortable with it. But by the second year we began to notice more lessons in which proportional reasoning came into play. Shey was the most taken with ideas Susan Lamon presented and immediately began focusing on proportional reasoning with his fifth graders, but initially used problems they did not understand. It took him a while to "feel out" where he could begin with these ideas.

Second, the teachers in this study came to have different expectations of their students' capabilities. Their goals for instruction became more focused on seeking conceptual understanding in addition to skill development. Over the 2 years, in all classrooms, we saw a gradual lessening of emphasis on carrying out procedures and more emphasis on conceptual understanding. For example, during the first year Cynthia taught a very procedurally oriented unit on decimal numbers. The focus was on rules for moving the decimal point, rules for operations, and rules for reading decimal numbers. During the second year, she asked if we had any instructional materials on decimal numbers that would help her teach them more conceptually. We gave her a unit (developed for an earlier project) that focused on first developing place value understanding, then using that understanding to compare and operate on decimal numbers. Cynthia was delighted with her students' abilities to work conceptually with decimal numbers on a district-required examination at the end of the unit. Yet we observed that a geometry unit she taught during the second year was again highly procedural; Cynthia lacked a deep understanding of the geometry content and information on students' thinking about geometry, and she slipped back to an earlier kind of instruction. As another example, during a seminar midway through the first year, Shey was asked what he would want his students to know about adding $\frac{5}{8}$ and $\frac{7}{9}$. He said that the first thing he wanted his students to be able to do was to find a common denominator. Yet midway through the second year, he complained about a substitute teacher who had taught his students to find the least common denominator; he did not want his students to know of this procedure until they could figure out how to add fractions with pattern blocks and explain their reasoning; he first wanted them to be able to estimate the sums using benchmarks for the fractions. He felt that by teaching them a ready-made procedure, the substitute teacher had lessened his students' motivation to understand what they were doing.

Third, the teachers' views about the role of curriculum materials changed. From the beginning, Tom and Linda bore as a badge of good teaching their dismissal of the textbook. (Linda appeared not to consider her piloting of new curriculum materials to be the same as using a text.) However, their instruction sometimes seemed to be more like a collection of unrelated problems than a carefully designed curriculum. Linda's instruction better approximated implementation of a curriculum when she piloted parts of a new curriculum project. Cynthia at first had disliked a fraction replacement unit (Corwin et al., 1990; its development was sponsored by the California Department of Education) because it did not "get kids to know the algorithms." Later in the project, though, she said that she liked using the unit but wished that it had better explicated the relationship of some of the fraction activities in the unit to the big ideas of fractions she had come to value. Shey frequently asked us to provide him with good instructional materials. Although we and our seminar speakers sometimes provided materials, our goal was for the teachers to be able to chose appropriate materials themselves or to adapt the textbook to their needs. But all of the teachers recognized as a major problem the lack of good instructional materials that would help them teach in such a way as to develop conceptual understanding on the part of their students.

Fourth, the manner of classroom discourse changed. The teachers were as aware of this change as we were. We watched as all teachers began to probe their students' understanding in ways we did not see during our first observations. In the final seminar we asked teachers why they now talked so much about questioning and its role in teaching as something they valued from the project; after all, we had never had a seminar in which we discussed the role of questioning.

Cynthia: But you ask us questions all the time.

Linda: Yeah. You're modeling, as we're the learners and you're in our position [as teachers] and we hear what you're asking us. I say, "Is that the kind of question I should ask a student? Why not? I should."

Shey: Yeah, and another thing is I think we're thinking deeper about what we're teaching, and we're coming up with things that we feel it's important for them to know.

Inv: And you're not afraid of the math anymore, I would hope.

Linda and Cynthia: *No.*

Darota: I guess it's not so much that I'm not afraid of the math as that I'm not afraid of the [students'] answers.

Cynthia later described with delight how, now that asking for explanations was habitual in her class, when her students went to the front of the classroom to use the overhead projector to demonstrate their work, they also refused to give direct answers; instead, they asked probing questions of the other students and demanded that their peers explain their thinking.

FINAL THOUGHTS

Our experiences with these teachers also changed us and provided opportunities for us to reflect more generally on teacher preparation and professional development. As is often the case with work such as this, we end with more questions than answers. Perhaps it is the formulation of questions that is of value—at least for us, and we hope for others too.

What Is Reasonable For Us to Expect Teachers of Middle-Grades Mathematics to Know?

What mathematics do teachers need to know to successfully change their instruction in ways that are currently recommended by the *Standards* documents (NCTM, 1989, 1991, 1995) and by the *California Framework* (California Department of Education, 1992)? There must be some middle ground between thinking teachers are successful because they can teach the procedures that lead to good scores on standardized tests and thinking that the mathematics is so complex that there is little hope that teachers will ever be prepared. The mathematics *is* complex, but perhaps teachers do not need to fully understand it all in order to be successful. Certainly the teachers should be able to reason multiplicatively and proportionally themselves. The teachers should understand that mathematical procedures and rules are human inventions that were intended to make mathematics efficient and easy to automatize, but that these same procedures and rules tend to hide the mathematical reasoning on which they are based, and so are often conceptually difficult. Sometimes technology makes these procedures no longer useful, and other procedures, less efficient but more transparent conceptually, should be the focus of instruction. Teachers must believe that they are capable of understanding all the mathematics they teach, given time and opportunity. It should be acceptable for teachers to teach procedurally if they recognize that they don't know a topic well enough to teach it conceptually, but they should be at the point at which to teach procedurally is a conscious decision they make for the time being. A teacher with this awareness is more apt to seek out a way to learn this mathematics at a later time.

Where Do Teachers Go for Help?

This is a major problem. There are few courses at universities that are appropriate for and available to middle-grades teachers who want to reach a deeper understanding of the mathematics they teach. Professional development offered through school districts rarely provides time and opportunities for teachers to explore some piece of mathematics in depth. Too often inservice is brief and superficial. This is not to say that such inservice is not of value. It is when teachers have the opportunity to explore the reform recommendations being made that some come to realize their own need for experiences that will lead them to a deeper understanding of mathematics.

Can Middle-Grades Teachers Be Expected to Teach Well in All Subject Areas?

Except for Tom, the teachers in our study all taught multiple subjects. To expect teachers both to have an in-depth understanding of all the subject areas they teach and to seek out multiple intense professional development opportunities comparable to that offered in this project seems to us to be unreasonable. The Knapp, Shields, and Turnbull report (1992) of mathematics, reading, and writing by disadvantaged children showed that teachers who excelled in teaching one of these subjects rarely excelled in others. There are many good arguments for having teachers specialize beginning in about fourth grade; the teachers in our project all felt, at the end of the 2 years, that specialization was necessary if teachers were to have a deep understanding of what they taught. In fact, Linda was sometimes able to trade courses with another teacher so that she could teach more mathematics and less social studies. Such scheduling is more easily accomplished in a small school such as the one in which Linda taught. Of course there are tradeoffs that must be weighed.

How is Teacher Preparation Different From Teacher Inservice?

Because all of us also prepare teachers, it was natural for us to have frequent discussions about the differences we found between teacher preparation and teacher inservice. Perhaps the major difference we found is that practicing teachers are very focused on their classrooms and on their students. Our teachers contextualized almost everything we did in terms of their own students. They would evaluate ideas in terms of how they would teach them and how their students would respond. In fact, it was sometimes difficult for us to discuss general issues across grade levels. But the teachers' own ideas of what their students were capable of understanding were often in error and changed when they themselves came to understand the mathematics more deeply. We came to understand that for the teachers with whom we worked, it was important that they engage as learners while still maintaining their roles as teachers and that when they engaged as teachers, they still maintained their roles as learners.

Preservice teachers do not often think in terms of what children can or cannot learn—and when they do, they are usually wrong. Although this difference may sound slight, we have come to believe that it profoundly affects what is possible with each of the two groups and has led us to a recommendation: Efforts should be made to take what is valuable in inservice teacher education and provide it to preservice teachers and to take what is valuable in preservice teacher education and provide it to inservice teachers. One important component of preservice teacher education that is often missing from inservice teacher education is the attention paid to learning mathematics content. We found that the teachers in this project came to value the focus our seminars had on the mathematics content, but that focus was always with an eye toward their own students. There are many lenses through which teachers view their students, and as the teachers spent more time with this project, they enriched the mathematical lenses through which they viewed their students. For the teachers, it was the *students* they were looking at, *through* the mathematics. When we asked them to look at mathematics, they would do so, but generally through their own students. Initially, it was the teachers' attention to and concern for their students that provided them the incentive to learn more mathematics, and as they learned more mathematics, they were better able to attend to and be concerned about their students in a new way. The teachers' understanding of the mathematics and their concern for their students' mathematical understanding supported each other. By the end of the project, the teachers had become more willing to engage in mathematical discussions without seeing direct implications for their students, but even at the end of the project they preferred to focus on content that they considered directly relevant to their own instruction.

Practicing teachers think about their students when they attend inservices. There is a lesson here to be learned by providers of preservice programs. We need to provide opportunities for preservice teachers to consider mathematics for teaching and learning in the context of work with children. One reason we consider this important is that it will provide students with an opportunity to take off their "student hats" and replace them with their "teacher hats." In time, perhaps they will begin to look like the teachers in our current project, who learned to wear both hats at the same time.

One caveat: These notions of viewing students through mathematics and viewing mathematics through students are not simple. Darota was so concerned about her students' living environments that she found it difficult to view her students through the mathematics, even when she was teaching mathematics. For Darota, viewing her students through the mathematics was a luxury that she did not feel she could afford.

What Are the Dangers of Activity-Based Instruction?

We learned that when classes are not textbook driven, but rather are focused on activities, it is easy for teachers to lose sight of their goals. In activities such as planning for an end-of-school picnic or planning a lesson that incorporated other subject areas, enormous amounts of time were lost to nonmathematical discussions. Teachers can sometimes lose sight of the academic goals of a lesson. We wonder whether this fact is the basis for some of the current backlash to the changes in mathematics instruction in California.

What Are Some of the Other Problems Teachers Face When They Try to Implement Change in Their Classrooms?

There are many we could mention, based on our experiences with these teachers. Lack of administrative support, lack of both parental support and understanding of what the teacher is attempting to do, lack of appropriate instructional materials, lack of access to people who can help teachers when they do not understand the mathematics, lack of time to research and reflect and reshape instruction are but a few. One that perhaps many do not think to mention is that teachers can also lose sight of the reasons they are in the classroom. For example, Darota's felt need to be a role model, to teach values, to teach manners, to be a social worker for her students, all seemed to constantly take time and energy away from helping her students learn academic subjects.

Are Our Perceptions of These Teachers Shared by Others in the Mathematics Education Community?

We found that our own perceptions of the teachers were not necessarily in agreement with how others viewed them. Linda and Tom were both invited to take leadership roles in large teacher-inservice projects in mathematics. Both of these teachers were poised and outgoing. But we worried, in Tom's case in particular but also with Linda, about their abilities to guide other teachers' mathematical development when they both seemed to us to be only beginning their own development. Shey probably had the best understanding of middle school mathematics and had extraordinary ability to interact with students, but he seemed unknown outside of his own classroom.

How Should Teachers Be Evaluated?

While we watched teachers develop and grow professionally, we sometimes asked ourselves this question. Certainly, it would be difficult on a visit to a classroom to know what stage of development a teacher is in. It is still all too easy to evaluate a teacher on the basis of student interest and motivation, and on classroom management. Yet we know that students can be highly motivated to work on an activity that has very little value as a site for learning. We are reminded of what Ed Silver once told us: A good task taught poorly is usually of more value than a poor task taught well.

What is the Role of Classroom Observations in a Study of Teacher Change?

We realized how important our classroom observations were in helping us understand where the teachers were; the seminar discussions, on their own, were not enough. Certainly no teacher set out to deceive us— their descriptions of their instruction were certainly accurate in their own minds. But those who had participated in more inservice projects and had begun to pick up the rhetoric of reform would have led us to believe, without our observations, that these teachers were at a different level than they actually were.

And Last But Not Least, What Kinds of Teacher Expectations Are Reasonable?

This question is particularly important because large sums of money are being allocated for teacher professional development to try to reach all teachers with brief inservice projects. But we were shown, once again, that change is gradual. Teachers need help over an extended period. We had not thought it would take us 2 years to reach the level of change we had reached when the project ended. As researchers, we can talk about gradual change with some objectivity. But for teachers, and for those involved in professional development of teachers, there is often disappointment and pain involved. If we recognize and accept that change is gradual, that old habits of teaching and old beliefs about mathematics are deeply ingrained and are based not only on our own teaching experiences but on our experiences as students as well, then acceptance of the ups and downs of change is easier and discouragement is less likely to hinder growth.

Our work with these teachers over 2 years also changed us. We too are developing as teachers of teachers. We are profoundly grateful to the teachers for all they taught us.

REFERENCES

Armstrong, B. E., & Bezuk, N. S. (1995). Multiplication and division of fractions: The search for meaning. In J. T. Sowder & B. P. Schappelle (Eds.), *Providing a foundation for teaching mathematics in the middle grades* (pp. 85–119). Albany, NY: State University of New York Press.

Armstrong, B. E., & Larson, C. N. (1995). Students' use of part-whole and direct comparison strategies for comparing partitioned rectangles. *Journal for Research in Mathematics Education, 26,* 1–19.

Armstrong, B. E., Philipp, R. A., & Sowder, J. T. (1993). Assessment of fraction understanding: Student performance and teacher reactions. In J. R. Becker & B. J. Pence (Eds.), *Proceedings of the fifteenth annual meeting of the North American Chapter of the International Group for the Psychology of Mathematics Education* (Vol. 2, pp. 103–109). San José, CA: The Center for Mathematics and Computer Science Education, San José State University.

Ball, D. L. (1990). Reflections and deflections of policy: The case of Carol Turner. *Educational Evaluation and Policy Analysis, 12,* 263–275.

Behr, M. J., Harel, G., Post, T., & Lesh, R. (1992). Rational number, ratio, and proportion. In D. A. Grouws (Ed.), *Handbook of research on mathematics teaching and learning* (pp. 296–333). New York: Macmillan.

Behr, M. J., Harel, G., Post, T., & Lesh, R. (1993). Rational numbers: Toward a semantic analysis—Emphasis on the operator construct. In T. P. Carpenter, E. Fennema, & T. A. Romberg (Eds.), *Rational numbers: An integration of research* (pp. 13–47). Hillsdale, NJ: Erlbaum.

Behr, M. J., Lesh, R., Post, T. R., & Silver, E. A. (1983). Rational-number concepts. In R. Lesh & M. Landau (Eds.), *Acquisition of mathematics concepts and processes* (pp. 91–126). New York: Academic Press.

Bezuk, N. (1987). Variables affecting seventh-grade students' performance and solution strategies on proportional reasoning word problems. *Dissertation Abstracts International, 47,* 2932A. Doctoral dissertation, University of Minnesota, 1986.

Bezuk, N. S., & Armstrong, B. E. (1993). Activities for understanding division of fractions. *Mathematics Teacher, 86,* 43–46, 56–60.

Borko, H., Eisenhart, M., Brown, C. A., Underhill, R. G., Jones, D., & Agard, P. C. (1992). Learning to teach hard mathematics: Do novice teachers and their instructors give up too easily? *Journal for Research in Mathematics Education, 23,* 194–222.

Brown, C. A. (1993). A critical analysis of teaching rational number. In T. P. Carpenter, E. Fennema, & T. A. Romberg (Eds.), *Rational numbers: An integration of research* (pp. 197–218). Hillsdale, NJ: Erlbaum.

California Department of Education. (1992). *Mathematics framework for California public schools: Kindergarten through Grade Twelve.* Sacramento, CA: Author.

Carpenter, T. P., Fennema, E., Peterson, P. L., Chiang, C. -P., & Loef, M. (1989). Using knowledge of children's mathematics thinking in classroom teaching: An experimental study. *American Educational Research Journal, 26,* 499-531.

Cassell, J. (1982). Harms, benefits, wrongs, and rights in fieldwork. In J. E. Sieber (Ed.), *The ethics of social research: Fieldwork, regulation, and publication* (pp. 7–31). New York: Springer-Verlag.

Cazden, C. B. (1986). Classroom discourse. In M. C. Wittrock (Ed.), *Handbook of research on teaching* (3rd ed., pp. 432–463). New York: Macmillan.

Chazan, D., & Ball, D. (1995). Beyond exhortation not to tell: The teacher's role in discussion-intensive mathematics classes. Unpublished manuscript. East Lansing, MI: Michigan State University.

Clark, C. M., & Peterson, P. L. (1986). Teachers' thought processes. In M. C. Wittrock (Ed.), *Handbook of research on teaching* (3rd ed., pp. 255–296). New York: Macmillan.

Cohen, D. K. (1990). A revolution in one classroom: The case of Mrs. Oublier. *Educational Evaluation and Policy Analysis, 12,* 327–345.

Corwin, R. B., Russell, S. J., & Tierney, C. C. (1990). *Seeing fractions: A unit for the upper elementary grades.* Sacramento, CA: California Department of Education.

Cramer, K. A., Post, T. R., & Behr, M. J. (1989). Cognitive restructuring ability, teacher guidance, and perceptual distracter tasks: An aptitude-treatment interaction study. *Journal for Research in Mathematics Education, 20,* 103–110.

Cronbach, L. J. (1975). Beyond the two disciplines of scientific psychology. *American Psychologist, 30,* 116–127.

Deyhle, D. L., Hess, G. A., Jr., & LeCompte, M. D. (1992). Approaching ethical issues for qualitative researchers in education. In M. D. LeCompte, W. L. Millroy, & J. Preissle (Eds.), *The handbook of qualitative research in education* (pp. 597–641). San Diego, CA: Academic Press.

Diener, E., & Crandall, R. (1978). *Ethics in social and behavioral research.* Chicago: University of Chicago Press.

Eisenhart, M. A. (1991). Conceptual frameworks for research circa 1991: Ideas from a cultural anthropologist: Implications for mathematics education researchers. In R. G. Underhill (Ed.), *Proceedings of the thirteenth annual meeting of the North American Chapter of the International Group for the Psychology of Mathematics Education* (Vol. 1, pp. 202–219). Blacksburg: Division of Curriculum & Instruction, Virginia Polytechnic Institute & State University.

Eisenhart, M. A., & Howe, K. R. (1992). Validity in educational research. In M. D. LeCompte, W. L. Millroy, & J. Preissle (Eds.), *The handbook of qualitative research in education* (pp. 643–680). San Diego, CA: Academic Press.

Flores, A., Sowder, J. T., Philipp, R. A., & Schappelle, B. P. (1995). Orchestrating, promoting, and enhancing mathematical discourse in the middle school: A case study. In J. T. Sowder & B. P. Schappelle (Eds.), *Providing a foundation for teaching mathematics in the middle grades* (pp. 275–299). Albany, NY: State University of New York Press.

Greeno, J. G. (1991a). *Notes toward semantics of rational numbers.* Unpublished manuscript.

Greeno, J. G. (1991b). Number sense as situated knowing in a conceptual domain. *Journal for Research in Mathematics Education, 22,* 170–218.

Greer, B. (1992). Multiplication and division as models of situations. In D. A. Grouws (Ed.), *Handbook of research on mathematics teaching and learning* (pp. 276–295). New York: Macmillan.

Harel, G. (1993). On teacher education programs in mathematics. *International Journal of Mathematics Education in Science and Technology, 25*(1), 113–119.

Harel, G. (1995). From naive-interpretist to operation-conserver. In J. T. Sowder & B. P. Schappelle (Eds.), *Providing a foundation for teaching mathematics in the middle grades* (pp. 143–165). Albany, NY: State University of New York Press.

Hart, K. M. (1984). *Ratio: Children's strategies and errors.* Windsor, England: NFER-NELSON.

Hiebert, J., & Behr, M. (1988). Introduction: Capturing the major themes. In J. Hiebert & M. Behr (Eds.), *Number concepts and operations in the middle grades* (pp. 1–18). Hillsdale, NJ: Erlbaum & Reston, VA: National Council of Teachers of Mathematics.

Johnson, C. G. (1982). Risk in the publication of fieldwork. In J. E. Sieber (Ed.), *The ethics of social research: Fieldwork, regulation, and publication* (pp. 71–91). New York: Springer-Verlag.

Kaput, J. J. (1985, August). *Multiplicative word problems and intensive quantities: An integrated software response* (Technical Report). Cambridge, MA: Educational Technology Center, Harvard Graduate School of Education.

Kaput, J. J., Luke, C., Poholsky, J., & Sayer, A. (1986). *The role of representation in reasoning with intensive quantities: Preliminary analyses* (Technical Report 869). Cambridge, MA: Harvard University, Educational Technology Center.

Karplus, R., Pulos, S., & Stage, E. (1983). Proportional reasoning of early adolescents. In R. Lesh & M. Landau (Eds.), *Acquisition of mathematics concepts and processes* (pp. 45–90). New York: Academic Press.

Kerslake, D. (1986). *Fractions: Children's strategies and errors*. Windsor, England: NFER-NELSON.

Kieren, T. (1976). On the mathematical, cognitive and instructional foundations of rational numbers. In R. Lesh (Ed.), *Number and measurement* (pp. 101–144). Columbus, OH: ERIC/SMEAC.

Kieren, T. (1980). The rational number construct—Its elements and mechanisms. In T. Kieren (Ed.), *Recent research on number learning* (pp. 125–149). Columbus, OH: ERIC/SMEAC.

Kieren, T. E. (1993). Rational and fractional numbers: From quotient fields to recursive understanding. In T. P. Carpenter, E. Fennema, & T. A. Romberg (Eds.), *Rational numbers: An integration of research* (pp. 49–84). Hillsdale, NJ: Erlbaum.

Kieren, T. E. (1995). Creating spaces for learning fractions. In J. T. Sowder & B. P. Schappelle (Eds.), *Providing a foundation for teaching mathematics in the middle grades* (pp. 31–65). Albany, NY: State University of New York Press.

Kieren, T. E., & Pirie, S. E. B. (1991). Recursion and the mathematical experience. In L. P. Steffe (Ed.), *Epistemological foundations of mathematical experience* (pp. 78–101). New York: Springer Verlag.

Knapp, M. S., Shields, P. M., & Turnbull, B. J. (1992). *Academic challenge for the children of poverty*. Washington, DC: U.S. Department of Education Office of Policy and Planning.

Lamon, S. J. (1991, April). *Ratio and proportion: Cognitive foundations in unitizing and norming*. Paper presented at the annual meeting of the American Educational Research Association, Boston.

Lamon, S. J. (1993a). Ratio and proportion: Children's cognitive and meta-cognitive processes. In T. P. Carpenter, E. Fennema, & T. A. Romberg (Eds.), *Rational numbers: An integration of research* (pp. 131–156). Hillsdale, NJ: Erlbaum.

Lamon, S. J. (1993b). Ratio and proportion: Connecting content and children's thinking. *Journal for Research in Mathematics Education, 24*, 41–61.

Lamon, S. J. (1995). Ratio and proportion: Elementary didactical phenomenology. In J. T. Sowder & B. P. Schappelle (Eds.), *Providing a foundation for teaching mathematics in the middle grades* (pp. 167–198). Albany, NY: State University of New York Press.

Leinhardt, G., & Greeno, J. G. (1986). The cognitive skill of teaching. *Journal of Educational Psychology, 78*(2), 75-95.

Lesh, R., Post, T., & Behr, M. (1988). Proportional reasoning. In J. Hiebert & M. Behr (Eds.), *Number concepts and operations in the middle grades* (pp. 93–118).

Hillsdale, NJ: Erlbaum & Reston, VA: National Council of Teachers of Mathematics.

Livingston, C., & Borko, H. (1990). High school mathematics review lessons: Expert-novice distinctions. *Journal for Research in Mathematics Education, 21,* 372–387.

Mack, N. K. (1993). Learning rational numbers with understanding: The case of informal knowledge. In T. P. Carpenter, E. Fennema, & T. A. Romberg (Eds.), *Rational numbers: An integration of research* (pp. 85–105). Hillsdale, NJ: Erlbaum.

Mack, N. K. (1995). Critical ideas: Informal knowledge and understanding fractions. In J. T. Sowder & B. P. Schappelle (Eds.), *Providing a foundation for teaching mathematics in the middle grades* (pp. 67–84). Albany, NY: State University of New York Press.

Markovits, Z., & Sowder, J. (1991). Students' understanding of the relationship between fractions and decimals. *Focus on Learning Problems in Mathematics, 13,* 3–11.

Markovits, Z., & Sowder, J. T. (1989). Effects of instruction on number magnitude. In C. A. Maher, G. A. Goldin, & R. B. Davis (Eds.), *Proceedings of the eleventh annual meeting of the North American Chapter of the International Group for the Psychology of Mathematics Education* (pp. 105–110). Rutgers: Center for Mathematics, Science, and Computer Education, Rutgers – The State University of New Jersey.

Markovits, Z., & Sowder, J. T. (1994). Developing number sense: An intervention study in Grade Seven. *Journal for Research in Mathematics Education, 25,* 4–29.

Marshall, S. P. (1988, May). *Assessing schema knowledge.* Paper presented at the annual meeting of the American Educational Research Association, New Orleans, LA.

Marshall, S. P. (1993). Assessment of rational number understanding: A schema-based approach. In T. P. Carpenter, E. Fennema, & T. A. Romberg (Eds.), *Rational numbers: An integration of research* (pp. 261–288) Hillsdale, NJ: Erlbaum.

Marshall, S. P., Pribe, C. A., & Smith, J. D. (1987). *Schema knowledge structures for representing and understanding arithmetic story problems.* San Diego: San Diego State University Center for Research in Mathematics and Science Education.

Merriam, S. B. (1988). *Case study research in education.* San Francisco: Jossey-Bass.

National Council of Teachers of Mathematics. (1989). *Curriculum and evaluation standards for school mathematics.* Reston, VA: Author.

National Council of Teachers of Mathematics. (1991). *Professional standards for teaching mathematics.* Reston, VA: Author.

National Council of Teachers of Mathematics. (1995). *Assessment standards for school mathematics*. Reston, VA: Author.

Noelting, G. (1980). The development of proportional reasoning and the ratio concept. Part I—Differentiation of stages. *Educational Studies in Mathematics, 11*, 217–253.

Ohlsson, S. (1988). Mathematical meaning and applicational meaning in the semantics of fractions and related concepts. In J. Hiebert & M. Behr (Eds.), *Number concepts and operations in the middle grades* (pp. 53–92). Hillsdale, NJ: Erlbaum & Reston, VA: National Council of Teachers of Mathematics.

Peterson, P. L. (1990). Doing more in the same amount of time: Cathy Swift. *Educational Evaluation and Policy Analysis, 12* , 277–296.

Philipp, R., Sowder, J., & Flores, A. (1992). The act of teaching mathematics: A case study. In W. Geeslin & K. Graham (Eds.), *Proceedings of the sixteenth PME Conference* (Vol. 3, pp. 27–34). University of New Hampshire, Durham, NH: Program Committee of the 16th PME Conference.

Philipp, R. A., Armstrong, B. E., & Sowder, J. T. (1993). Assessment of fraction understanding: Student performance and teacher reactions. In J. R. Becker & B. J. Pence (Eds.), *Proceedings of the fifteenth annual meeting of the North American Chapter of the International Group for the Psychology of Mathematics Education* (Vol. 2, pp. 103–109). San Jose, CA: Center for Mathematics and Computer Science Education.

Philipp, R. A., Flores, A., Sowder, J. T., & Schappelle, B. P. (1994). Conceptions and practices of extraordinary mathematics teachers. *Journal of Mathematical Behavior, 13*, 155–180.

Philipp, R. A., Sowder, J. T., & Flores, A. (1993). Conceptualizing rate: Four teachers' struggle. In I. Hirabayashi, N. Nohda, K. Shigematsu, & F. Lin (Eds.), *Proceedings of the seventeenth international conference for the Psychology of Mathematics Education* (Vol. 3, pp. 178–185). University of Tsukuba, Tsukuba, Ibaraki, Japan: Program Committee of the 17th PME Conference.

Philipp, R. A., Sowder, J. T., Flores, A., & Schappelle, B. P. (1995). A responsible mathematics teacher and the choices she makes: A case study. In J. T. Sowder & B. P. Schappelle (Eds.), *Providing a foundation for teaching mathematics in the middle grades* (pp. 301–325). Albany, NY: State University of New York Press.

Piaget, J., Grize, J. B., Szeminska, A., & Bang, V. (1977). *Epistemology and psychology of functions*. Dordrecht, The Netherlands: D. Reidel.

Resnick, L. B., Nesher, P., Leonard, F., Magone, M., Omanson, S., & Peled, I. (1989). Conceptual bases of arithmetic errors: The case of decimal fractions. *Journal for Research in Mathematics Education, 20*, 8–27.

Resnick, L. B., & Singer, J. A. (1993). Protoquantitative origins of ratio reasoning. In T. P. Carpenter, E. Fennema, & T. A. Romberg (Eds.), *Rational numbers: An integration of research* (pp. 107–130). Hillsdale, NJ: Erlbaum.

Schifter, D., & Fosnot, C. T. (1993). *Reconstructing mathematics education reform: Stories of teachers meeting the challenge of reform.* New York: Teachers College Press.

Schwartz, J. L. (1988). Intensive quantity and referent-transforming arithmetic operations. In J. Hiebert & M. Behr (Eds.), *Number concepts and operations in the middle grades* (pp. 41–52). Hillsdale, NJ: Erlbaum & Reston, VA: National Council of Teachers of Mathematics.

Shulman, L. S. (1987). Knowledge and teaching: Foundations of the new reform. *Harvard Educational Review, 57*(1), 1–22.

Silver, E. A. (1981). Young adults' thinking about rational numbers. In T. R. Post & M. P. Roberts (Eds.), *Proceedings of the third annual meeting of the North American Chapter of the International Group for the Psychology of Mathematics Education* (pp. 149–159). Minneapolis, MN: University of Minnesota.

Silver, E. A. (1985). Research on teaching mathematical problem solving: Some underrepresented themes and needed directions. In E. A. Silver (Ed.), *Teaching and learning mathematical problem solving: Multiple research perspectives* (pp. 247–266). Hillsdale, NJ: Erlbaum.

Silver, E. A., Shapiro, L. J., & Deutsch, A. (1993). Sense-making and the solution of division problems involving remainders: An examination of middle school students' solution processes and their interpretations of solutions. *Journal for Research in Mathematics Education, 24,* 117–135.

Simon, M. A., & Blume, G. W. (1994). Mathematical modeling as a component of understanding ratio-as-measure: A study of prospective elementary teachers. *The Journal of Mathematical Behavior, 13,* 183–197.

Soltis, J. F. (1990). The ethics of qualitative research. In E. W. Eisner & A. Peshkin (Eds.), *Qualitative inquiry in education: The continuing debate* (pp. 247–257). New York: Teachers College Press.

Sowder, J. (1992). *A conceptual framework for research on teaching and learning in the multiplicative conceptual field.* Unpublished manuscript. Center for Research in Mathematics and Science Education, San Diego State University, San Diego, CA.

Sowder, J. T. (1993). Making sense of numbers in school mathematics. In G. Leinhardt, R. Putnam, & R. A. Hattrup (Eds.), *Analysis of arithmetic for mathematics teaching* (pp. 1–51). Hillsdale, NJ: Erlbaum.

Sowder, J. T. (1995). Instructing for rational number sense. In J. T. Sowder & B. P. Schappelle (Eds.), *Providing a foundation for teaching mathematics in the middle grades* (pp. 15–30). Albany, NY: State University of New York Press.

Sowder, J. T. (1998). Ethics in mathematics education research. In A. Sierpinska & J. Kilpatrick (Eds.), *Mathematics education as a research domain: A search for identity* (pp. 427–441). Dordrecht, The Netherlands: Kluwer.

Sowder, J. T., & Philipp, R. A. (1995). The value of interaction in promoting teaching growth. In J. T. Sowder & B. P. Schappelle (Eds.), *Providing a foundation for teaching mathematics in the middle grades* (pp. 223–250). Albany, NY: State University of New York Press.

Sowder, J. T., Philipp, R. A., Flores, A., & Schappelle, B. P. (1995). Instructional effects of knowledge of and about mathematics: A case study. In J. T. Sowder & B. P. Schappelle (Eds.), *Providing a foundation for teaching mathematics in the middle grades* (pp. 253–274). Albany, NY: State University of New York Press.

Sowder, J. T., & Schappelle, B. P. (Eds.). (1995). *Providing a foundation for teaching mathematics in the middle grades.* Albany, NY: State University of New York Press.

Sowder, L. (1988). Children's solutions of story problems. *Journal of Mathematical Behavior, 7,* 227–238.

Sowder, L. (1995). Addressing the story-problem problem. In J. T. Sowder & B. P. Schappelle (Eds.), *Providing a foundation for teaching mathematics in the middle grades* (pp. 121–142). Albany, NY: State University of New York Press.

Stake, R., Cole, C., Sloane, F., Migotsky, C., Flôres, C., Merchant, B., Miron, M., & Medley, C. (1994). *The burden: Teacher professional development in Chicago school reform: Inter-institutional collaboration with the Teachers Academy for Mathematics & Science.* Champaign, IL: CIRCE, University of Illinois.

Stake, R. E. (1994). Case studies. In N. K. Denzin & Y. S. Lincoln (Eds.), *Handbook of qualitative research* (pp. 236–247). Thousand Oaks, CA: Sage.

Streefland, L. (1991). *Fractions in realistic mathematics education: A paradigm of developmental research.* Boston: Kluwer Academic Press.

Streefland, L. (1993). Fractions: A realistic approach. In T. P. Carpenter, E. Fennema, & T. A. Romberg (Eds.), *Rational numbers: An integration of research* (pp. 289–325). Hillsdale, NJ: Erlbaum.

Thompson, A. G. (1991). The development of teachers' conceptions of mathematics teaching. In R. G. Underhill (Ed.), *Proceedings of the thirteenth annual meeting of the North American Chapter of the International Group for the Psychology of Mathematics Education* (Vol. 2, pp. 8–14). Blacksburg: Division of Curriculum & Instruction, Virginia Polytechnic Institute & State University.

Thompson, A. G. (1992). Teachers' beliefs and conceptions: A synthesis of the research. In D. A. Grouws (Ed.), *Handbook of research on mathematics teaching and learning* (pp. 127–146). New York: Macmillan.

Thompson, A. G., Philipp, R. A., Thompson, P. W., & Boyd, B. A. (1994). Calculational and conceptual orientations in teaching mathematics. In D. B. Aichele (Ed.), *Professional development for teachers of mathematics* (pp. 79–92). Reston, VA: National Council of Teachers of Mathematics.

Thompson, P. W. (1992). Notations, conventions, and constraints: Contributions to effective uses of concrete materials in elementary mathematics. *Journal for Research in Mathematics Education, 23,* 123–147.

Thompson, P. W. (1993). Quantitative reasoning, complexity, and additive structures. *Educational Studies in Mathematics, 25,* 165–208.

Thompson, P. W. (1994). The development of the concept of speed and its relationship to concepts of rate. In G. Harel & J. Confrey (Eds.), *The development of multiplicative reasoning in the learning of mathematics* (pp. 181–234). Albany, NY: State University of New York Press.

Thompson, P. W. (1995). Notation, convention, and quantity in elementary mathematics. In J. T. Sowder & B. P. Schappelle (Eds.), *Providing a foundation for teaching mathematics in the middle grades* (pp. 199–221). Albany, NY: State University of New York Press.

Thompson, P. W., & Thompson, A. G. (1994). Talking about rates conceptually, Part I: A teacher's struggle. *Journal for Research in Mathematics Education, 25,* 279–303.

Vergnaud, G. (1983). Multiplicative structures. In R. Lesh & M. Landau (Eds.), *Acquisition of mathematics concepts and processes* (pp. 127–174). New York: Academic Press.

Vergnaud, G. (1988). Multiplicative structures. In J. Hiebert & M. Behr (Eds.), *Number concepts and operations in the middle grades* (pp. 141–161). Hillsdale, NJ: Erlbaum & Reston, VA: National Council of Teachers of Mathematics.

Wiemers, N. J. (1990). Transformation and accommodation: A case study of Joe Scott. *Educational Evaluation and Policy Analysis, 12,* 297–308.

Wilson, S. M. (1990). A conflict of interests: The case of Mark Black. *Educational Evaluation and Policy Analysis, 12,* 309–326.

Yin, R. K. (1984). *Case study research: Design and methods.* Beverly Hills, CA: Sage.

Appendix A

TEST OF TEACHERS' PEDAGOGICAL CONTENT UNDERSTANDING

The purpose of having you answer these questions is not to evaluate you. The results will be used in planning our work with you in the seminars. Many of the questions are not easy to answer and we do not expect you to be able to answer every one.

Part I—Short Answer Questions

If you use a **calculator** on any of these items, please say so.

1. What number is one third of the way between ½ and ⅞?
2. Write a decimal between 3.1 and 3.11.
3. Order these fractions from smallest to largest:*
   ⅝, ³⁄₁₀, ⅗, ¼, ⅔, ½
   Briefly explain your strategy.
4. If this □□□ □□□ is ³⁄₂ of one unit, how many squares are in the unit?
   (Show or tell how you obtained your answer.)
5. Place the decimal point in the correct place:
   4.5 × 51.26 = 02306700 (Show or tell how you obtained your answer.)
6. Marissa bought 0.43 pounds of wheat flour for which she paid $0.86. How many pounds of flour could she buy for $1.00?
7. The small square in this tangram puzzle is what fractional part of the larger square?

* Adapted from a teacher-observation form from the Center for Learning and Teaching of Elementary Subjects at Michigan State University. Permission obtained from Penelope Peterson, Co-director of the Center.

8. This is 120% of some smaller figure. Shade an area equivalent to 100% of the smaller figure.

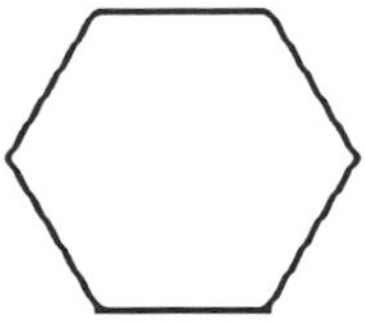

9. Three identical pizzas are to be fairly shared by 8 people. How much will each person get? Explain your reasoning.

10. What is a good *estimate*
   a. of ⁶⁄₁₃ + ⅝?
   b. of 15% of $49?

11. What happens to the value of the fraction ³⁄₁₆ if the numerator and denominator are both increased?

12. Find a fraction, if possible, between ¼ and ⅕. If it cannot be done, tell why.

13. Work these problems, showing all *written* work on this paper. **If a calculator is used, say so. Mentally calculated answers are accept-able, and can be given without writing anything down about how they were obtained.**
   14¾ − 5½ = _____
   ⅝ + ⁹⁄₁₈ =   _____
   12 ÷ ⅙ =   _____
   97 − 0.4 =   _____
   ½ ÷ 0.5 =   _____
   7.2 ÷ 12 =   _____
   ⅞ ÷ 2 =   _____

14. Three fourths of the seventh-grade class went to the football game. Of the ones who went to the game, one third went by car. What part of all of the seventh graders went to the game by car? Explain your answer.

15. This segment is ¾ of a whole:  Draw the whole.

16. Shade ⅝ of this rectangle:

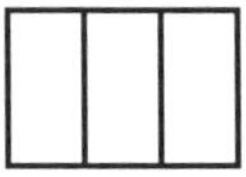

17. If Nick drove fewer miles in more time than he did yesterday, his average driving speed is:
   a. faster than yesterday.   b. slower than yesterday.
   c. the same as yesterday.   d. There is not enough information to tell.

18. What fractions give an infinite repeating decimal expansion? What can you say about nonrepeating decimals?

19. A biker rides at a speed of 20 km/hr for half an hour and then jogs at a speed of 15 km/hr for half an hour. What is her average speed?

20. A biker rides at a speed of 20 km/hr for a few km, and then turns around and walks home (same route) at a speed of 5 km/hr. What is his average speed?

21. Two people make 243 parts in 9 hours. One makes 13 parts each hour. How many does the second person make per hour?

22. Two fellows, Brother A and Brother B, each had a sister, Sister A and Sister B. The two fellows argued about which one stood taller over his sister. It turned out that Brother A won by 17 centimeters.

     Brother A was 186 cm tall.

     Sister A was 87 cm tall.

     Brother B was 193 cm tall.

     How tall was Sister B?

Part II: Pedagogical Content Understanding

1. A student solves this problem, "If cheese is $1.89 per pound, how much is 0.78 pounds?" by $1.89 ÷ 0.78. Why might the student be doing this? How would you respond?

2. a. Place the following three numbers in order from smallest to largest:
   0.5, 0.42, 0.423

   b. Margaret, Sammy, and Maria placed them in order as follows. What might each of the students be thinking? How could you find out?

      | Margaret: | 0.5, 0.42, 0.423 |
      | Sammy: | 0.423, 0.42, 0.5 |
      | Maria: | 0.42, 0.423, 0.5 |

3. In 1990, Mary received a 10% raise. In 1991, due to budget cuts, Mary's manager wanted to cut back salaries to the 1990 rates, so he reduced Mary's salary by 10%. Comment on this.

4. Make up an interesting story problem or situation in which the following could reasonably arise: $\frac{3}{4} ÷ \frac{1}{8} = n$.

5. Conversation among students who drew their own representations (for comparing $\frac{1}{4}$ and $\frac{1}{8}$):
   Student 1 drew

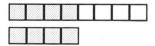

   and claimed that $\frac{1}{4} = \frac{1}{8}$.

Student 2: You must make the whole rectangles the same size.

Student 3: It doesn't matter how big you make the rectangle because you can see that ¼ takes up all of the rectangle while ⅛ takes up only half of it.

One teacher's analysis:

They should have used fraction bars. Then this problem would not have arisen.

What is your analysis?

6. "A recipe calls for ¾ cup of flour. How much flour is needed if the recipe is doubled?"

   Student A represents this problem as ¾ × 2. Student B represents it as 2 × ¾. Are both representations satisfactory? Why or why not?

7. A student is shown cards with these two parts of equal-sized cakes. The first cake has orange (shaded) frosting and the second cake has green (dotted) frosting. He is asked which pan has more cake left or whether the amounts left are the same.

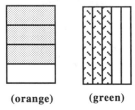

(orange)   (green)

He responds by putting the shaded card on top of the dotted card and comparing the widths of leftover shaded parts, but ignoring the lengths. He says, "I think they're the same because when I put this one over here [shaded area over dotted area], it was like I took the extra part from here [nonoverlapped shaded area] and put it here [nonoverlapped dotted area], and it's about the same."

Comment on this response.

Appendix B

INITIAL INTERVIEWS
WITH TEACHERS

Part I. Background questions

1. Tell me about your background. How have you been prepared to teach mathematics?

   What mathematics courses did you take in college?

   Do you feel that your college courses were useful? Why/Why not?

   In what inservice activities have you participated?

   What "turned you on" to teaching mathematics?

   What people, materials, and so on have had an influence on your teaching of mathematics? Why?

   How familiar are you with the *Mathematics Framework*? How has this document influenced your thinking and teaching?

   How familiar are you with the two NCTM Standards documents? How have they influenced your thinking and teaching?

   Do you belong to any mathematics teacher organizations (NCTM, CMC, GSDMC, etc.)?

2. Do you find mathematics easier or harder to teach than other subjects? Why?

   Do you think the majority of your students find mathematics easy to learn or hard to learn? Why?

   Is it important to you that your students enjoy mathematics?

3. What would you say is your primary focus when teaching mathematics?

   What is the role of problem solving in your class?

How do you balance conceptual development with skill development?

Do you do any "drill" in your class? What skills do you want your students to have by the end of the school year, and how do you go about making sure students have those skills?

4. How do you plan for instruction in mathematics?

What type of long-range planning do you do?

What type of short-range planning do you do?

Do you always have a clear objective for each class?

How important is it to you to "stay with" your plan for a lesson?

Has there ever been a time when you have not stayed with your lesson plan because of something that happened that led you in a different direction?

Can you describe a lesson that turned out to be very different from what you expected but that you felt was very successful?

How does classroom management influence your planning?

5. Describe a typical math class in your classroom.

Do you assign homework? For what purpose? What do you do with the homework assigned?

Do you ever teach to the whole class? How do you decide when to keep everyone together or break them into groups?

How would you describe the types of questions you ask? The kinds of responses your expect?

Do you have students work together? If so, what is the most successful way you've had students work together? Do you use cooperative groups? How? Every day?

Do you use manipulatives? How do you decide to use them? How do you decide when to use them? Which manipulatives have you found most useful? Least useful? Why?

What is the role of the textbook in your classroom?

6. What does it mean to "learn" mathematics?

What is the teacher's role in the mathematics classroom?

Who is ultimately responsible for the mathematics learned?

7. How important is it that teachers have a deep understanding of the mathematics they teach?

As your understanding of a mathematical concept or topic has changed, how has this changed the way in which you taught that concept or topic? Can you give an example?

Has there been a student question or response that made you go back and rethink the mathematics involved?

8. How do you assess the mathematical learning of your students?

   What role does student understanding, as assessed by you, play in your decisions when you plan instruction?

   How much attention do you pay to standardized test taking and test reporting?

9. Describe some of the individual differences among students in your classroom. How do you accommodate these differences?

10. Do you ever observe others teach mathematics? Does anyone observe you, for the purpose of helping you improve your teaching? Do you ever videotape your classes?

    Would it be all right with you if we videotaped your class?

11. What do you find to be the primary problems or barriers to teaching mathematics the way you believe it should be taught?

Part II. Understanding *Of* and *About* mathematics

12. Are there some common errors or misconceptions that your students have that make it difficult for them to understand what fractions are?

    How do you explain "division by zero" to your students?

    A student says that $\frac{3}{8} + \frac{5}{12}$ is $\frac{8}{20}$ and justifies her reasoning as follows: If I made 3 out of 8 free-throws in the morning, and 5 out of 12 free-throws in the afternoon, then altogether I made 8 out of 20 free-throws." How would you respond to that student?

13. What does "rational number sense" mean to you? What role does it play in your teaching?

14. Rank the importance during your instruction on fractions in
    a. teaching algorithms.
    b. teaching for concepts.
    c. teaching estimation.
    d. following the textbook.

    Which concepts are important for students to learn at the grade level you teach?

15. Why do we teach mathematics in school? What is its role in the lives of our students?

16. Here are two views of what mathematics is and how it should be taught. Read them, then use them to describe what *you* think about mathematics and how it should be taught.

The "Knowing Mathematics" View

Mathematics is a discipline characterized by accurate results and infallible procedures. It is more accurate to say that mathematics is discovered than to say it is created. Knowing mathematics means being able to apply basic concepts and being skilled in performing procedures. It follows then that a good teacher of mathematics presents concepts and procedures as clearly as possible and gives students opportunities to identify and apply concepts and to practice procedures.

The "Making Mathematics" View

Mathematics is socially constructed and involves conjectures, proofs, and refutations. The results are subject to change, and therefore their validity must be judged in relation to a social and cultural setting. It follows then that the primary aim of teaching mathematics is to engage students in the processes of doing mathematics, through activities that grow out of problem situations. The problem situations require reasoning and creative thinking, gathering and applying information, discovering, inventing and communicating ideas, and testing those ideas through critical reflections and argumentation.

17. Are there other questions you think I should have asked in this interview?

Appendix C

REFLECTIONS OF TEACHERS AT
CONCLUSION OF YEAR 1

Some questions for you to reflect upon, in writing, are given below. Browse through the seminar transcripts first (25 pages of seminar transcripts accompanied the questions). Take your time to reflect on these questions. When you have answered them, please send your response to us together with the enclosed invoice (signed, dated, and with the date filled in on the blank). You will be paid for 1 full day (6 hours) of work for this final summer assignment.

1. As you think back over our seminars, what things stand out in your mind? Why do you think those things stand out rather than other things?

   As you meander through the transcripts of seminars, what strikes you as surprising? Were there discussions or comments made that you see differently, reading them now, than you did hearing them for the first time? What are the highlights of the seminars, for you? (Do not feel confined to these excerpts.)

   There is also the human aspect of the seminars to consider. What has been the impact on you of your interaction with others (e.g., the other four teachers, project staff, invited speakers, last year's teachers)?

2. Give an example of one mathematical concept that you have come to understand more fully this past year. Has this yet had any effect on the manner in which you teach that concept? If not (perhaps you taught it before we discussed it), then how do you think your teaching of that topic might change in the future?

3. What do you perceive to be the teacher's role in the mathematics classroom? Is this a role you feel comfortable playing? If not, what kinds of experiences would make you more comfortable with it?

4. Do you find it any easier than before to understand the difficulties students are having with mathematics? If so, can you provide any examples? Are your students any more willing to become involved in mathematical discussions, rather than just finding answers? Do you think any of them perceive mathematics differently than they did at the beginning of the year?

5. We have spent a great deal of time this past year on the topic of fractions. Describe how you now see fractions as part of the curriculum; what you think to be the essential features you want your students to learn (generally speaking); the role of manipulatives in teaching fractions; the role of the textbook; and finally, the role of your own understanding of fractions and fraction operations. (We realize you may have answered part of this earlier.)

6. How have you changed as a mathematics teacher this past year? What aspects of that change do you think are directly related to this project? What other influences have there been on your teaching (in math or other areas)? Have they been complementary with this project or not?

   As you have probably realized, classroom change is a gradual, slow process, some of it quite painful and some of it very rewarding. (Maybe it is even unhealthy to change too much, too fast!) Keeping this in mind, where do you see yourself a year from now? Five years from now? What kinds of support and help do you need along the way?

7. We had thought, at the beginning of the year, that this year we would have a series of seminars, coupled with some classroom visits. However, any changes in the instruction and student learning would be a little more likely the second year. We therefore thought we would focus much more during our second year on observing you in classroom settings, rather than on seminars. It is our perception, though, that the discussions during seminars are very rich and lead to some deep exploration of mathematical content. We are therefore willing to continue with seminars (frequency and time is open). But perhaps your perceptions differ from ours. What would be most useful to you over the next year? What would you like to participate in doing? And what level of involvement would you like to have?

Appendix D

TEACHER OBSERVATION FORM

Teacher   _____   Date   _____

Observer _____   Class _____

PART I: SUMMARY/DESCRIPTION OF THE LESSON. INCLUDE TRANSCRIBED SECTIONS AS APPROPRIATE. NUMBER THE PARAGRAPHS.

PART II: NOTES FOR REFLECTION ON LESSON. REFER BACK TO NUMBERED PARAGRAPHS AS APPROPRIATE; COMPLETE WHEN NOT COVERED IN PART I; LEAVE BLANK IF NOT APPLICABLE.

1. **Mathematical Content**
   a. What was being taught? Was the class time partitioned into discrete parts? (If partitioned, give an approximate time line.)
   b. What seemed to be the goal? (What are students supposed to be learning to be able to do, to understand, etc.?)
   c. Were the underlying mathematical meanings of the content being emphasized in this lesson, or were procedural steps and facts being emphasized? Give specific examples.
   d. Was the emphasis on "doing mathematics" (e.g., framing problems, making conjectures, looking for patterns, examining constraints, determining whether an answer is valid or reasonable, knowing when a problem is solved, justifying, explaining, challenging), or was the emphasis on getting right answers? Give specific examples.
   e. Was the content of this lesson connected to other things that the class has been dealing with? Give specific examples.
   f. How was understanding assessed?

2. **Instructional Representations and Mathematical Tools**
   a. What instructional representations (concrete, pictorial, real-world, or symbolic) did the teacher or the students use in this lesson and what mathematical ideas were they targeting?

Describe each instructional representation, noting whether it was introduced by the teacher or by a student. If given by a student, describe how the teacher responded to it. Describe the strengths and weaknesses (in your opinion) of each representation. (Provide evidence for your assessment, considering how the representation fits with the mathematics, how helpful it seems to be as a learning tool—that is, does it focus attention on the central idea? Does it model significant components or aspects of the idea or the thinking that underlies it?)

b. Itemize the mathematical tools that teacher or students used in this lesson.

Concrete pedagogical materials

Pictorial tools

"Real-world" situations or stories

Measurement tools and other mathematical objects

Calculators

Mathematical language (special terms used to refer to the substance of mathematics—e.g., "quotient," "parallelogram," "negative number")

Mathematical symbols and notation

Language and skills of mathematical discourse (e.g., formulating hypotheses, challenging solutions, providing counterexamples, supporting a result with an alternative justification)

c. What was the role of the textbook?

3. **Classroom Discourse**

   a. Did the teacher frequently verbalize reasons, understandings, and solution strategies him- or herself? Did the students do this frequently in response to prompting/encouragement from the teacher or spontaneously? How did the teacher respond to students when they did this? Give examples.

   b. Did the teacher frequently make conjectures, challenge ideas, validate and justify solutions him- or herself? Did the students do this frequently in response to prompting/encouragement from the teacher or spontaneously? How did the teacher respond to students when they did this? Give examples.

   c. What were the students doing and what was the teacher's role during discussions? How much freedom did the teacher allow in student answers? In what ways was the discourse convergent? In what ways was the press toward consensus? In what ways was the discourse divergent? Were there space and time to disagree, to remain unconvinced?

d. Were there times during the lesson when a significant number of students seemed exceptionally engaged in the mathematics at hand? What were they engaged in?

Were there times during the lesson when a significant number of students seemed to be engaged in something other than the mathematics at hand? What were they engaged in?

4. **Intellectual Space**
   a. Were the problems or tasks problematic to students (i.e., was there no immediately obvious solution path)?
   b. Did students seem to be confused about anything? If so, about what? How did the teacher treat the confusion?
   c. What routines seemed to be in place in the class, and how well did students seem to know these?
   d. What role did classroom management problems seem to play?

PART III. POST-OBSERVATION QUESTIONS

1. How do you think the lesson went?
2. Why was this lesson taught? Where did you get the ideas for this lesson? How is it connected to what you have done and to what you plan to do?
3. Was any part of the lesson influenced by this project? Has anything from the project influenced your teaching since we last observed you?
4. Are you left with any questions about the teaching/learning that went on today?
5. How is this lesson similar to or different from your usual mathematics lesson?

Other Possible Post-Observation Questions
1. What were your objectives in teaching this lesson?
2. What previous lessons relate to this lesson?
3. What do the students already know about this topic?
4. Why is it important for students to learn this content?
5. How is it related to other content they have learned?
6. Why did you
   a. Select the activities/behaviors for the students?
   b. Choose the classroom organization?
   c. Select the examples, definitions, and analogies used?
   d. Select the modes of representation used?
   e. Select the techniques used (e.g., individual vs. group, guided discussion vs. didactic, manipulatives vs. paper and pencil, procedural vs. meaningful instruction)?

7. What are common student misconceptions about this content?
8. What are/were your expectations about
    a. Students' abilities to understand the content?
    b. Especially difficult aspects of the lesson?
    c. How students would feel/felt about the lesson?
9. How comfortable do you feel about teaching this topic?
   About questions students may ask?
   About how this topic is related to other topics?

Also ask specific questions about particular decisions made during the class.

Appendix E

TEACHER/TEACHER OBSERVATION FORM

Part I: To be completed by the observing teacher

Observation of:

Observer:

Date:

1. What was the mathematical content of the lesson you observed? What were the goals of the lesson, as perceived during the observation?

2. Was there an opportunity to talk about the lesson before the observation? If so, how did the teacher relate the lesson to what went on before today? What was the general focus of the discussion and the questions?

3. Provide a brief description of the approach the teacher took in teaching the lesson. (Class discussion? Group work? Teacher explanations? Manipulatives used? Writing? etc.)

4. What was the emphasis of the lesson? Conceptual understanding? Learning procedures/ skills? Problem solving?

5. Was any assessment undertaken during the class? If so, was it used to guide the lesson in any way? Or does it appear that it will be used in future planning?

6. Are there aspects of beliefs about mathematics, of teaching, of planning, of discipline, of organization, etc., where your approach is fundamentally different from that of the teacher you observed?

7. Were there any points during this lesson when you thought that the teacher's remarks or responses reflected an understanding that differed from your own with respect to

   a. the mathematics involved?
   b. the instructional approach to this mathematics?
   c. children's thinking about this mathematics?
8. What were the "high points" of the lesson?
9. Did you have any suggestions for the teacher?
10. What were the major points of discussion after the lesson?

Any other comments are welcome.

Part II: To be completed by the teacher who was observed

   Your name:

   Visitor-Observer:

   Date:

1. What was the mathematical content of the lesson you taught? What were the goals of your lesson?

2. Was there an opportunity to talk about the lesson before the observation? What was the general focus of the discussion and the questions?

3. Provide a brief description of the approach you took in teaching the lesson. (Class discussion? Group work? Teacher explanations? Manipulatives used? Writing? etc.)

4. What did you emphasize the day of the observation? Conceptual understanding? Learning procedures/skills? Problem solving?

5. What were the major points of discussion after the lesson?

Any other comments are welcome.

Appendix F

FRACTION UNDERSTANDING AND PROPORTIONAL REASONING TEST

Name _____ Grade _____

Teacher _____ Date _____

Directions: Some of these problems may be easy and some may be difficult. Do your best on all of the problems.

1. Look at each pair of numbers. IF one is LARGER than the other, circle it. IF the numbers are the SAME, put = between them.

    a. $7/7$ 1
    b. $5/4$ 1
    c. $2/7$ $3/7$
    d. $1/6$ $1/8$
    e. $5/7$ $5/9$
    f. $3/4$ $6/8$
    g.   0.7 $1/7$
    h.   0.5 $6/12$

2. Circle the fraction CLOSER in size to $1/2$: $5/8$ or $1/5$

3. Erin won $5/8$ of the games he played; Pat won $3/4$;
   Val won $9/16$; and Kelly won $2/3$.
   Which of the players had the best record? _____
   Which of the players had the worst record? _____

4. **About** how much is $9/10 + 11/12$?
   Circle the closest answer: 1, 2, 20, 22, 42

5. Jane said that $12 \div 1/2$ is 6, but Sammy said no, it is 24. Which is right?
   _____ How do you know?

6. Hadad ate $2/3$ of a candy bar. This much is left. Make a drawing of how big the candy bar was before Hadad ate any.

7.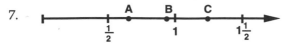

Which number goes best with A? ⅝, ⅓, ²⁄₇   Circle the answer.
Which number goes best with B? ¹⁄₁₀, ¹¹⁄₁₂, ¹³⁄₁₀   Circle the answer.
Which number goes best with C? ¼, ⁵⁄₄, 3   Circle the answer.

8. Circle the correct answer for: 5 + ½ + 0.5
   a. It can't be done.   b. 5   c. 5.5

   d. 6   e. 1

9. John found ¾ of a pie in the refrigerator. He sat down and ate ⅔ of
   the pie that was left.
   What fractional part of a whole pie did he eat?   _____

10. Shade in ¾ of this rectangle.

11. There are three baby eels in fish tanks. Eels are long fish. The eel in
    fish tank A is 10 cm long. In fish tank B the eel is 20 cm long. In fish
    tank C the eel is 25 cm long. The number of food balls each eel gets
    depends on the length of the eel. Eel A gets two food balls each
    day.

    How many food balls should the eel B get? (Show how you got
    your answer.)
    How many food balls should eel C get? (Show how you got your
    answer.)

12. Jean and Carla each bought the same kind of bubble gum at the
    same store. Jean bought 2 pieces of gum for 6¢. If Carla bought 8
    pieces of gum, how much did she pay? (Show how you got your
    answer.)

13. At Bank A, John put in $4 and after 1 year got back $8. At Bank B,
    Maria put in $10 and after 1 year got back $15. If you had $7 to put
    in a bank, would you put it in Bank A or Bank B? Why?

14. On the left you see some girls and some pizzas. On the right you see some boys and one pizza. The girls share their pizzas fairly, and the boys share their pizza fairly. Who gets more pizza, a boy or a girl?

(Show how you got your answer.)

AUTHOR INDEX

SUBJECT INDEX